First World War
and Army of Occupation
War Diary
France, Belgium and Germany

15 DIVISION
45 Infantry Brigade
Royal Scots Fusiliers
6/7th Battalion
6 May 1916 - 31 January 1918

WO95/1947/2

The Naval & Military Press Ltd
www.nmarchive.com
Published in association with The National Archives

Published by

The Naval & Military Press Ltd

Unit 10 Ridgewood Industrial Park,

Uckfield, East Sussex,

TN22 5QE England

Tel: +44 (0) 1825 749494

www.naval-military-press.com

www.nmarchive.com

This diary has been reprinted in facsimile from the original. Any imperfections are inevitably reproduced and the quality may fall short of modern type and cartographic standards.

© **Crown Copyright**
Images reproduced by permission of The National Archives, London, England, 2015.

Contents

Document type	Place/Title	Date From	Date To
Heading	1947/2 6/7 Battalion Royal Scotts Fusiliers		
Heading	15th Division 45th Infy Bde. 6/7th Bn Roy. Scots Fus. 1916 May-Jan 1918 To 59 Div (Pioneers). 6 Bn 1915 May-1916 Mar. 9 Div. 27 Bde. 6/7 Bn Amalgamated May 1916		
Heading	6/7th Royal Scots Fusiliers. May 1916.		
Miscellaneous	In The Field D.A.G., G.H.Q. 3rd Echelon.	10/06/1916	10/06/1916
War Diary	Vermelles.	06/05/1916	07/05/1916
War Diary	Hohenzollern.	08/05/1916	19/05/1916
War Diary	Sailly La Bourse.	20/05/1916	31/05/1916
Heading	6/7th Royal Scots Fusiliers June 1916.		
War Diary	Hulluch.	01/06/1916	11/06/1916
War Diary	Labourse.	12/06/1916	19/06/1916
War Diary	Holenzohen.	20/06/1916	30/06/1916
Heading	6/7th Royal Scots Fusiliers. July 1916.		
Heading	Confidential. War Diary 6/7th Battn. Royal Scots Fusiliers. 1st July 1916 to 31st July 1916. Volume.3.		
War Diary	Hohenzollern.	01/07/1916	06/07/1916
War Diary	Bethune.	07/07/1916	13/07/1916
War Diary	Hulluch Sector.	14/07/1916	21/07/1916
War Diary	Houchin.	22/07/1916	23/07/1916
War Diary	Bours.	24/07/1916	28/07/1916
War Diary	Le Meillard.	29/07/1916	31/07/1916
Heading	45th Brigade. 15th Division. 6/7th Battalion. Royal Scots Fusiliers August 1916.		
War Diary	Vignacourt.	01/08/1916	03/08/1916
War Diary	Mirvaux.	03/08/1916	03/08/1916
War Diary	Bresle.	04/08/1916	07/08/1916
War Diary	Trenches.	08/08/1916	08/08/1916
War Diary	Peak Wood Soull Conta Lmaison.	09/08/1916	11/08/1916
War Diary	Trenches.	12/08/1916	13/08/1916
War Diary	Albert.	14/08/1916	14/08/1916
War Diary	Albert at E 8a Reference Map. Albert 1/40000.	15/08/1916	17/08/1916
War Diary	Albert (E8a).	17/08/1916	18/08/1916
War Diary	Trenches.	19/08/1916	31/08/1916
Heading	6/7th (S) Battn, The Royal Scots Fus. September, 1916.		
Map	15th Division Map No. 5.		
War Diary	Trenches.	01/09/1916	03/09/1916
War Diary	Albert.	04/09/1916	04/09/1916
War Diary	Lavieville.	05/09/1916	11/09/1916
War Diary	X.26.d.	12/09/1916	12/09/1916
War Diary	Trenches.	13/09/1916	17/09/1916
War Diary	Martin Puich.	17/09/1916	17/09/1916
War Diary	Trenches.	17/09/1916	18/09/1916
War Diary	Millencourt Baizieux Wood.	19/09/1916	19/09/1916
War Diary	Baizieux Wood.	19/09/1916	30/09/1916
Map	15th Div. Map No 8 A. 1:10,000.		
Miscellaneous	Appendix I.		
Map			
Miscellaneous	Appendix II.		

Heading	6/7th Royal Scots Fusiliers October 1916.		
Heading	Confidential. War Diary. Of 6/7 Royal Scots Fusiliers. 1st to 31st October 1916. Volume. VI.		
War Diary	Boizieux	01/10/1916	03/10/1916
War Diary	Bresle.	04/10/1916	07/10/1916
War Diary	Lozenge Wd Martin Puich.	08/10/1916	08/10/1916
Miscellaneous	Martinpuich.	08/10/1916	12/10/1916
War Diary	Le Sars Front.	13/10/1916	15/10/1916
War Diary	Area X27a	16/10/1916	18/10/1916
War Diary	Martinpuich.	19/10/1916	24/10/1916
War Diary	Frontlines W. Le Sars.	24/10/1916	24/10/1916
War Diary	Area X27a	25/10/1916	31/10/1916
Map	15th. Division. Map. No.10. Appendix. I.		
Map	15th Div: Map No.15. Appendix. II.		
Heading	6/7th Royal Scots Fusiliers. November 1916.		
Heading	Confidential. War Diary of 6/7th Royal Scots Fusiliers. From 1st Novr. 1916. To 30th Novr 1916. Vol.17.		
War Diary	Martinpuich.	01/11/1916	02/11/1916
War Diary	X 27a Albert.	03/11/1916	03/11/1916
War Diary	Albert.	04/11/1916	06/11/1916
War Diary	Franvillers.	06/11/1916	30/11/1916
Heading	6/7th Royal Scots Fusiliers. December 1916.		
Heading	Confidential. War Diary of 6/7th (Service) Batt. Royal Scots Fusiliers. From 1st Dec. 1916 To 31st Dec, 1916. Volume.VIII. Vol.18.		
War Diary	Nametz Wood.	01/12/1916	06/12/1916
War Diary	Albert.	07/12/1916	15/12/1916
War Diary	Le Sars Sector.	15/12/1916	19/12/1916
War Diary	Shelter Wood S.	19/12/1916	23/12/1916
War Diary	Martinpuich	23/12/1916	26/12/1916
War Diary	Le Sars Sector.	26/12/1916	27/12/1916
War Diary	Pioneer Camp.	28/12/1916	29/12/1916
War Diary	Le Sars Sector.	30/12/1916	31/12/1916
Heading	6/7th Battn. The Royal Scots Fusiliers. January, 1917.		
Heading	Operation Order file Oct 27th/15. G.R. XI. 19th Division.		
War Diary	Shelter Woods.	01/01/1917	06/01/1917
War Diary	Villa Camp.	06/01/1917	12/01/1917
War Diary	Shelter Wood N.	12/01/1917	16/01/1917
War Diary	Support. Right Sector Le Sars.	17/01/1917	17/01/1917
War Diary	Left Front.	18/01/1917	19/01/1917
War Diary	Pioneer Camp.	20/01/1917	22/01/1917
War Diary	Le Sars.	22/01/1917	24/01/1917
War Diary	Bazentin Camp.	25/01/1917	28/01/1917
War Diary	Le Sars (Left Sector).	29/01/1917	31/01/1917
War Diary	Le Sars Left Sector. Villa Camp etc.	31/01/1917	31/01/1917
Heading	6/7th (S) Battn, The Royal Scots Fusiliers. February, 1917.		
Heading	Confidential. War Diary From 1/2/17 To 28/2/17. (Volume.XX). Vol.19.		
Heading	Confidential. War Diary of 6/7th (Service) Battn. Royal Scots Fusiliers. From 1st February 1917 To 28th February 1917. Vol. X. Vol.20.		
War Diary	Villa Camp.	01/02/1917	02/02/1917
War Diary	Fricourt Camp.	03/02/1917	04/02/1917
War Diary	Franvillers.	05/02/1917	15/02/1917

War Diary	Ferraincourt.	16/02/1917	16/02/1917
War Diary	Nuncq.	17/02/1917	18/02/1917
War Diary	Gouy-En-Ternois.	19/02/1917	27/02/1917
War Diary	Duisans.	28/02/1917	28/02/1917
Heading	Confidential. War Diary of 6/7 Royal Scots Fusiliers From 1st March 1917 To 31st March 1917. Vol. XI.		
War Diary	Duisans.	01/03/1917	02/03/1917
War Diary	Arras.	03/03/1917	17/03/1917
War Diary	Duisans.	18/03/1917	18/03/1917
War Diary	Izel Le Hameau	19/03/1917	30/03/1917
Heading	Confidential. War Diary of 6/7th Royal Scots Fusiliers From 1st April 1917 To 30th April 1917. Vol. XI. Vol. 22.		
War Diary	Izel-Le-Hameau.	01/04/1917	02/04/1917
War Diary	Arras.	02/04/1917	03/04/1917
War Diary	Front Line.	04/04/1917	05/04/1917
War Diary	Arras Front Line.	05/04/1917	11/04/1917
War Diary	Arras.	12/04/1917	18/04/1917
War Diary	Monchy South.	19/04/1917	27/04/1917
War Diary	Arras.	24/04/1917	29/04/1917
War Diary	Berneville.	30/04/1917	30/04/1917
Miscellaneous	Operations of April 9,10 & 11, 1917. Mon. April 9, 1917.	09/04/1917	09/04/1917
Miscellaneous	Report on Operations 19th April-28th April 1917.	19/04/1917	19/04/1917
Miscellaneous			
Map	The Triangle. Scale 1/5000.		
Heading	Confidential. War Diary of 6th/7th Royal Scots from 1st to 31st May 1917. Vol.23.		
War Diary	Berneville.	01/05/1917	06/05/1917
War Diary	Wanquetin.	07/05/1917	07/05/1917
War Diary	Ivergny.	08/05/1917	20/05/1917
War Diary	Bonnieres.	21/05/1917	21/05/1917
War Diary	Cherienne.	22/05/1917	31/05/1917
Heading	To go with diary 6/7 RSF.		
Heading	Confidential. War Diary of 6/7th (Service) Battn. Royal Scots Fusiliers. From 1st June 1917. To 30th June 1917. Vol. XIII.		
War Diary	Cherienne.	01/06/1917	21/06/1917
War Diary	Blangerval.	22/06/1917	22/06/1917
War Diary	Hestrus.	23/06/1917	23/06/1917
War Diary	Febvin Palfart.	24/06/1917	25/06/1917
War Diary	Lambres.	26/06/1917	26/06/1917
War Diary	Borre.	27/06/1917	27/06/1917
War Diary	Wotau Area.	28/06/1917	30/06/1917
Heading	Confidential. War Diary of 6/7th (Service) Battn Royal Scots Fusiliers. From 1st July 1917 To 31st July 1917. Vol. XIV.		
Heading	Confidential. War Diary of 6/7th Royal Scots Fusiliers. 1st to 31st July, 1917. Volumn.25.		
War Diary	Broxeele Area.	01/07/1917	13/07/1917
War Diary	H 16a.	14/07/1917	18/07/1917
War Diary	Front Lines Ypres.	19/07/1917	21/07/1917
War Diary	Camp.	22/07/1917	25/07/1917
War Diary	St Laurence Camp.	26/07/1917	31/07/1917

Heading	Confidential. War Diary of 6/7th (Service) Battn. Royal Scots Fusiliers. From 1st August 1917 To 31st August 1917. Vol.XVI.		
War Diary	Frezenburg Line.	01/08/1917	02/08/1917
War Diary	H.16.a.	03/08/1917	03/08/1917
War Diary	Winnezeele.	04/08/1917	12/08/1917
War Diary	C Camp Winnezeele.	13/08/1917	19/08/1917
War Diary	H.16.a.	20/08/1917	20/08/1917
War Diary	Ypres.	21/08/1917	30/08/1917
War Diary	H.7.C.	31/08/1917	31/08/1917
Miscellaneous	Report On Operations-Ypres 1917. (Phase 2.11). 6/7th. Royal Scots Fusiliers. Appendix. 1.		
Miscellaneous	Clearing Up Parties.		
Heading	Confidential. War Diary of 6/7th (Service) Battn. Royal Scots Fusiliers. From 1st Sept 1917 To 30th Sept 1917.		
War Diary	Pioneer Camp Worm Houdt.	01/09/1917	01/09/1917
War Diary	Wormhoudt	02/09/1917	02/09/1917
War Diary	Yhutments Etrun.	03/09/1917	06/09/1917
War Diary	Roeux.	06/09/1917	10/09/1917
War Diary	Stirling Camp.	11/09/1917	14/09/1917
War Diary	Baroosa Camp.	15/09/1917	23/09/1917
War Diary	In the Line.	24/09/1917	30/09/1917
Miscellaneous	Routine Orders Issued By Lt. Col. F.L.D. Gordon Comdg 6/7th. Royal Scots Fusiliers. Appendix. 1.	00/09/1917	00/09/1917
Operation(al) Order(s)	Operation Orders No.9. In the Field 13th. Sept.17. Appendix. II.	13/09/1917	13/09/1917
Operation(al) Order(s)	6/7th. Royal Scots Fusiliers. Operation Orders No.10. In the Field. Appendix. III.	22/09/1917	22/09/1917
Miscellaneous	Table Of Working Parties. Appendix. 14.		
Heading	Confidential. War Diary of 6/7th (Service) Battn. Royal Scots Fusiliers. From 1st Oct 1917 To 31st Oct 1917. Vol.XXVII.		
War Diary	In the Line.	01/10/1917	01/10/1917
War Diary	Wilderness Camp.	02/10/1917	09/10/1917
War Diary	Oil Factory Arras.	10/10/1917	15/10/1917
War Diary	Arras.	16/10/1917	17/10/1917
War Diary	In the Line.	18/10/1917	21/10/1917
War Diary	Middlesex Camp.	22/10/1917	25/10/1917
War Diary	Rt Sub Sector-Roeux.	26/10/1917	30/10/1917
War Diary	Support Roeux Sector.	31/10/1917	31/10/1917
Operation(al) Order(s)	6/7th. R.S.F. Operation Orders No.177.	25/10/1917	25/10/1917
Operation(al) Order(s)	6/7th. R.S.F. Operation Order No.16.	04/10/1917	04/10/1917
Heading	Confidential. War Diary of 6/7th (Service) Battn. Royal Scots Fusiliers. From 1st Novr. 1917 To 30th Novr 1917. Vol.XVIII. Vol.29.		
War Diary	Support Roeux Sector.	01/11/1917	01/11/1917
War Diary	Arras.	02/11/1917	10/11/1917
War Diary	Right Sub Sector. Monchy.	11/11/1917	14/11/1917
War Diary	Stirling Camp.	15/11/1917	18/11/1917
War Diary	Right Sub. Sector Monchy.	19/11/1917	23/11/1917
War Diary	Wilderness Camp.	24/11/1917	26/11/1917
War Diary	Arras.	27/11/1917	27/11/1917
War Diary	Greenland Hill Sector.	28/11/1917	30/11/1917
Operation(al) Order(s)	6/7th R.S.F. Operation Order No.20. Appendix. I.	01/11/1917	01/11/1917
Operation(al) Order(s)	6/7th. R.S.F. Operation Orders. No.21. Appendix. II.	08/11/1917	08/11/1917

Operation(al) Order(s)	Operation Orders No. 23. 6/7th. Royal Scots Fusiliers. Appendix. III.		
Operation(al) Order(s)	Operation Orders No. 23. 6/7th. Royal Scots Fusiliers.		
Operation(al) Order(s)	6/7th. Royal Scots Fusiliers. Operation Orders No.4. Appendix.IV.	18/11/1917	18/11/1917
Operation(al) Order(s)	6/7th R.S.F. Operation Orders No.30. Appendix. V.	25/11/1917	25/11/1917
Heading	6/7th Royal Scots Fusiliers. War Diary. From 1st December 1917 To 31st December 1917. Vol. XIX.		
War Diary	Arras.	01/12/1917	07/12/1917
War Diary	Arras. & Monchy Sector.	08/12/1917	08/12/1917
War Diary	Monchy Sector.	09/12/1917	15/12/1917
War Diary	Gavrelle Switch.	16/12/1917	19/12/1917
War Diary	Roeux Sector.	20/12/1917	22/12/1917
War Diary	Arras.	23/12/1917	31/12/1917
Operation(al) Order(s)	0/7. R.S.F. Operation Order No.31. Appendix. 1.	01/12/1917	01/12/1917
Miscellaneous	Relief Table-Issued With 6/7th R.S.F. Operation Order No.31.		
Operation(al) Order(s)	6/7th Ref. Operation Order No.32. Appendix. 11.		
Miscellaneous	Relief Table. issued with 6/7th R.S.F. Operation Order No.		
Operation(al) Order(s)	R.S.F. Operation Order No.36. Appendix. III.	15/12/1917	15/12/1917
Operation(al) Order(s)	R.S.F. Operation Order No.36.		
Operation(al) Order(s)	6/7th R.S.F. Operation Orders No.35. Appendix. IX. War Diary.	19/12/1917	19/12/1917
Miscellaneous			
Operation(al) Order(s)	6/7th R.S.F. Operation Orders No.37. Appendix. V.	22/12/1917	22/12/1917
Heading	6/7th B. Royal Scots Fusiliers. War Diary from 1st Jan. 1918 to 31st. Jany. 1918. Vol. XXXI.		
War Diary	Arras.	01/01/1918	01/01/1918
War Diary	Wanquetin.	02/01/1918	31/01/1918

1942/2
6/7 Batteria Royal
Scotts Fusiliers

15TH DIVISION
45TH INFY BDE

6/7TH BN ROY. SCOTS FUS.
JULY 1915 - JAN 1918

TO 59 DIV (Honce...)

6RN 1915 May - 1916 Mar   9 Jun 27 DE

6/7 BN Autogether may 1916

MAPS/PLANS
RECORDED

Index

SUBJECT.

6/7th Royal Scots Fusiliers.

No.	Contents.	Date.

May 1916

In The Field 45/15
10/6/16

D.A.G., G.H.Q. 3rd Echelon

1. I beg to forward the last volume of the War Diary of the 7th R. Scots Fusiliers.

2. Also Volume I of the War Diary of the 6/7 R. Scots Fusiliers up to and including 31.5.16

The 6th and 7th Battalions were amalgamated on 13.5.16 on which date I have opened the War Diary of the amalgamated Battalions.

I took over command of the amalgamated Battalion yesterday and find that the War Diary has not been rendered punctually. This will not recur.

J. Scott Lt. Colonel
Cmd: 6/7 R.S. Fus.

WAR DIARY or INTELLIGENCE SUMMARY

Army Form C. 2118.

7th R. Scots Fusiliers

Place	Date	Hour	Summary of Events and Information	Remarks and references to Appendices
VERMELLES	MAY 6		2 Reserve trenches. Enemy shelled trenches but not heavily. Working parties that night.	
	7		Quiet. Working parties K.B.52. Moved up and took over Right sub-section HOHENZOLLERN SECTOR	
HOHENZOLLERN	8		2 trenches right sub-section HOHENZOLLERN SECTOR	
	9		do — do —	
	10		do — do — 11th moved into reserve trenches	
	11		Headquarters VERMELLES. Germans attacked 10/Royal Scots who returned me, about 5 p.m. A & D Coys moved to RESERVE TRENCH N of HULLOCH ALLEY. support Royal Scots. C & B Coys occupied LANCASHIRE TRENCH. 7PM. A Coy less bombing party moved into OB1. D Coy less bombing party 7 Hears in GORDON ALLEY. Bombers of D coy under 2/Lt Cooper started to bomb up GORDON ALLEY, party under 2/Lt Watson. A Coy bombed at HULLOCH ALLEY. 2 Platoons from B coy reported to CO Royal Scots for bomb carrying from batt. Stores forward. 2 Platoons B coy, 2 Platoons C coy went into VILLAGE LINE N. Junction KEEP. Junction KEEP occupied by 2 Platoons "C" coy under an officer. Batt. Hqrs were established in VILLAGE LINE N of JUNCTION KEEP. 2nd in Command	

Army Form C. 2118.

WAR DIARY
or
INTELLIGENCE SUMMARY.

(Erase heading not required.)

7 Royal Scots Fusiliers

Place	Date	Hour	Summary of Events and Information	Remarks and references to Appendices
HOHENZOLLERN	MAY 11		Capt Paton went up to Front Line to take command of operations line P.M. Bombardment & bombing continued. C.O. & Adjutant went up 10 P.M. & took up a position in O.B.2. with telephone communication to rear. Communication to front was by runner. At 1.30 A.M., 7 R.S.F. bombed counter attack with 'A' Coy. from SACKVILLE ST. between GORDON ALLEY & HOLLOCH ALLEY. The attack was made on ANCHOR TRENCH & though carried out with almost gallantry, failed on account of heavy enfilade fire from enemy machine guns. Word was received from Brigade to consolidate where we were. This was done & the line stood from left: KAISERIN TRENCH, POTER ST, CLIFFORD ST, SACKVILLE ST. Our extreme Rt was junction of latter with HOLLOCH ALLEY, our extreme left, SAVILLE ROW. We established bombing posts in KAISERIN TRENCH, CLIFFORD ST, GORDON ALLEY. The rest of the day was quiet.	
	12			

WAR DIARY
or
INTELLIGENCE SUMMARY.
(Erase heading not required.)

Army Form C. 2118.

Instructions regarding War Diaries and Intelligence Summaries are contained in F.S. Regs., Part II. and the Staff Manual respectively. Title pages will be prepared in manuscript.

Place	Date	Hour	Summary of Events and Information	Remarks and references to Appendices
	13		Amalgamation with 6th Battn, who formed no 2 in the trenches. The consisting Coy of the one batt. formed the corr. Coy of the other.	
	14		Day quiet until evening. About 4.15 P.M. we received instructions from Brigade re counter attack at night. The main attack was being carried	

Amalgamation
6/7th Roy Scots Fusiliers

Vol I. 6/7 R.S. Fusiliers V OP

Army Form C. 2118.

WAR DIARY
or
INTELLIGENCE SUMMARY.
(Erase heading not required.)

Place	Date	Hour	Summary of Events and Information	Remarks and references to Appendices
HOHENZOLLERN	MAY. 14		Out by 46th Brigade on our right. At 6PM, our machine guns enfiladed Boyau 99 held by enemy. At same time our Artillery opened heavy fire on Boyau 99, & ALEXANDER TRENCH. At 6.30 PM our bombers cleared our barricade in GORDON ALLEY & commenced to bomb at trench. They were held up at enemy bay head, but continued bombing till 8 PM which time we received orders from Bgde to return to our original post & hold fast there. The enemy bombardment was heavy, SACKVILLE St & parts of GORDON ALLEY being levelled to the ground - also VIGO St. Conditions became normal by 9.30 PM, & work in trenches was done by both sides.	
	15		Occupied night sub-sector with 2 Coys in firing line, 1 in SUPPORT (OB1) 1 in Reserve (RESERVE TRENCH).	
	16 17		Day quiet.	
	18		11AM - 11.30AM, heavy shelling on VIGO St., & field guns OB1. otherwise quiet. 1AM - 2AM - wired SACKVILLE St between GORDON ALLEY & HULLOCH ALLEY. VIGO St built up where blown up.	
	19.		Relieved by 8/10th Gordons. Proceeded by Coys & billets in SAILLY LA BOURSE.	

WAR DIARY
INTELLIGENCE SUMMARY
(Erase heading not required.)

Army Form C. 2118.

6/7 R. Scots Fusiliers

Place	Date	Hour	Summary of Events and Information	Remarks and references to Appendices
SAILLY LA BOURSE	20	Noon	Battn. inspected by Brig Gen. Allgood, on ground adjacent to Chateau de Bois, SAILLY.	
		6PM	RC Chaplain in Church, SAILLY, for convenience of the troops. Protestants allotted Coys as follows A Coy 20th and B 21st, C 22nd, D 23rd 9 pm.	
	21		Church Parade – C of England 8AM. Presbyterian 10.30AM RC. 11AM. Working Party – 1 Officer & 40 O.R. 17.45PM at 73 Field Coy RE store SAILLY Labour.	
	22		Parade – 3½ hour Physical drill, 1 hour drill by Coy, 2½ hours drill by coys in arranging bombing & wiring squads. Working party as on previous day.	
			Drinking water delivered. Octane 3PM.	
	23		Parade – Physical training 3½ hour. Baths in mine SAILLY 1 hour each coy. Bombing 1 hour each coy, Wiring 1 hour each coy. Inspection of "A" Coy 10AM by Commanding Officer. Working party as on previous day.	
	24		Parade as on previous day, except exception of bathing. Inspection of "B" Coy by Commanding Officer. Inspection with returns all coys 2PM–3 PM.	
	25		Parade – Wiring a Bombing Squads 1 hour each coy. Drill 1 hour each coy. Inspection of C & D coys by Commanding Officer. Working party as on previous day.	

WAR DIARY
or
INTELLIGENCE SUMMARY.

Army Form C. 2118.

6/7 R.S. Fusiliers

Place	Date	Hour	Summary of Events and Information	Remarks and references to Appendices
SAULTY L'ABOURSE	MAY 26		Parades:- 6.30 – 7.30 AM Cleaned – rifle inspection etc. The Battn. was inspected on Sports close to Chateau de bois at 10 AM. by G.O.C. 145th Bd. 11.30 – 12.30 practice for Cup in Wiring & Bombing. Working parts as on previous day.	
	27		Moved into the trenches occupying RIGHT Sub Sector. Extreme right VENDIN ALLEY extreme left WINGS WAY. Day quiet but at "Stand to" evening enemy active with grenades.	
	28.		RIGHT Sub Sector. Enemy active with grenades. A few sniper "Tearers" on STRAW ALLEY with intention of getting our "Snipers" shooting time. 5 P.M. Enemy mine TRALEE CRAOP.	
	29		11 AM enemy traversed our SUPPORT LINE with field guns, also HAY ALLEY. At 8.30 AM enemy exploded a mine behind Tralee Craoh. At points H13c65 & H13c67 our snipers claim hits. 4 P.M. Enemy shelled our front with field guns in reply to our artillery fire.	
	30		Day quiet but enemy still active with rifle grenades.	
	31		Enemy working in his front & SUPPORT LINE. We shelled him at frequent intervals. Our snipers active claiming 6 hits.	

Index................ ....

1.G.

SUBJECT.

6/7 Royal Scots Fusiliers

No.	Contents.	Date.
	June 1916	

WAR DIARY

Army Form C. 2118.

VOL II

6/7 Royal Scots Fusiliers

JUNE 15

Place	Date	Hour	Summary of Events and Information	Remarks and references to Appendices
HULLUCH	June 1		Enemy rifle & MG and rifle grenades. Response to trench mortars. D co. between HOLLY LANE and VERDUN ALLEY. C Co. between HAY ALLEY (Boyan/BA) and HOLLY LANE. B co. between KINGSWAY and HAY ALLEY. A co. in reserve in B cov. with heavy trench mortars (Rumfords).	
	2		Day fairly quiet. Shelling of support and reserve lines between 11AM & 11.30 AM. In afternoon about 4 hrs enemy retaliation from trench mortars. Fair work fired from Flight Quad.	
	3		"Stand to" being other and left front. At artillery & silenced him. About 3PM a team trench mortar was brought up to bear on our front & support lines. Two direct shots on left front and flanked well deployed & at 3.30pm the enemy expended himself in the Inales Quad. Fire died down to constant sniper fire.	
	4		Rest of day normal.	
	5		Quiet day, intermittent shelling of right support. A co. relieved B co. in left front. Dug new line being knocked. Combined strafe on enemy front lines Crater, deepened Leinster Lane.	

WAR DIARY
or
INTELLIGENCE SUMMARY.

Army Form C. 2118.

Vol II

6/7 Royal Scots Fusiliers.

Place	Date	Hour	Summary of Events and Information	Remarks and references to Appendices
HULLUCH	Jan 5		Our supports took trench mortar & rifle grenades. Night quiet.	
	6		Enemy working hard behind MARSH & FAITH WOOD of Craters firing. 2 snipers. Our snipers had good work in these parties chances & hits. Right Coy very quiet. Night normal.	
	7		Relieved by 13th Royal Scots. Batt. moved back into Batt. reserve distribution. 2 Coys between Devon Lane & Vendin Alley in 10th Avenue. 2 Platoons in LONE TREE REDOUBT. 2 Coys in CURLEY CRES. and OB1. Batt. Hqrs in FOSSE WAY near junction with Curley Cres. Working parties about mining fatigues by day. Conditions normal.	
	8		As on previous day.	
	9		As on previous day. Major Pugh 10th WSH arrived & took over command. Major Pinch left for Batt. Hqrs.	
	10		Battalion relieved by 7th Camerons. Whole Brigade went into reserve. Marched to billets in LABOURSE. Day spent in cleaning equipment	

WAR DIARY
or
INTELLIGENCE SUMMARY.
(Erase heading not required.)

Army Form C. 2118.

Vol. II

1/7 Royal Scots Fusiliers

Place	Date	Hour	Summary of Events and Information	Remarks and references to Appendices
Laboursse	June 12		Working parties by night & day.	
	13		Memorial Service. Coy Kitchens in Church tested. Sadly laborious. Major Watt 2nd in command Capt McDonald & 4 officers and 250 men attached from B.O.T.T. Remainder of Batn. Cleaned equipment & billets.	
	14		C & D coys inspected by Commanding Officer. Working parties R.E. 3 officers 8 NCOs + 110 men. Lecture at noon by Commanding Officer on Company Administration. Bath 2 coys.	
	15		A & B coys inspected by Commanding Officer. Working parties 2 officers 8 NCOs + 180 men. Bath A & B coys & Grenadiers (3).	
	16		A Coy training. Bombing & practice in carrying smoke helmets (Oth. coys). Practice smoke helmets. Bombing 9.21. Lecture by 1/Lt Boag on "Hohenzollern front".	
	17		A Coy as on previous day. Working parties R.E. Lecture 1/Lt Bryson on "Intelligence Summaries" & Signal Sgt on Communication between an officer & Artillery & vice versa.	
	18		A Coy as on previous day. Working parties. Demonstration by 2/Lt Robertson	

Army Form C. 2118.

WAR DIARY
or
INTELLIGENCE SUMMARY.
(Erase heading not required.)

6/7 Royal Scots Fusiliers.

Instructions regarding War Diaries and Intelligence Summaries are contained in F.S. Regs., Part II. and the Staff Manual respectively. Title pages will be prepared in manuscript.

Place	Date	Hour	Summary of Events and Information	Remarks and references to Appendices
Laboure	June 18		of Smoke bombs & candles. Arrival of New Mexican Officer for duty. Th. Ralston R.A.M.C.	
	19		Cleaning of billets. Advance party left for trenches.	
	20		Batt. moved up with the trenches and took on right front and Reserve. Bombardment. Coy M.H.L.I. attached for instruction. 1 Platoon each coy. Distribution: D Coy on right, B in centre, A on left, C in Reserve.	
Molenjaecker	21		Rifles reported enemy working on new trenches with 9 machine guns fire opened on them — caused casualties. Bombing at Maidens Crater. Enemy Snipers in retaliation. Rest of day quiet.	
	22		Lt. Col Scott commanding left for 2nd Batt. A & S.H. Major Tabor took command. Capt Despuch acting 2nd. M.H.L.I. moved out. Coy & took over from D Coy on right. Day quiet.	
	23		Day normal — Enemy shelled ALEXANDRA TRENCH & O.P.s of front with intervals with SHRAPNEL — Little damage. H.A. & S.H. (?) relieved in H.L.	
	24		Moved into Batt. Reserve, relieved 13th Royal Scots. 3 Coys + 1	

WAR DIARY
or
INTELLIGENCE SUMMARY.
(Erase heading not required.)

Army Form C. 2118.

Place	Date	Hour	Summary of Events and Information	Remarks and references to Appendices
HULLUCH TRENCHES	June 24.		Coys A & 3H in Lancashire Trench and one Coy in Reserve, Nash Road + 1 Platoon in Central Keep + on Nation - Junction Keep. Working parties to R.E. + Tunnelling Coys.	
	25.		Working parties R.E. + Tunnelling Coys - day normal. Major Gordon Royal Scots Fusiliers arrived + took command.	
	26.		Working parties as before. Relaxation made for demonstration + raid but same it not suitable so cancelled. Artillery fired on fixed points on enemy wire to cut gap - return active stop this night + occasion damage.	
	27.		Working parties as before. Artillery cut wire at selected points + patrols reconnoitre to locate same about mid-night. Shots bombs were discharged + smoke candles alight that the enemy day front between SAVILLE ROW + BOYER REDOUBT. Between same redoubt and HAIRPIN CRATER. Two Waves (gas cylinders) were discharged at 1.10AM. At 1.40 AM 2 May 9 + 20 other ranks attempted a raid at above C 11 & 48, but had heavy rifle & MG fire [...]	

WAR DIARY or INTELLIGENCE SUMMARY

Army Form C. 2118.
Vol. IX
6/7 Royal Scots Fusiliers

Place	Date	Hour	Summary of Events and Information	Remarks and references to Appendices
Henyhiton	June 27		Working parties to R.E. & Tunnelling Coys. Capt McLennan Lieuts & 2/Lt Moon rejoined from sick furlough. 2 went to "C" & "D" Coys respectively.	
	28		Bns moved into trenches 11th A&M on left, just passed Wakenzielen Cab. A & H Bns in. A on left, C & D Coys took to relieve 4 Gordons, bombing Coys on left. New comms being done by 151st Brittles at G.6.c.8.5, G.b.c.1.5, & C.4.6.4.1. Night normal.	
	29		Day normal. Artillery fairly active from 3.15 am to 5 am & from 12 noon to 4 PM. Pilots sent out to reconnoitre but had to return owing to bombardment by enemy. About 9 PM a heavy bombardment was opened by enemy on our front, RAILWAY & reserve trench. At 9.45 pm. Runner report about 9.30 PM bombardment lifted from front line and then lights were sent up, indicated the enemy in to then attacking. Machine Gun fire came at once opened on them & they took to flight. Evidently taking cover of long grass nearest our line and drew a 3 bombs. One was shot at by an officer who turning to retreat and men on returning found Germans had left, leaving one rifle behind	

Army Form C. 2118.

WAR DIARY
or
INTELLIGENCE SUMMARY.
(Erase heading not required.)

Vol. II.
6/7 Royal Scots Fusiliers

Place	Date	Hour	Summary of Events and Information	Remarks and references to Appendices
Wulverghem	June 29		them. The enemy left about 6 here of known on our front. 9 unidentified. Next morning 100 were carried out. The rest of the enemy was quiet.	
	30		Day normal. At 10.30 pm this time took our ration to relieve 6th Gordon Hdrs killed known's wounded. The rifle from and machine gun nests occupied take [indef] personnel to Dugouts. 12 no one 2 known were relieved by us on the front occupied to Dawn our next heavy bombardment followed by Bosch area and lasted till about 2 am. Remainder of night was quiet	

P.S. Jordan
Lt-Col.

SUBJECT.

45/15

6/7th Royal Scots Fusiliers

No.	Contents.	Date.

July 1916

CONFIDENTIAL.

WAR DIARY

6/7th Battn. Royal Scots Fusiliers.

1st July 1916 to 31st July 1916.

VOLUMN. 3.

WAR DIARY
or
INTELLIGENCE SUMMARY

Army Form C. 2118.
Vol III.
6/7 Royal Scots Fusiliers

Place	Date	Hour	Summary of Events and Information	Remarks and references to Appendices
HOHENZOLLERN	July 1		D Coy. in reserve. C, B, A coys. in the firing line. A coy. being on the left & C on the right. Weather conditions very bad, and at night the 33rd Div. on our left was heavily bombarded. A coy was also involved in this front-attachment.	
	2		A Coy was relieved by D Coy on the left. The day was quiet. At 10 p.m. we let off a minnie of smoke-bombs, and this was followed by heavy front-bombardment. Our posts as a result of which our trenches (front & support) were badly damaged. At 12 midnight all was quiet.	
	3		The day was fairly quiet. A most of the work consisted in clearing the trenches damaged by the preceding bombardment. At 11.30 p.m. 9 at 1 am. two mines on either front-attachment, one left to the 33rd Div. & firing started. D coy. on the left coy. caught the fringe of this bombardment.	
	4		During the quiet, a mode front attack no attempt on clearing trenches.	

WAR DIARY or INTELLIGENCE SUMMARY

Army Form C. 2118.

VOL III — 7 Royal Scots Fusiliers

Place	Date	Hour	Summary of Events and Information	Remarks and references to Appendices
HOHENZOLLERN	July 5		Quiet during the day; officers from 7th Bn Leins. one tackd over line at night our trench were reoccupied. 8 1st Lg Glos.Fus. and the bomb & gun positions.	
	6		Battln was relieved by 9th (Cameron) trenches were very wet. Relieved men served in PHILOSOPHE; at LABOURSE Hq was not by the pipe band & marched to BETHUNE; the rest of Battn were billeted in the Palais Festing, the officers in Rue de Lille, & the Fierman.	
Beluine	7		The day was spent in cleaning clothing & equipment. Capt. Garnier, Lt & D.M. Corbetts reported for duty. reported for duty from the 11th Yorks Batt. Lt & D.M. Coberts reported for duty. B Coy., the company for training, instruct. of Hotchkiss rifles. C Coy. parade for fatigue.	
	7		Scott de Jeune Fille, 9-11.30am, Transport, 11.30am-1pm. B Coy 2-4.30pm. Bioneers 1.30pm – 5.30pm.	
	8		D Coy Parade for baths 2 o/c A Gunners' fille 9am-10 noon. B Coy 2-4 pm. Machine Gunners 4pm – 5.30pm. R.E. working parties were found as follows. D Coy Officer, 2 N.C.O's 5 men. B Coy Capt. for the officer, 1 N.C.O & 7 men. C Coy 2 officers 6 N.C.O's & 73 men, the remainder of the	

WAR DIARY
or
INTELLIGENCE SUMMARY.

Army Form C. 2118.

VOL III

(9) Royal Scots Fusiliers

Place	Date	Hour	Summary of Events and Information	Remarks and references to Appendices
BETHUNE	July 8		Batt^n formed up in column on foot. The army Physical drill qualification test at 5.30 p.m. a lecture was given by the Coys officers in the Voices of Instructor when an also attended by few officers at Salty Lebanon on "Employment of graphs; how to read them."	
	9		Parade: Rev. Voltaire Sartey 10.15 a.m. R.C. Bethune Cath^l 10.30 a.m. C of E. Municipal Theatre 10.30 a.m. Holy Communion 7.0 a.m. 58 men.	
BETHUNE	10		R.E. working party 1 off. 3 N.C.O's. Captn Shaw. 3 off. 12 N.C.O's. 150 men. & paraded at Tobacco factory at 4.45 a.m. Remainder of Coy furnished ordinary and mark from the Schools physical exercises, Bombing, Lewis Gun, Sniper etc. No operation instruction.	
	11		An inspection of gas helmets was held by Lieu^t Orr officer Div^nal gas officer RE, pay 2 off, 8 N.C.O's. & 100 men paraded at Tobacco factory at 4.45 p.m. Members of 6th C of B Staff reconnoitred approaches to Hohenzollern trench. Sniper visited by 4/7 R.S.F.	
	12		Nos not specified on our Somme Bombs, in applied exercises, in Tonberg.	

Army Form C. 2118.

WAR DIARY
or
INTELLIGENCE SUMMARY.
(Erase heading not required.)

Vol III 6/7 Royal Scots Fusiliers

Place	Date	Hour	Summary of Events and Information	Remarks and references to Appendices
BETHUNE	July 12		Snipers & observers were trained in the use of telescopic compass, rain gauges & treated telescopes & targets; machine gunner worked under the M.G.O. & information party of 1 officer, 2 N.C.O.'s & 23 men attended a presentation of mineral rocks by the Corps Commander. (Majors M.W Crawford C.E. & major Hislop.)	
	13		Notes were written on the sloping of shelters, front Hautmyon. Party consisting of 1 officer, 4 N.C.O.'s, 16 men went to Sailly-la-Bourse for instruction in firing of rifle grenades. Party consisting of O.C. C Coy. worked over & down the Devonshire Sector Battalion relieved 10th H.L.I. in the trenches. Began left A in the center, C on the right, C Coy in reserve. Dug. Lent forgon into front. at night the enemy raided Brecon Sap. as a result of raid 2 men were missing.	
HULLUCH SECTOR	14		Heavy shelling of border. Enemy unsuccessfully attempted by patrol at night with a view to a raid on the receiving trenches.	
	15		Enemy was quiet. During the evening about 9.45 p.m. a severe enemy of found our front. 2nd Lt. Hutcheson & 2nd Lt. Smith joined a Coy from 11th Yorkshire Bn.	
	16		Plane, went out. Reconnoitering ground with a view to recover. Front & thing over.	
	17			

Army Form C. 2118.

WAR DIARY
or
INTELLIGENCE SUMMARY.
(Erase heading not required.)

Vol III

6/7 Royal Scots Fusiliers

Place	Date	Hour	Summary of Events and Information	Remarks and references to Appendices
HULLOCH SECTOR	July 17		Army Lewis gun School. Saw we had fine light.	
	18.		Batt⁰ was relieved by 11 A. & S. H. in the trenches. Batt⁰ HQ. in early Coln. Decoy in 10 Eleven. A Coy in Curly Coln. B.H.Q. Coy. O.B.S. Batt⁰ warned to be ready. Preparations made by us for a raid, in co-operation with Special Mortars.	
	19.		Raid was made at night and was not a success.	
	20		Royal Scots Rifles took over trenches from Tatanyover. Day was somewhat quiet. Batt⁰ was relieved and moved off. They alive. Thence to Houchin, where they were billeted in camp Proff Harboltum & Mr. Mutrie joined for duty.	Murphy. LENS II.
HOUCHIN	22		Batt⁰ left Houchin at 10.10 a.m. + marched via Bray, Divion Ourton, Dieval, to Bours. A halt was made on the way for dinner, not arrive Divion, and arrived about 4.30 at Bours, where billets were taken up. Many rich some in the adjoining villages J Caucourt of Monneville	
	23		Batt⁰ rested at Bours. Fet. inspected Church parade.	
BOURS	24		Parades. Physical Drill, Squad Drill, Musketry, Manoeuvre for attack, Signalling Observers been leadership & practices men in the screen. Yesterday night with the lamp. 2nd Lieut Laurie reported for duty from hospital.	

Army Form C. 2118.

WAR DIARY
or
INTELLIGENCE SUMMARY.
(Erase heading not required.)

Vol III

6/7 Royal Scots Fusiliers

Place	Date	Hour	Summary of Events and Information	Remarks and references to Appendices
Bours	25		Barracks. C.O. & 2/Lt. Thompson proc. Company Dress Intended Dress Drill & Musketry instruction. March lecture by Bn. Major on Musketry	Shrapnel LENS.11
	26		Bat. marched to MONCHIEAUX, departing from Bours at 8 a.m., arriving at 1 p.m. Bat. was billeted in the village, stayed there overnight.	
	27		Bat. left MONCHIEUX for BONNIERES. Bat. arrived & billeted in the village, stayed overnight	
	28		The Battalion left BONNIERES & arrived at LE MEILLARD. The system followed on the march was raw men transport marching ground intervening. So far no rain up until today. The men marching to LE MEILLARD form their particular Stations do ... by the Company officers.	
LE MEILLARD	29		The Bat. arrived at LE MEILLARD. Parade. Holy Communion 7.30 a.m. R.C. LE MEILLARD Church 11 a.m. Pres. 11.30 a.m. C.E. 9.30 a.m.	
	30		Instruction of rifle by Lawrence Sgt. at 9 a.m. Instruction of all men in use of Lewis gun bomb, N.C.O.s in village fighting	
	31		Bat. paraded at 4.30 a.m. & left for VIGNACOURT, where they arrived about 9.45 a.m. The whole brigade was billeted in the	

Army Form C. 2118.

WAR DIARY
or
INTELLIGENCE SUMMARY.

Vol III of Royal Scots Fusiliers

(Erase heading not required.)

Place	Date	Hour	Summary of Events and Information	Remarks and references to Appendices
	31		village. At 6 p.m. parades of N.C.O's were company arrangement were held in the harbour of instructing in village fighting	

1.8.16

L.I. Gordon Lieut. Col.
Commanding 7th Battn Royal Scots Fusiliers.

45th Brigade.
15th Division.

6/7th BATTALION

ROYAL SCOTS FUSILIERS

AUGUST 1 9 1 6

Instructions regarding War Diaries and Intelligence Summaries are contained in F.S. Regs., Part II. and the Staff Manual respectively. Title pages will be prepared in manuscript.

INTELLIGENCE SUMMARY
August 1916
(Erase heading not required.)

Vol IV 6/7 (R) Batt. Royal Scots

Place	Date	Hour	Summary of Events and Information	Remarks and references to Appendices
	August			Insertions
VIGNACOURT	1		Assault course was used by all companies from 7am till 10.30am. Harness-makers Company arrangements in July event draft, five center and organisation - transport passed for special instructors. Altought the machine gun sector-paraded reserved out night-manoeuvres. The signallers responded to trump-work.	
	2		Manoeuvres, Coy. Drill. Instructions on usage of lifting-strong village fighting within formations, respective position & tactical uses. Draft of 30 arrived Note Battalion paraded this morning to proceed to MIRVAUX.	AMIENS 17
	3		So over the heat of the day, a start was made at 4.45 A.M. to restrain arriving at MIRVAUX, ahead MOLLIENS in BOIS, about 8.30am, men being fallen out.	
MIRVAUX	4		This morning the Battalion proceeded to BRESLE, leaving at 3.45am. & arriving at 8.30am. The Battalion again marched well, no one falling out.	17
BRESLE	5		OC Coys, L.G.O. and Signal Officer proceeded to trenches on tour of inspection, but did not enable to push further than Corbie-Liaison on account of bombardment. Coy. drill.	

INTELLIGENCE SUMMARY.

VOL. IV 6/7 Royal Scots Fusiliers

Instructions regarding War Diaries and Intelligence Summaries are contained in F.S. Regs., Part II and the Staff Manual respectively. Title pages will be prepared in manuscript.

(Erase heading not required.)

Place	Date	Hour	Summary of Events and Information	Remarks and references to Appendices
BRESLE	August 6		Divine Service. Joint meeting with 13th Royal Scots for Presbyterian Parade at 11 A.M. Voluntary Service in the evening at 6 P.M. Church of England Service at 10 A.M. Between the hours of 6 A.M. & 7 A.M. this area occupied by the Battn. was thoroughly cleaned. Draft of 83 Other Ranks arrived from 11th Entrenching Battn. Captain J. Smith (9th Green Howards [Pioneer]) joined for duty as 2nd in Command. OC Coys, LO visited the trenches. Formations in attack practised by whole Battn. between 10 A.M. and 12 noon.	
"	7			
TRENCHES	8		Marched from BRESLE via ALBERT & FRICOURT [F. Trenches relieving 8th YORKS, in left sector of Divisional front. From occupied from S.10.2.8. + X.5.4.2.] A coy on Right C in centre D on left. B in support.	MAP Reference ALBERT 1/40000
PEAK WOOD South CONTALMAISON	9		Relieved by 11th A+S.H. - heavily shelled whilst relieving - good few casualties resulting. Marched & Brigade Reserve in PEAK WOOD S of CONTALMAISON. Quiet day.	
"	10		Shelled occasionally resulting in a few casualties. Working party of 4 officers and 200 men for SAP digging in BUTTERWORTH TRENCH (front line).	
"	11		Again shelling - working party of 1 NCO & 40 men carrying ammunition to front line. About 12 midnight 4 German Prisoners (1 an NCO) brought in. Captured by Lt. Gault whilst on patrol. He entered German front line trench - Lt. Gault wounded	176+

INTELLIGENCE SUMMARY.

(Erase heading not required.)

Instructions regarding War Diaries and Intelligence Summaries are contained in F.S. Regs., Part II. and the Staff Manual respectively. Title pages will be prepared in manuscript.

Vol. IV 6/7 Royal Scots Fusiliers

1916

Place	Date	Hour	Summary of Events and Information	Remarks and references to Appendices
TRENCHES	August 12	—	Moved up into Front & Support Line. B coy leading at 5PM. Distribution: A coy right, C coy in Centre, B coy on left. D coy in SUPPORT. A.Coy & B Coys going over the open in two waves attacked the German front line trench (known as SWITCH LINE) at 10.32 P.M. 6th Camerons on our immediate left doing likewise. Also 4th & 9th G.B. on our right. At 11.10 PM. SWITCH LINE occupied and consolidation commenced. 11.45PM — German prisoners of 139th Regt. brought in. 4th G.B. were not successful and a defensive flank was formed on our Right along CLOSTER SAP. By 7AM our original front line was connected with our new line by a communication trench at that time 3' deep — the deepening was continued. Casualties 12 Officers and other ranks (approx). Officers 2/Lt Warner (Killed) 2/Lt Kerr (Killed) 2/Lt Jones 2/Lt Austin, 2/Lt Blackstone, 2/Lt Mackie, 2/Lt Strang, Lt. Dingwall and 2/Lt Hutchison Wounded. Missing Capt Fowler, 2/Lt Nicolson and 2/Lt Carr. Remainder of day quiet. Targets presented in shell holes which Machine guns took advantage of. Shelling of rear front line & CLOSTER ALLEY faint. heavy at night. Relieved about 5AM by 8/10th Gordons. Marched to Caml (E8a) where bivouacked	1774
	13			
ALBERT	14		Draft of 119 ORanks joined & were posted to 16 Coys.	Reference ALBERT 1/40,000

INTELLIGENCE SUMMARY

1916 — VOL. IV — 6/7 Royal Scots Fusiliers

(Erase heading not required.)

Place	Date	Hour	Summary of Events and Information	Remarks and references to Appendices
ALBERT at E8a Reference MAP ALBERT 1/40000	August 15		Thorough inspection of all equipment & arms — particular attention being paid to Smoke helmets and Iron Rations. Batteries took place in the new Arena. Boots & small kit issued. 2nd Lt. Strang Hutcheson Bothwell died of wounds 13=7=16	Reference ALBERT 1/40000
	16		Bombing squads reorganized. Company work included Extended order drill from order picking up of targets, physical drill etc. 5 extra men in any attached to Machine Gunners for training purposes whilst the Battn was out. Circulars practice flag work & aeroplane screen took 1 Officer and 50 O.Ranks whole at E8d Central at 8am. Note published in Battn order of 12/13th inst.	
	17		Parades under Coy arrangements. Particular attention paid to training of section leaders & NCO's in word of command and control for extra etc. Circulars under L.G.O. Schemes under 1L.Q.M. Working Party. 3 Officers 200 O.Ranks reported at FIELD guides this from 7th H.A.G. About 4pm and were received from Bde to "STAND TO" & send Liaison Officer to BHQ. 2/L. Scott went. About 4.45 pm Bde asked when we would be ready to move.	1284

INTELLIGENCE SUMMARY. VOL IV 6/7 RSF

Instructions regarding War Diaries and Intelligence Summaries are contained in F. S. Regs., Part II and the Staff Manual respectively. Title pages will be prepared in manuscript.

(Erase heading not required.)

Place	Date	Hour	Summary of Events and Information	Remarks and references to Appendices
ALBERT (E8a)	August 17		Reported ready to move 5.40 P.M. At 5.50 PM 2/L Scott returned stating we were to "STAND DOWN" but be prepared to move on half an hours notice — At 7.35 PM "STAND TO" again ordered from Bde. About 8.45 PM wire from Bde to "STAND DOWN". Draft of 17 arrived & posted to Coys. Inspection of GAS HELMETS and BOX RESPIRATORS by Divisional Gas Officer. A coy 9.30am B coy 10.30am C coy 11.15am D coy 12.15 PM. M.O. renewed with their Coys for this inspection. Working party of 1 Officer and 50 O. Ranks	
"	18		reporting at E9d Central at 6 a.m. Marched from E8a to trenches A coy, leading at 5.45am. Relieved 10/11th A.&.S.I in SUPPORT being situated around SHELTER WOOD, with Batn HQ in SHELTER WOOD (X22c4.1) Working party of 2 Officers and 100 men.	By ALBERT /wow By Trenches Shell S70SE
Trenches	19		All quiet. 4 working parties of 1 Officer and 30 men at intervals throughout the day — our artillery active between 6PM and 7PM.	
"	20			
"	21		Relieved 11th A.&.S.H. in Front Line having 1st Devs on our RIGHT and HH & Bde Y.13th RS on our left. Disposition A coy on right, B coy in centre, "C" coy on left, D coy in SUPPORT. Much work done in consolidating line — night fairly quiet	17/7

INTELLIGENCE SUMMARY.

AUGUST 1916 VOL IV 6/7 Royal Scots Fusiliers

Place	Date	Hour	Summary of Events and Information	Remarks and references to Appendices
Trenches	1916 Aug. 21		Except for intermittent shelling of Lancs SAP. A Patrol of Lewis gun team with gun and 6 o'clock went out about 80 yds. to its East of extent Right. Established a post there which was eventually linked up with main front line, thus adding an additional 80 yds to our front line. Came in. Salvage collected and taken to Bde dump.	
"	22		Day normal took 100% of anti-aircraft (machine?) trenches cleared of Theads strengthened. "A" Coy on night relieved by D coy from SUPPORT. Large working parties on at night from A&SH and R.S. B&C companies commenced 6 strong points out in front of FRONT LINE - B coy doing 3 & C coy 3. B coy completed theirs linking up with FRONT LINE. LEWIS GUN placed in No 1 & No 3. C coy having further to go out and more to do did not complete but made substantial progress. LANCS SAP again shelled during the night.	187
"	23		Relieved by 6th Camerons, relief commencing about 7.30am. B interior went with SUPPORT 2 coy in O.G.1 2 in O.G.2. Batn HQ VILLA WOOD. Night quiet	
"	24		Relieved by 11th A&SH, & moved to Reserve. Relief over by 9AM.	

INTELLIGENCE SUMMARY.

VOL IV 6/7 Royal Scots Fusiliers

August 1916

Place	Date	Hour	Summary of Events and Information	Remarks and references to Appendices
Trenches	August 1916 24		Batn. HQ in SHELTER WOOD (X.22.c.4.). 2 Coys in SHELTER WOOD and 2 in CUTTING. Gas Shells put over in neighbourhood of VILLA WOOD and CUTTING about 9.15 PM. – Helmets put on about 9.30 PM – All Clear sounded 12 midnight.	Ref. t/Nat. France Chart 57DSE
	25		No change in Dispositions. Working parties 3 parties of 1 NCO & 10 men throughout the day. 2 parties of 1 Officer & 50 ORanks at 7.30 P.M. Coys worked by day in cleaning out trenches and general sanitation of area – 2 incinerators built (2 incinerators 10' x 2' x 10'). No 16986 Sgt Headley arrived from England (9th RSF) and posted to "D" Coy. Enemy shelled area NE of SHELTER WOOD between 11.45 am & 12.30 pm – 4 Casualties. Working party of 75 mm exclusive of officers & NCOs at junction of PEARL ALLEY & THE CUTTING.	
	26			
	27		At 2 am working party of 2 officers & 75 ORanks left for front line trenches – returned about 8.30 am. Warning order received that our troops probably relieve Robin Frontline tomorrow	1 M +

INTELLIGENCE SUMMARY.

Vol IV 6/7 Royal Scots Fusiliers

(Erase heading not required.)

Instructions regarding War Diaries and Intelligence Summaries are contained in F. S. Regs., Part II. and the Staff Manual respectively. Title pages will be prepared in manuscript.

August 1916

Place	Date	Hour	Summary of Events and Information	Remarks and references to Appendices
Trenches	Aug 1916 27		Draft of 48 Officers and 2/Lieut James Thomson Robertson, 2/Lieut John Henry Stark & 2/Lieut Matthew Wallace today joined for duty and were posted to companies.	
"	28		Moved up into Support, relieving 11th A&SH. Relief complete about 2.15P.M. Batt. HQ in VILLA WOOD. Received warning that we would probably relieve 13 R.S. in front line tomorrow – also orders bombs would be discharged at 2 PM on 29th and again at 10am & 30th.	
"	29		Moved up and relieved 13th R.S. in front line – relief was by 10.15am. Batt. HQ in O.C.I. about 200 yds. E. of PEARL ALLEY. Smoke bombs discharged. Attack working party at front 600 yds NE. of S2 a 9.1. about 12.45P.M. Artillery informed who fired on party – result not known. Work was resumed about 6PM that H Strong points 400 yds apart, were to constructed E of front right of SWITCH TRENCH. Work commenced at 10PM. D Coy 11th A & S.H. supplying covering party – from N & S. 9th Gordons working party on sinking up S2 d 4.5 and S2 d 4.7. (French front line with INTERMEDIATE TRENCH) & B Coy supplied covering party. Barrage by enemy on our front & support lines between 11.15PM & 12 midnight – again 1.30am – 1.30am.	Py 15" Div Sig 18[?] Py 15" Div Sig Py 15" Div Trench Mort

1577 Wt W10791/1773 500,000 1/15 D. D. & L. A.D.S.S./Forms/C. 2118.

INTELLIGENCE SUMMARY. Vol IV 6/7 (W)Bn Royal Scots Fusiliers

August 1916

(Erase heading not required.)

Place	Date	Hour	Summary of Events and Information	Remarks and references to Appendices
Trenches	Aug. 30		By daylight the new work was overnight was as follows:- From the E end of SWITCH LINE an additional 90 yards of trench was dug with 2 strong points constructed therein. 2 Lewis guns in one strong point and 1 in the other. By 5am trench work on our right about 150 yards East renewed (unremoved) during night a party of officers & any obtainable men to do. A party from A Coy (Gordons) (Thorpe's) linked up the INTERMEDIATE between points S2 d.4.5 and S2 d.4.7. Ref. Point S86 5.8 and vicinity was shelled intermittently all day, shrapnel and 5.9s. About 1.30 PM B Coy (Capt Watson) whose company dug the strong points referred to above reports that a German leading corresponding rank (our sergeant) had announced and states that the officer had sent him over to state they accepted by called and proposed arrangements under which they would surrender unconditionally themselves at about 6PM. The first of them came out about 3PM and coming over in three's and four's all afternoon by 7PM the neighbouring trench (INTERMEDIATE) was entirely evacuated & prisoners in our hands. 107 Germans gave themselves up to us and 4 officers, 2 Warrant officers & 13 men gave themselves up to 46th Bde on our right. During evening work commenced detail of which will be in tomorrows report. Wh to J 12 midnight – night normal. Watson wounded slightly. Shrapnel.	By mch. 1500 Trench Mch. 183+

1577 Wt.W10791/1773 500,000 1/15 D.D.&L. A.D.S.S./Forms/C. 2118.

INTELLIGENCE SUMMARY.

Vol IV 6/7 (S)Ra Royal Scots Fusiliers

Place	Date	Hour	Summary of Events and Information	Remarks and references to Appendices
In Trenches	August 31		Night fairly quiet. Enemy barrage along road in X12d. An additional 100 yards along at E end of SANDERSON TRENCH known as H6. Bell boundary — roughly along 50 yard left & completely lunk up to the new front line. Gordon trench between S2d 4.5 and S2d 4.7 deepened from 2' to 4½'-5'. This is now a fairly good communication trench to new front line (MANSEA TRENCH). Relieved by 6th Cameron Highlanders and 11th A&SH. 6th Camerons relieved our two right coys and also placed 3 platoons in Support with 3 coys. 11th A&SH relieved our two left coys. Batt. moved into SHELTER WOOD. Relief complete 12.30PM. Batt. HQ in SHELTER WOOD. Men rested — no working party. At 9.25PM it was reported by oc coy in CUTTING that enemy were shelling that place with TEAR Shells. 1-9-16 A. S. Tralor Lieut Col 6/7th (SERVICE) BATTn. ROYAL SCOTS FUSILIERS.	ref 15th November

6/7TH (S.) BATTN,
The Royal Scots Fus.

September, 1916

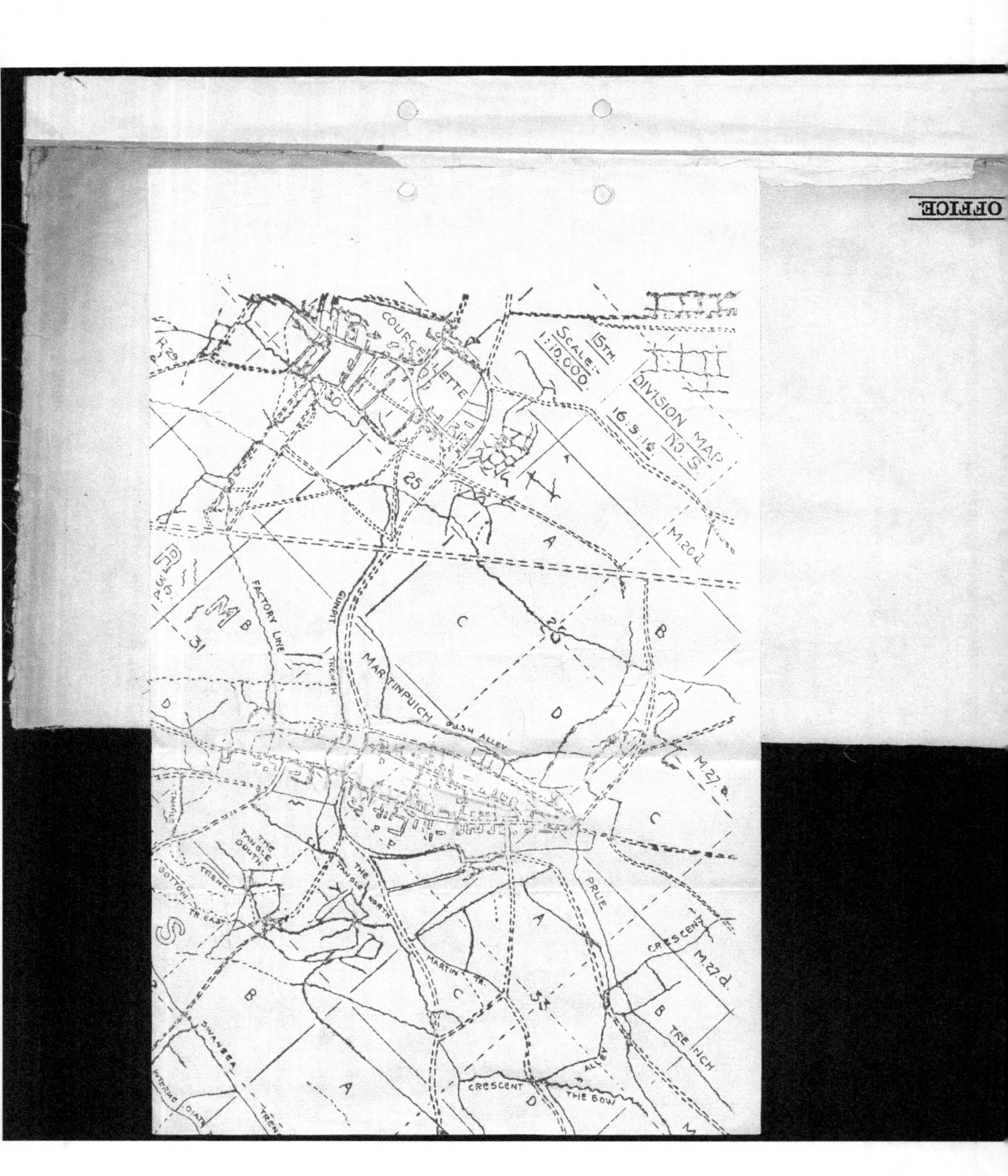

WAR DIARY

Army Form C. 2118.

1/7 (Ser) Bn. Royal Scots Fusiliers

INTELLIGENCE SUMMARY. Vol. V September 1916

Place	Date	Hour	Summary of Events and Information	Remarks and references to Appendices
Trenches	Sept. 1		Batn. disposition. 3 companies around SHELTER WOOD, 1 company in the CUTTING. Batn. HQ. Shelter Wood (X22.c.4.1). Day quiet. Working parties 1 officer & 50 o'Ranks at 1.45PM guides from 9th R.E. 1 officer 50 o'Ranks at 2.15PM guides from 9th R.E. parties on their way up to trenches carried up from MIDDLE WOOD 20 Boxes S.A.A. & New bomb store in SCOTCH ALLEY, 2nd party carried up from same place 50 boxes Mills Bombs to same store.	Ref to MAP. FRANCE Sheet 57d SE
	2		About 4.15AM enemy shelled the CUTTING with S.9's and Shrapnel. 2/Lieut. G.H. Stubbs wounded. Working parties 1 officer & 35 o'Ranks paraded at junction of PEARL ALLEY & THE CUTTING at 2PM - Guide from 9th R.E. 1 officer & 35 o'Ranks at Batt. HQ at 2.15PM. Guide from 9th R.E. Day quiet. Received warning of probable relief of 11th A & S.H. by us on 3rd inst. Attack on HIGH WOOD by 1st Bde, estimated to take place on 3rd. Zero hour 12 noon.	167
	3		Relieved 11th A & S.H. in left of Bde front. 1st Coy. moved off 7.50AM. Batn. Right Road running N & S. - S2d. Batn. left NEWCH ALLEY.	Ref 15 Div Trench MAP. E.M.J.

Army Form C. 2118.

WAR DIARY or INTELLIGENCE SUMMARY.

Vol V. 6/7 (At) Bn Royal Scots Fusiliers

(Erase heading not required.)

Instructions regarding War Diaries and Intelligence Summaries are contained in F. S. Regs., Part II. and the Staff Manual respectively. Title pages will be prepared in manuscript.

September 1916.

Place	Date	Hour	Summary of Events and Information	Remarks and references to Appendices
Trenches	Sept 3		Relief complete by 10.30 a.m. Situation D Coy on right, A Coy on left, C Coy in SUPPORT occupying ROYLE TRENCH and 1 Platoon in ROYLE REDOUBT. B Coy in Reserve in OG1 with 1 Platoon in PIONEER ALLEY. Heavy bombardment on both sides about 12 noon, on our extreme right about HIGH WOOD. Enemy shelled SANDERSON TRENCH at that time with field guns	
ALBERT	4		Relieved by 2nd Northumberland Fusiliers. Guides met Reliefs at the CUTTING at 4 a.m. Relief over 8.30 a.m. Batn breakfasts at FRICOURT CIRCUS and marched by Platoons at 100 yards distance to outskirts of ALBERT. Carried for remainder of day men cleaning themselves as far as possible	N7+ SB
LAVIEVILLE	5		Marched off at 6 a.m. to LAVIEVILLE. Bivouacked on ground adjacent the Village. Bde HQ in the Village. Day spent in cleaning up & Coy inspections as to Kit etc.	
	6		Lists of Coy deficiencies collected — Parties of Boots leaving turns etc. All NCOs of the Battn paraded at 2 PM under RSM & Bros	2.1.8.J.

WAR DIARY
INTELLIGENCE SUMMARY

Army Form C. 2118.

VOL V 6/7 Royal Scots Fusiliers

September 1916

Place	Date	Hour	Summary of Events and Information	Remarks and references to Appendices
LAVIEVILLE	6		Lecture given by the latter on "Duties of NCO's". FOEDEN Pamphlet issued	
	7		Routine under Coy arrangements. Work included close order drill, handling of arms and indication of targets. Rifle range Coy to Coy used by Coys. B Coy 9am, C Coy 10am, A Coy 11am, D Coy 12 noon. FOEDEN Disinfector used by A Coy at 9AM. Lewis Gun Sgts and non 1 or 2 of each team paraded under L.E.O. Draft of 7/10 Royal Scots who joined Bath. on 12/8/16, paraded for duties under R.S.M. at 2 PM. All drafts who joined since 1st May 1916 examined by M.O. as to Inoculation.	
	8		Routine as for previous day with the 7/10th Royal Scot draft again drilled by RSM. 6 Officers joined for duty. Lieuts. James McLeish Gray Alexander Massie James Neil McEwan Julian Hart Winsor Rowan Nimmo and Frederick James Worsley Williams.	
	9		Working party 7AM. 1 officer & 50 O Ranks working on new flying ground in Dib. Batn. paraded as strong as possible and practised the attack. Batch drill. Draft 6 O Ranks received & posted to Coys?	Reference Mao AM15/15 D.D.J.

WAR DIARY
INTELLIGENCE SUMMARY

Army Form C. 2118.

Vol V C/7 Royal Scots Fusiliers

September 1916

Place	Date	Hour	Summary of Events and Information	Remarks and references to Appendices
LAVIEVILLE 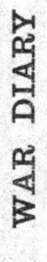	Sept 10		Divine Service. Church of England Service at 9.10am. Roman Catholic Service in LAVIEVILLE CHURCH at 10am. Presbyterian service at 10am. Lieut Col E.I.D Gordon (Commanding Officer) to Hospital. Went thro' Water reported from Hospital. Major J. Smith assumed Temporary Command.	
"	11		Practice Brigade attack on ground W. of LAVIEVILLE. Adjutant with 8 orderlies and 8 signallers with flags reported to Bde Major at 8.15am. Ground allotted to Battn. marked out. Battn. paraded on Battn. parade ground at 9am and proceeded to above ground about 9.15am. Battn. occupied defensive lines having A coy in 1st line, B coy with 3 Platoons in the 2nd line and 1 Platoon in a redoubt line slightly to left rear. C & D coys of Battn. all seen on final objective in the rear. The attack was carried out by 11th A & SH and 13th RS with 6th Cameron H. in support and was done twice. Armourer Sgt. inspected all rifles of the Battn. in the afternoon - 20 requiring repair and were replaced. Evening spent in cleaning up Camp. Elevation orders received from Bde for move on following day. M/r 9b Cooper returned from a training course & resumed duty with "D" coy. E.V.S.T.	

WAR DIARY or INTELLIGENCE SUMMARY.

Army Form C. 2118.

Vol V 6/7 Royal Scots Fusiliers September 1916

Place	Date	Hour	Summary of Events and Information	Remarks and references to Appendices
X.26.d.	Sept. 12		Batn. paraded at 6am and marched to Reserve location in X.26.d. Route MILLENCOURT - Road junction D.6.b - ALBERT - BECOURT. Took over trenches & 6 tents from 10th Scottish Rifles. Conference of Commanding officers at Bde. HQ (W.29.d) at 4PM. Operation orders received for move next day at MESNICOURT. Draft of 191 ORs + 2Lts. Generally in support.	Reference MAP ALBERT 1/40,000
Trenches	13		Moved off at 3AM to relieve 7th Cameron Highlanders in RIGHT Section of Div. Front. Relief complete by 7.10AM. Disposition B coy on right, A coy on left, D coy in SUPPORT, C coy in Reserve. Batn HQ X.12.c.4.6. Night quiet. "Strafe" by our own Artillery - SANDERSON TRENCH for a distance of 200 yards from junction of H.L.I. Trench deepened 2' - 6 new firesteps made. EGG TRENCH 150 yards on new front lines & SANDERSON TRENCH proceeding. Information deepened 1'. - Trench improved generally. HAM TRENCH defended to an average depth of 4'6". Communication trench between EGG TR & HAM TR. dug down to an average depth of 5'6". Eastern end of EGG TR continued on & linked up with SANDERSON to depth 4½'. Relieved by 11th A & SH on our Right & 13th R.Scots on our left. 6th Camerons moved into SUPPORT. Disposition at 3AM. 2 Coys (B & A) in " C	At FRANCE 57.d.S.E. Reference 1:10,000 TRENCH MAP
	14			
	15			

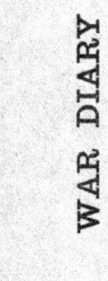

WAR DIARY or INTELLIGENCE SUMMARY.

Army Form C. 2118.

Vol V 6/7 Royal Scots Fusiliers
Sept 1916

Place	Date	Hour	Summary of Events and Information	Remarks and references to Appendices
Trenches	Sept 15		WELCH ALLEY (2 coys (B & D) in KOYLI TRENCH. Batn HQ in O.G.1.) All quiet & arrangements in hand for assault on enemy lines in accordance with Brigade instructions. Steady bombardment by our Artillery. Zero hour 6.20a.m. At Zero Companies moved into following positions B coy in Post TRENCH with left resting on road boundary (see Appendix 1) C coy in SANDERSON TRENCH with left on road boundary. A coy LANCS TRENCH between HLI TRENCH and road and D coy 'Matoon' in LANCS TR. to be used for conducting prisoners from there to MIDDLE WOOD. The other 3 Platoons were used for carrying purposes. 1 Platoon under 2/Lt 2nd Booker to Right dump (4 oaks of SANDERSON TR) all attendie 1 and Matoon under 2/Lt R.a. Clark to Left dump. (see Att) These Platoons were to carry forward to new position SAA Bombs Rations Water etc. 1 Platoon under an officer carried from Bole Bank store in WELCH ALLEY to the forward dumps. At 8.10 am a message was received from HQ A.P Kiel (OC A coy) that dispositions were as follows:-	APPENDIX 1.

WAR DIARY
or
INTELLIGENCE SUMMARY

Army Form C. 2118.

Vol V

6/7 Royal Scots Fusiliers

Sept 1916

Place	Date	Hour	Summary of Events and Information	Remarks and references to Appendices
Trenches	Sept 15		B Coy EGG TRENCH, "C" Coy Post TRENCH, "A" Coy SANDERSON TR (west of WELCH ALLEY) D Coy LANCS TR (east). Platoon 3 Platoons carrying). At 9.30am message was received from Capt Gardner "B Coy" that all was quite right — that Div (50th) on our Right were well advanced and likewise 2nd Canadian Div on our Left, up to this line (9.30am) 3 officers and about 200 German prisoners had passed our HQ. 9.55am — Order sent to send up 2 Platoons to HAM TRENCH to replace 2 Platoons of Camerons gone forward — this order sent by "B Coy" 10am for Confidence. Personal effort of a prisoner killed. 10.40am word received from Capt Gardner that 2 Platoons of this coy, are in position in HAM TRENCH in hand rendered by 6th Camerons. At 2.20 PM, orders were received from Bde and added to by telephone conversation to the effect that the 50th Div on our right were now in PRUE TRENCH (NE corner of MARTINPUICH) and 2nd Canadian Div on our Left in SUNKEN RD just NE of GUN TRENCH. The 15th Div. at 3PM will attack POSH ALLEY and thus link	Appendix II Appendix MAP P.S.B.

WAR DIARY or INTELLIGENCE SUMMARY

Army Form C. 2118.

Vol V 6/7 (Sco) Royal Scots Fusiliers

Sept 1916

Place	Date	Hour	Summary of Events and Information	Remarks and references to Appendices
TRENCHES	Sept 15		up till now 2 Divisions & at same time envelope & take MARTINPUICH. The H5th QHB took the Right half attack, the 46th QHB the Left. At 3PM, O.C. Camerons advanced from TANGLE TRENCH and will be assisted by 2 Platoons B Coy RSF. The latter will report to senior Cameron officer by 3PM – these Platoons are to clear dug-outs & cellars in MARTINPUICH and to act as escorts to prisoners. After 6th Camerons have moved to TANGLE TR. remaining 2 Platoons of B Coy under Capt Gardiner and the whole of C Coy under 2/Lt Wright move forward & occupy TANGLE TR. At same time 2 Lt A Coy (2/Lt Akins) will move forward & occupy HAM TRENCH and also OC D Coy (2/Lt Lee) will move into HAM TRENCH also. Word has just been received (5 PM) from Capt Gardiner that the two platoons detailed did not moved with 6th Camerons – OC of Cameron party considered his party strong enough for work in hand. Disposition therefore was B & C Coys in TANGLE TR and A & D Coys in HAM TRENCH. There was heavy intermittent shelling of the TANGLE TR., with occasional bursts on HAM TR.	
	16		Early in the morning Capt Gardiner with about 2 Platoons from TANGLE Tr.	E.C.S.F.

WAR DIARY
or
INTELLIGENCE SUMMARY

Army Form C. 2118.

Vol V C/7 Royal Scots Fusiliers
Sept 1916

Place	Date	Hour	Summary of Events and Information	Remarks and references to Appendices
Trenches	Sept 16		1/6 HAM TR. Disposition now C coy & ½ B coy in TANGLE. A coy & ½ B in HAM TR. D coy carrying — word received from Bde that as soon as our rations are up A B C & D coys move forward to front line (POSH ALLEY) and relieve 6th Cameron Highlanders. 2/Lieut (J.W.) James Thomson Hodierson and Lieut Mathew Wallace wounded — 2/Lieut Jas Laurie (A.C.O.) to hospital (sick) arrival of 2/Lt. 9/B Scott and 2/Lt. Shanks as Reinforcement each. HERICOURT. Relief of 6th Cameron Highlanders commenced about 5PM. Complete 9.30PM. Disposition FRONTLINE POSH ALLEY "C" coy on right occupying CUTTING. B coy in centre "A" coy on left. D coy in SUPPORT in cellars in MARTINPUICH. Night quiet. About 9.30PM word was received from Bde that much movement had been seen in the afternoon in & around LESARS. A captured prisoner states that a counter attack on MARTINPUICH was contemplated and would be about 3AM. and was sent the coys to this effect & all precautions taken. Right flank was particularly guarded.	Appendix III
	17		Night normal all the shelling practically going into MARTINPUICH	Appx?

WAR DIARY
INTELLIGENCE SUMMARY.

Army Form C. 2118.

Vol V 6/7 Royal Scots Fusiliers.

Places	Date	Hour	Summary of Events and Information	Remarks and references to Appendices
Trenches	Sept 16		About 9am report was received from OC "A" Coy, stating that he had gone forward from his left about 300 yards to the crest of the rise and found what took to be a German trench about 200-250 yards away - a little movement could be seen there. Two sniper holes were also found which were unoccupied. "C" Right coy reported about same time that the dispositions was as follows:- 2 Platoons CUTTING and 2 Platoons in forward trench. The CUTTING being found too wide & a prominent mark, a trench was jumped 30 yds forward & dug & linked up with B Coy. This trench was 5' feet and connected by C.T. to CUTTING. Two Lewis guns on it & on Stokes Mortar. The latty fires half right & commanded LE SARS ROAD. Word was received from Bde that our extreme right rested near the junction of MARTIN ALLEY with PRUE TRENCH (?) M'Hodge was informed by an Artillery officer who had been observing that a battery of about 8 guns was lying out about 100 yds in front his extreme right - H Elwards (engaged?) and 1 wounded were taken - also the guns - these certainly were the property of the Artillery officer G.O.C.	

WAR DIARY
INTELLIGENCE SUMMARY.

Vol V 6/7 Royal Scots Fusiliers

Sept 1916

Army Form C. 2118.

Place	Date	Hour	Summary of Events and Information	Remarks and references to Appendices
MARTIN PUICH	Sept 19		were the who first it was to discover them. Word was received from Bde that trenches in & around the WINDMILL (N of the CUTTING) was unoccupied according to report & that we were to push forward claims patrols & of this was so occupy them. Capt Gardner sent up an old C Trench from Centre of PUSH ALLEY & 7/N Stops sent several patrols out towards WINDMILL. This they reached & occupied but enemy must have observed them as they opened a heavy fire on this part. One machine Gun of the 45th M.G. Coy received a direct hit and two men buried & killed. A gunpit close by was set on fire and this caused the forward parties to retire to their original position. Capt Gardner however established a bombing post in one of his advanced the enemy to be at about 15 yards away. Orders received for relief by 8th Seaforths. Guides to be at the junction of WELCH ALLEY & SANDERSON TRENCH at 7 PM. A from C Coy & from "A" Coy - 2 Coys Seaforths took over our line. D Coy moved from Cellars in MARTIN PUICH at 8 PM. On relief A C & D Coys	E.O.J.

WAR DIARY
INTELLIGENCE SUMMARY

Army Form C. 2118.

Vol V 6/7 (Royal Scots Fusiliers)

Sept 1916.

Place	Date	Hour	Summary of Events and Information	Remarks and references to Appendices
Trenches	Sept 17		Occupied LANCS TRENCH with B Coy in 6th AVENUE Bath Hd remained this same (KOYLI TRENCH). Cooks were in MIDDLE WOOD and had hot tea ready for the men when they came out. Also 9 rations were dealt out immediately, 9 men given a meal. Night quiet.	
	18		Warning received from Bde that we were being relieved by 68th Infantry Bde today — guides (1 per platoon) to be at CONTALMAISON X road to TRAKE WOOD at 12.30 P.M. — Advance party would proceed at 10 a.m. to MILLENCOURT and report to Town Major there for billets & area. — Lent pph Left and was to collect guides to collect 911 dgts at ALBERT. Batn was relieved by 11th Northumberland Fusiliers and was completed 2.30 P.M. On relief coys moved by platoons at 200 yards interval E of ALBERT to bwk in MILLENCOURT. Route PEARL ALLEY FRICOURT man ALBERT ROAD, ALBERT ESC MILLENCOURT. Cooks came cutting & collected dinner & tea was got ready for men on arrival in billets. Batn was in billets by 6.30 P.M. — Adv billek Bde HQ at 10 a.m. being the 6/7 R. Scots Fus in reserve	
MILLENCOURT BAIZIEUX WOOD	19		purchased for men's tea — Batn paraded on road outside Bde HQ at 10.20 am and marched	

WAR DIARY
or
INTELLIGENCE SUMMARY. Vol V 6/7 Royal Scots Fusiliers

Army Form C. 2118.

Sept. 1916

Place	Date	Hour	Summary of Events and Information	Remarks and references to Appendices
BAIZIEUX WOOD.	19		Off at 10.30am for BAIZIEUX WOOD — Route Starting Point MILLENCOURT Reference	ALBERT 1/40,000
			LAVIEVILLE ROAD D5a3.8. LAVIEVILLE — BRESLE ROAD Junction D9c4.3	
			Arrived BAIZIEUX WOOD 12.15PM by found my Cookers/Limbers over the	
			Cooking Ground till 3 PM — 6th W.I.CK (Kinross) moved our ten. —	
			2/Lieut Jas B Scott taken on the strength as from 15th Sept 1916.	
	20		Lieut Col E.I.D. Gordon returned from Hospital	
			Corps spent the forenoon in having a thorough cleaning of all Clothes	
			Equipment etc. Coy Commanders held an inspection. Fee that this was	
			so. Deficiencies taken and return rendered to Qmaster. Draft of	
			5 ORanks received 4/5th Inf Bde memo C.154 was read to all ranks	
			on parade "Following from 15th Div. begins Commander in Chief has	
			received the following telegram from His Majesty the King and Requests	
			I congratulate you and my brave troops on the brilliant success	
			just achieved and have no doubt that complete victory will	
			ultimately crown our efforts and the splendid result of the fighting	
			yesterday confirmed this views. AAA George R.I. AAA Ends.	

Army Form C. 2118.

WAR DIARY
or
INTELLIGENCE SUMMARY.

Vol V 9/7 Royal Scots Fusiliers

Sept. 1916

(Erase heading not required.)

Instructions regarding War Diaries and Intelligence Summaries are contained in F.S. Regs., Part II. and the Staff Manual respectively. Title pages will be prepared in manuscript.

Place	Date	Hour	Summary of Events and Information	Remarks and references to Appendices
BAZIEUX WOOD	21		Parade 9AM – 12.30PM. Routine to include Coy drill Nature & Squad drill Marching, Arms, Physical Exercise – Subordinate commanders exercised as far as possible. Signallers & Lewis Gunners under their respective Commanders. Then 2PM – 3PM Short route march by coys. East of Gardine. Was admitted to Hospital (sick).	
"	22		9AM – 12.30PM – Forenoon was spent by Companies in thoroughly cleaning Equipment and Clothes – the former was washed and cleaned, boots and oil and a dubbin applied. 10AM – Inspection of all subaltern officers on Inch Marching Order by Brigadier. 2PM – 3PM – Route March by Companies. Roll of B reported and taken on strength.	
"	23		9AM All officers & Brigadiers inspection of previous day inspected by Major Smith. 9.30 AM. Inspection by OC Coys of the Coys, dress drill marching order. Parade thereafter till 12.30PM. included range (OSCOy 8 and C5 C7.5) Physical exercises Coy drill 2PM – 3PM – Bombing (all Coys).	France Sheet 62
–	24		Divine Service. Presbyterian 10AM in field next to Transport. Church of England at 9.30 AM. Church service thereafter. Roman Catholic	

WAR DIARY
INTELLIGENCE SUMMARY.

VOL V C/7 Royal Scots Fusiliers

Title pages Sept 1916

Place	Date	Hour	Summary of Events and Information	Remarks
BAIZIEUX WOOD	24		10am in the Village.	
"	25		9AM – 10AM All coys Coy drill. 10am – 11am All coys Bombing. 11am Inspection by Brigadier. Bat. Major inspected rifles & small kit. Inspection over 1.10 P.M.	
"	26		9AM – 12.30PM – 2PM – 3PM Routine included Physical exercise, Musing Musketry, Making of Strong Points, Bombing and Bayonet work. 2/Lt N. Taylor "H" coy & 2/Lt G. Gordon (scouts) attached here for instructional purposes. 1 officer & 100 furces paraded for instruction under CSM WYNTER Army Instruction School hours 9am – 12.30pm – 2pm – 4pm. Mns. Gas NCO's transferred from "A" coy to "B" coy + 2/Lt Gregg Allan Major Stansberge late C.R. Edward and 2/Lt 2/D Goodall – 20th I.B.D. also Lieut h O'Kan to arrived from France.	
"	27		Routine as per previous day. Lewis Gunners for the whole of range. Commanding Officer Medical Officer each Coy Commander + 2 NCOs per coy attended an instruction course at Div HQ Montigny at 9.30am in the use of new Small box – respirator. Capt A.W. McGrew Shaw and Lieut.	France Sept 25

WAR DIARY or INTELLIGENCE SUMMARY

Army Form C. 2118.

Vol V 1/7 Royal Scots Fusiliers Sept. 1916

Place	Date	Hour	Summary of Events and Information	Remarks and references to Appendices
BAZIEUX WOOD	27		Bivouacing resumed from Hospital and Base respectively. Routine as for previous day. – At disposal relieved with box resp. Lewis Gunners under L.C.O. Between 11am and 12 noon 30 min from "A" coy threw live bombs under supervision of Lieut. McKean 11th A&SH. At the Officers & Warrant Officers of the Batt. attended a lecture 9 Glenurquhart on "Bayonet Fighting" by the Superintendent of Army Physical Training & Bayonet Fighting at 3 PM on recreation ground close to Camp. Draft of 5 O.R.anks arrived from 3rd G.B.D	
	28			
	29		Routine as for previous day – Between 11am – 12 noon 30 men from "A" coy threw live bombs under supervisory Lieut McKean 11th A&SH. During the wet weather the routine of the previous day was unable to be adhered to – men were retained in tents. N.C.O's were given repeat instruction in use of Contors by officers. The mechanism of the mills bomb was explained in detail to all officers by 2/Lt Cooper and 1/Lt 9/13 Scott. Capt J Gardner rejoined from Hospital and resumed command of A coy. T.O.S.	

WAR DIARY
INTELLIGENCE SUMMARY. 6/7 Royal Scots Fusiliers

Sept 1916

Army Form C. 2118.

Place	Date	Hour	Summary of Events and Information	Remarks and references to Appendices
BAIZIEUX WOOD	30		Routine included, Physical training, Strong Point fighting, Extended order drill & Musketry - Bombing, Bayonet fighting. Battns were alloted the Baths between 8am - 10am - Each Coy had half an hour sending 1 Platoon. 30 men from "B" Coy threw live bombs between 11am - 12 noon - unfortunately they were late in arriving & the whole party was not completed in the throwing. Lieuts A.B. Hodge & H Hanks left for short rest in camp at AULT.	

1.10.16

L.V.O. Jordan
Lieut Col.
Comdg. 6/7 R.S.F.

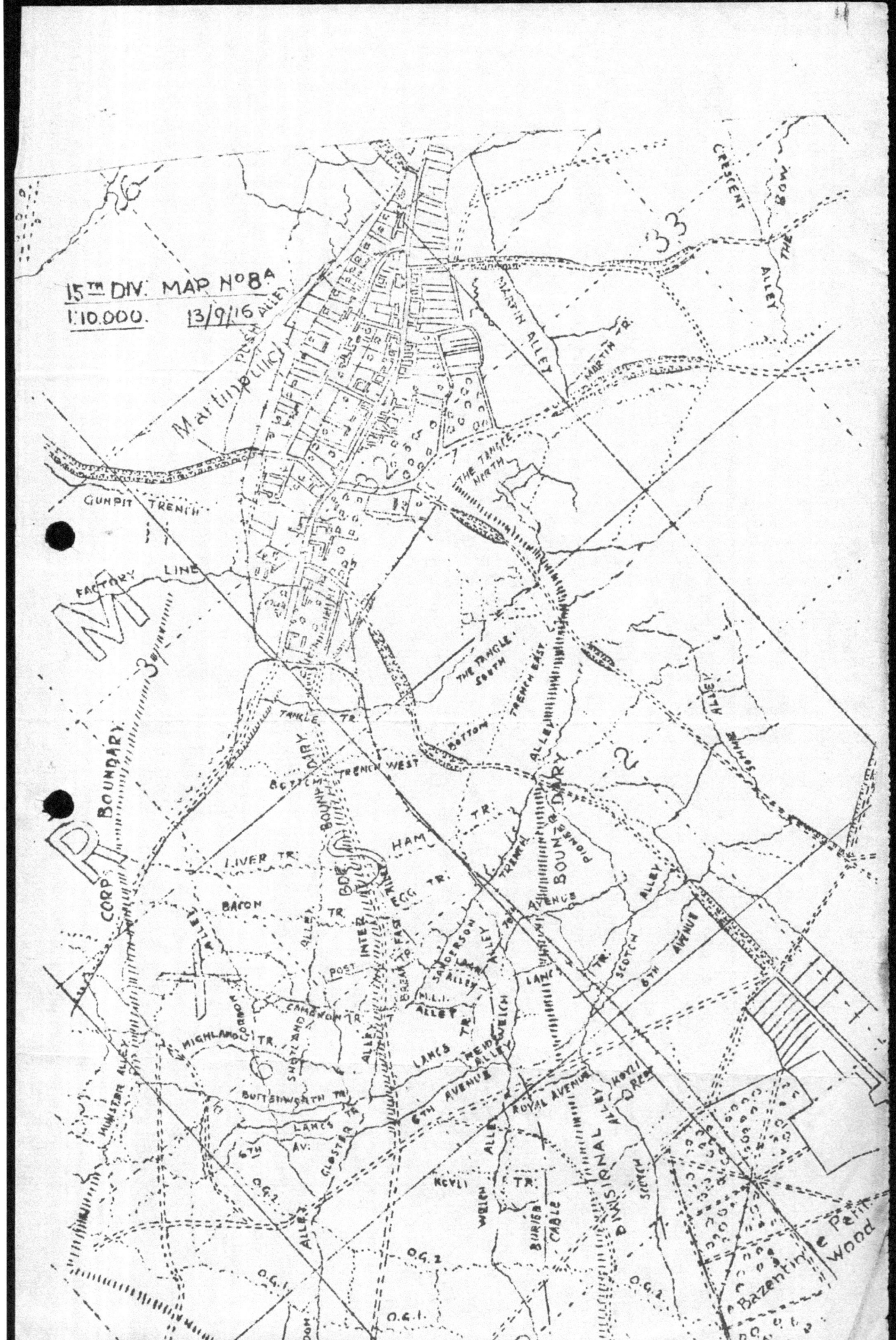

APPENDIX T

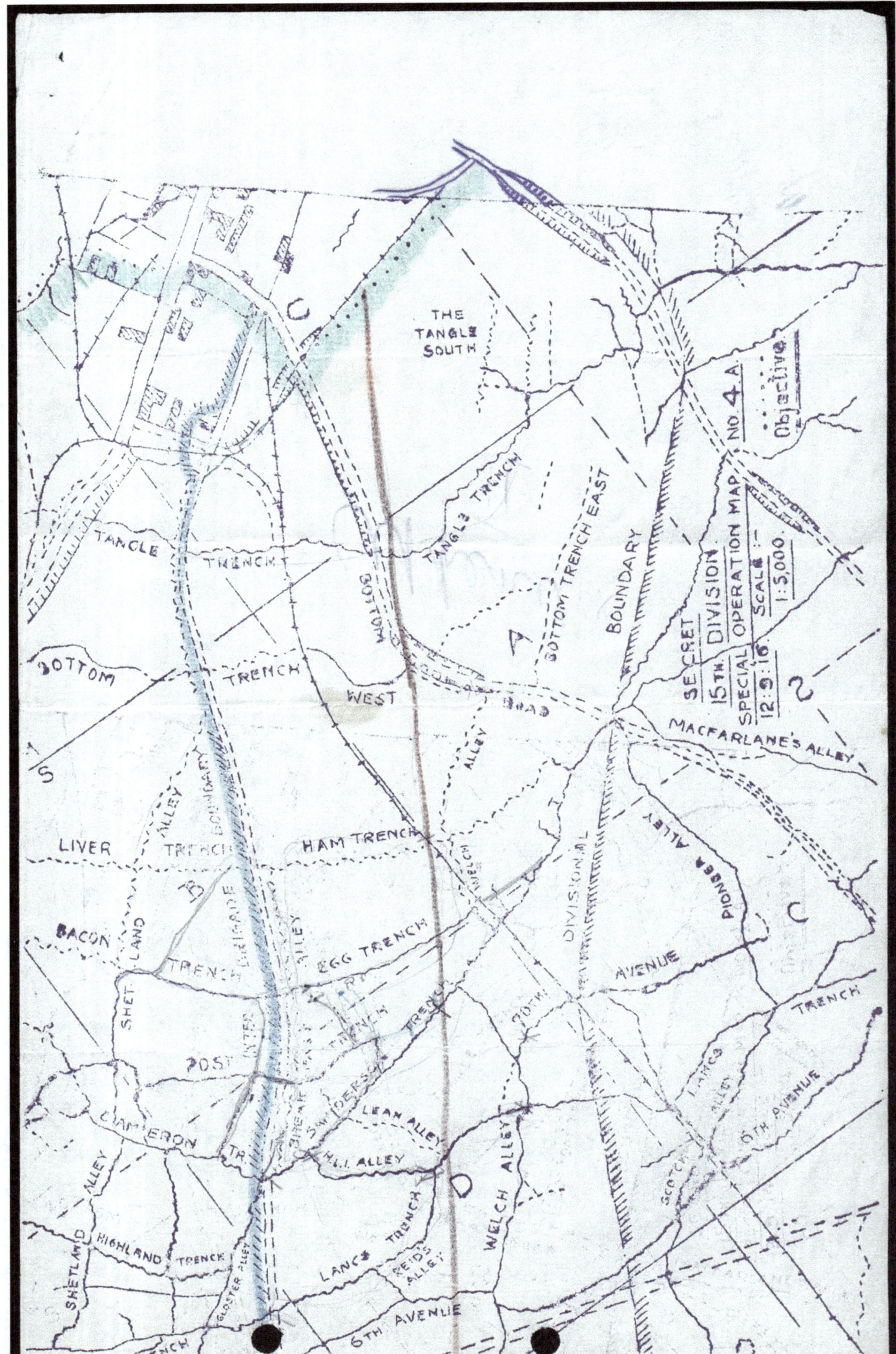

Appendix II

Index

SUBJECT.

6/7th Royal Scots Fusiliers

No.	Contents.	Date.

October 1916

Index

CONFIDENTIAL.

WAR DIARY.

OF
6/7 Royal Scots Fusiliers

1st to 31st October 1916.

VOLUME VI

Army Form C. 2118.

WAR DIARY
or
INTELLIGENCE SUMMARY.

(Erase heading not required.)

October 1916 — 6/7 Royal Scots Fusiliers — Vol VI

Place	Date	Hour	Summary of Events and Information	Remarks and references to Appendices
Catterick	Oct. 1		Divine Service Presbyterian 10am - Church of England 10am - and Roman Catholics 11.30am. Report received on a recent inspection of Transport - Establishment Animals & Vehicles complete. Condition of Vehicles Good. of Animals Excellent. of Harness Excellent of Shoeing Very Good.	
"	2		Weather was very bad and companies were confined to tents - Lectures and instruction given in mechanism of bomb, compass work bearings etc. Night Operations cancelled owing to weather.	
"	3		Weather again interfered with parade - OC & Coy however had to run throwing bombs under 2/Lt McLean. Bn Bombing Officer Coys had use of Baths at intervals during the forenoon - All coys paraded at 3PM under CSM Wynter Gray Gymnastic Staff for Physical exercise & Bayonet Fighting. In the evening Coy Officers & NCOs laid out stop posts with tapes under supervision of Lieut Jigsis & Lt Gordons. Operation orders were received for route next day to BRESLE, also a practise attack. Draft 50 Ranks Arrived.	EHS

WAR DIARY or INTELLIGENCE SUMMARY.

Army Form C. 2118.

Vol VI 6/7 Royal Scots Fusiliers

Month: October 1916

Place	Date	Hour	Summary of Events and Information	Remarks and references to Appendices
BRESLE	Oct. 4		Weather very bad and owing to rain & condition tracks attack was postponed. Left DAIZIEUX at 9.20 AM and marched to BRESLE. Batt in billets at Bresle abt opposite church. Operation orders received from Bde for practise attack next day.	
"	5		Batt. marched off at 10 AM and took up position approx between D3C0.1 – D3C3.6. with 2 advancing waves in front & support lines respectively. A Coy Right front. B Coy Left front. C Coy Right Support – D Coy Left Support. 1st Objective was D3b5.1 – D9a.99. 2nd Objective D4c2.6 – D9C.9.6. Final objective. D4c9.4 – D10a8.2. Zero hour hour was 11.15 am. Batt: also went attacked at D20h.1. The attack was done twice. Zero hour for second practise 1.45 PM. Batt. returned to billets 3 PM. Lecture given in the "Agincourt" Cinema Hall by commander of 47th Division.	FRANCE SHEET 62D 1/40000
"	6		Between 9AM and 11AM Coys practise the attack, especially the simultaneous action at Zero hour. Route march (all coys) to BUIRE where 2nd RSF are at present situated was commenced shortly after 11AM. Wiring 10 new per coy. Test.	"

Army Form C. 2118.

WAR DIARY
or
INTELLIGENCE SUMMARY.
(Erase heading not required.)

Vol VI 6/7 Royal Scots Fusiliers

October 1916

Place	Date	Hour	Summary of Events and Information	Remarks and references to Appendices
BRESLE	Oct. 6		was held at the following times A coy 8.30 am B coy 9.30 am C coy 10.30 am & D coy 11.30 am. C & D coys again in the afternoon C coy 2 pm, D coy 3 pm. Draft of 5 O.Rank reported from 20th Infy Base Depot.	
"	7		Bayonet fighting all coys from 7.15 am – 7.45 am – Musket attack from 9 am – 10.30 am Coy drill 10.30 am – 11 am. Bomb Mort 11 am – 1 pm. Their 1020 a Conference of all Commanding Officers at Brigade H.Q. at 9.30 am. Warning was received from Bde that Batn. would probably move early tomorrow.	
LOZENGE WD – MARTIN PUICH	8		Battalion paraded by Coys, in order ABCD HQ. Batn moved from Bresle to Reserve Area (LOZENGE WOOD). Movement was by National Railways. Interval No 1 Platoon leading – Arrived LOZENGE WOOD 12 noon and rested – 1 tool per man given out and bombers supplied with 12 bombs each other rank two bombs – Orders from Bde to move into line. Coy Cdrs off at 4.40 pm – Guides were at CONTALMAISON VILLA from 8th YORK & LANCS REGT. at 6 pm but on arrival they were not found. Proceeded to MARTINPUICH pushing to Light Railway Track – C & D coys dropped out on the way occupied EGG TRENCH.	RSF

WAR DIARY or INTELLIGENCE SUMMARY

Army Form C. 2118.

(Erase heading not required.) VOL VI **6/7 Royal Scots Fusiliers.**

October 1916

Place	Date	Hour	Summary of Events and Information	Remarks and references to Appendices
MARTINPUICH	Oct. 8		A & B Coys work as follows A Coy FACTORY LINE, B Coy SUNKEN ROAD, (also MARTINPUICH) Batt. HQ. in MARTINPUICH approx. M.33.c.2.9. – Night quiet – a few guards on dumps found.	15 Div. Trench Map No 10.
"	9		Day spent in supplying fatigue parties – Parties to carry rations from CONTALMAISON VILLA to forward positions of 6th Camerons – Parties carrying rations & water to and from dumps – two separate parties of 25 for burying dead – a few casualties from shrapnel with carrying parties approx. 12. Between 6PM & 6.30PM heavy artillery "strafe" on enemy lines on our left.	
"	10		Duties much the same as previous day – Fatigue parties carrying rations, ammunition etc. Draft of 5 came up from 20th G.O.D. 2/Lieut. Whitelaw returned from Fourth Army School of Instruction at FLIXECOURT. 32 other ranks leave the majority belonging to 10th Northumberland Fusiliers. Their effect forward.	
"	11		Warning received that 9th Division on our right would assault the enemy lines at Zero hour on the 12th. In preparation the artillery along the whole Corps front were bombarding the enemy lines & communications between 1.20PM and 3.35PM thereafter assuming their normal tasks. In the hope of the enemy manning his parapets machine gun fire periodically was placed on enemy lines	C.B.S.

Army Form C. 2118.

WAR DIARY
or
INTELLIGENCE SUMMARY.
(Erase heading not required.)

6/7 Royal Scots Fusiliers

October 1916   Vol VI

Instructions regarding War Diaries and Intelligence Summaries are contained in F.S. Regs., Part II. and the Staff Manual respectively. Title pages will be prepared in manuscript.

Place	Date	Hour	Summary of Events and Information	Remarks and references to Appendices
MARTINPUICH	Oct 11		and communications. Warning was received from Bde that 6/7 RSF would probably relieve the 6th Cameron Highlanders on night 11th/12th Oct 1916. Relief arranged to commence 12 midnight - guides at Bath HQ at that time. Each man carried out 1 full sized entrenching tool & bandolier. Rations for next day men later up - C Coy carried up rations for 13 R Scots, D Coy 50 tons water for same Batn.	Appendix "11"
—	12		Dispositions - all coys 26th Avenue - Bath HQ 26th Av. Between 10.10 am & 10.45 am enemy shelled 26th Av. with field guns - steady bombardment of enemy lines becoming intense at 2.5PM - slackened off & ceased about by 3PM - About 5PM after one of our aeroplanes came down in 26th Av - abandoned by pilot & observer - reason not quite known. Lieut (Act Capt) Gg M'Cro joined on 11th but remained with main stores at ALBERT. Orders for relief of 13th R Scots received - guides for 13 R Scots at their HQ to 26th Av. at 12 midnight - order of relief DCAB HQ. Advanced party for digging trenches of 50mm from C & D coys with 2 officers from D & 1 from C Coy proceeded up at 5.30 PM.	

WAR DIARY or INTELLIGENCE SUMMARY

Army Form C. 2118.

October 1916. Vol VI. 6/7 Royal Scots Fusiliers

Places	Date	Hour	Summary of Events and Information	Remarks and references to Appendices
LE SARS FRONT.	13		Relief was completed about 2.45 a.m. — Battn. H.Q. 26th AVENUE. Coys in OG1 & OG2 with garrisons in Strong Points W. of LE SARS. Day normal with intermittent enemy shelling — LE SARS & CAT TRENCH heavily shelled also 26th AVENUE (mostly Shrapnel) The latter owing chiefly to the fact that a large party of men came over the open to this trench then dispersed. 2/Lieut M.D. Goodall wounded — work was commenced shortly after 6 P.M. in connecting up Strong Points — 9 the clearing of OG.2 which badly blocked —	APPENDIX II
	14		Work done during the night fairly satisfactory but hampered slightly owing to the hard nature of the ground (chalk) Posts 1 & 2 were connected by a trench about 4' in depth — 1 German prisoner taken — same in about M15 a 6.7 — He had lost his direction — Patrols were sent out but found no enemy work objects no 9 no wire in front of LITTLE WOOD. — 2/Lt. D. McLean's body (6th Camerons) was found & effects taken & forwarded to 6th Cameron Highlanders — it is proposed to bury him this evening — night otherwise normal —	
	15		Much work done overnight CAMERON TR. Joining OG1 & OG2 deepened to depth of 5' and firestep made. — A large number of dead cleared. M.S.G.	

WAR DIARY
or
INTELLIGENCE SUMMARY

Army Form C. 2118.

Vol VI 6/7 Royal Scots Fusiliers

October 1916

Place	Date	Hour	Summary of Events and Information	Remarks and references to Appendices
LE SARS FRONT LINE	15		Another prisoner taken - Saxon - states situation or change in the troops opposite us. Strong points M16c1.8 & M15d7.7 were consolidated by a trench 3½ feet deep. Hard surface. Men suffered 6 casualties buried at M16c1.8. Day normal except for heavy shelling of CAT TR. & OC2 between 1.15 PM & 1.30 PM. Orders received for relief by 7/K.O.S.B. Guides at their HQ in CUTTING, MARTINPUICH at 7 PM - Advance parties came up at 3 PM. Relief somewhat slow and completed 12.30 am - Battn moved by	APPENDIX II
Area X27a.	16		Corps to Area X27a. (LOZENGE WOOD) - Not tea & biscuits and blankets were served out to the men as they came in. 2/Lieuts John Carran and William Orr taken on strength as from 13/10/16. Day spent resting and cleaning up. A fatigue party of 2 officers and 100 o'ranks reported to guides of 1st Northumberland Field Coy RE at S8C9.8 (NE corner of BAZENTIN LE PETIT WOOD) at 10.15 am. They worked on the road & finished at 2 P.M. 2/Lieut BC Brown proceeded to Corps H.ᵗ Army, FLIXECOURT Baths for the Baths at BECOURT WOOD	MAP ALBERT 1/40,000
"	17			MAP ALBERT 1/40,000

WAR DIARY or INTELLIGENCE SUMMARY

Army Form C. 2118.

6/7 Royal Scots Fusiliers Vol VI

October 1916

Place	Date	Hour	Summary of Events and Information	Remarks and references to Appendices
Area X27a.	Oct. 17		of the following hours B Coy 2PM, C Coy 3PM, D Coy 4PM & A Coy 5PM. Bathing Party as for previous day and found by "B" Coy. Rested in the morning who cancelled owing to wet weather.	
"	18		by Coys on sick parade adjacent to camp. Warning order of move tomorrow. Camp cleaned up — Blankets including those of the Argylls handed in to Divisional New Dumping Kit collected & taken to stores. Bathn moved off A coy leading at 4.20 PM — movement was by platoons at 200 yds interval — marching was heavy owing to sodden nature of ground — Battn in new position by 9 PM.	
" MARTINPUICH	19		Disposition A Coy 2 Platoons SUNKEN ROAD, 2 Platoons MARTIN ALLEY, B Coy 2 Platoons SUNKEN ROAD, 2 Platoons MARTIN ALLEY, C Coy, PRUE TRENCH, D Coy, STARFISH TRENCH. Battn HQ at Hut M15 c.2.3. Work party of 1 officer & 40 men returned to Bazentin at 9.15 PM.	
"	20		Day normal — Shelters constructed on E side of SUNKEN ROAD and in MARTIN ALLEY — Work party of 3 officers & 150 o.Ranks marched off at 6 PM for work on digging new track in front of present front line (CHALK TRENCH). RE Sub.spr Party from MERCOURT (1 NCO & 12 men) returned.	

WAR DIARY or INTELLIGENCE SUMMARY.

Army Form C. 2118.

Vol VI 6/7 Royal Scots Fusiliers

October 1916

Place	Date	Hour	Summary of Events and Information	Remarks and references to Appendices
MARTINPUICH	Oct 21		Day normal. Coys spent the day in improving the trenches they occupied & in constructing dugouts & shelters. 1 Latrine made in MARTIN ALLEY. Much salvage collected including equipment, arms, bombs (Mills & Stokes), rubbish buried in shell holes. 4 Officers & 150 men proceeded as a working party for front line at 6 P.M.	
"	22		Work done on front line considerable but still after amounts to - Coys continued the clearing of rubbish & collecting of salvage. Went RL McMurtrie arrived from the base - day normal.	
"	23		Conference for Commanding officers at Bat HQ 10 A.M. - orders received for relief of 5th Cameron Highrs in front line. Coys moved off in the following order B A C D HQ. First Coy moved off at 5.15 P.M. night hazy.	
"	24		Working parties on SCOTLAND TRENCH supplied by 13th Royal Scots - & 'B' Coy supplied covering parties - night was normal as regards shelling but the number of coloured very lights sent up by the enemy was above the average - day was wet & only work done was the clearing as far as possible of mud from	

Army Form C. 2118.

WAR DIARY
or
INTELLIGENCE SUMMARY.
(Erase heading not required.) Vol VI 6/7 Royal Scots Fusiliers

Instructions regarding War Diaries and Intelligence Summaries are contained in F.S. Regs., Part II. and the Staff Manual respectively. Title pages will be prepared in manuscript.

October 1916

Place	Date	Hour	Summary of Events and Information	Remarks and references to Appendices
Franklin N. LE SARS	Oct 24		Occupied trenches – order received that 13th Royal Scots would relieve us at night – this order cancelled and orders issued for relief by 10/11th HLI. guides were at junction of GILBERT ALLEY & GUNPIT ROAD at 6 P.M. Relief was completing at 12.30 a.m., being slow owing to intense very dark night – On relief Battn. moved to Area X.27.a. S. of CONTALMAISON. Hot tea was served to the men on arrival in camp.	
Area X.27.a.	25		Men rested – Baths were allotted at BECOURT as follows A coy 10 a.m. B coy 11 a.m. C coy 2 P.M. D coy 3 P.M. – 2/Lieut McMillan reported back from hospital –	
–	26		Inspection of equipment such as bombs tools sandbags – inclusion of feet – fatigue hats, puttees Drawn to two reliefs 8.30 a.m. & 2 P.M. 1 N.C.O. & 10 men – Baths between 2 P.M. – 3 P.M. for those who were unable to bath on previous day – Order received that Battn. would probably move up on the afternoon of 29th –	
–	27		Baths as follows D coy 10 a.m. C coy 10.30 a.m. B coy 11 a.m. A coy 12 noon. Order was received cancelling the relief today & later details as	

WAR DIARY or INTELLIGENCE SUMMARY

Army Form C. 2118.

Vol VI 6/7 Royal Scots Fusiliers

October 1916

Place	Date	Hour	Summary of Events and Information	Remarks and references to Appendices
Onex X27a	Oct 27		To relief of 7/6 KOSB in the Factory line the next day were received — Draft of 48 o'Ranks arrived from 204 I.B. Depot & allocated to Coys. Casualties for the week were 5 killed, 33 wounded, 2 to Hospital 32 from Hospital 18 — On comparison the casualties are still more than drafts received — At 10.30 PM notice was received from H.Q. Bde cancelling the proposed relief of next day —	
"	28		Working party of 1 NCO + 30 men in divis. relief 9AM + 1.30PM to 15th Division — Camp cleared up and pathways made —	
"	29		Divini Servici Roman Catholic 7.15 am — Church of England 9.30 am followed by celebration of Holy Communion — Presbyterian 11 am — Awaiting Party of 2 officers + 100 o'Ranks supplied to 73rd Field Coy RE for events Von Nada — they reported at 6 am at the "CUTTING" and finished work at 1.30 PM — Draft of 15 o'Ranks received from 20th I.B. Depot. Orders received from 45th Bde & H6a Bde for relief of 10/11th H.L.I. in the FACTORY LINE tomorrow (36-)	

WAR DIARY or INTELLIGENCE SUMMARY.

Army Form C. 2118.

Vol VI – 6/7 Royal Scots Fusiliers

October 1916

Places	Date	Hour	Summary of Events and Information	Remarks and references to Appendices
Area X 27a	Oct 30		Orders for move cancelled – about 1.30PM telegram received from 46th Bde that the Battn. would remain in its present area – draft of 43 O'Ranks received from 20th J.B. Depot.	
	31		Working party of 2 Officers & 100 O'Ranks reported to O.C. 73rd Field Coy R.E. at Contalmaison Cutting at the following times. 1 Officer 50 O'Ranks at Baths at Becourt 7.30am and 1 Officer 50 O'Ranks at 7.45 am – Baths allotted as follows C coy 8am, D coy 9am, A coy 10am, B coy 11am. Orders received that this Bn. would relieve 7/8 K.O.S.B. in FACTORY LINE at night – B coy, Rations having been sent out to all coys went the leading coy, 9 moved off by platoons about 5.45 PM – relief was completed by 10 PM and disposition was as follows – B coy SONKEN ROAD, A coy FACTORY LINE, C AD Coys HAM TRENCH, Batt HQ M 32 C 1.8.	APPENDIX 1

E.I. Gordon
Lt. Col.
Comdg. 6/7th Royal Scots Fusiliers

Index

SUBJECT.

6/7th Royal Scots Fusiliers

No.	Contents.	Date.

November 1916

CONFIDENTIAL

Vol VII

WAR DIARY

of

6/7th ROYAL SCOTS FUSILIERS.

FROM 1st NOVR 1916.

TO 30th NOVR 1916.

VOLUME VII

Army Form C. 2118.

WAR DIARY
or
INTELLIGENCE SUMMARY.

(Erase heading not required.)

6/7 Royal Scots Fusiliers
Vol. VII
November 1916.

Place	Date	Hour	Summary of Events and Information	Remarks and references to Appendices
MARTINPUICH	Nov. 1		Day quiet. Fatigue party of 1 officer & 20 men worked at Rly M.R. to the purpose of moving instructions re laying of duck boards along trench line. Word received that we would relieve 13th Royal Scots in Support and on following day would be relieved by 4th H. Oxford & Bucks L.I. Coy moved off the first at 5PM in the following order "C", D.B.A. H.Q. Destremont Trench and 1 platoon in Destremont Farm. "A" Coy 70th Avenue. "C" & "D" Coys 26th Avenue. Batn HQ. 26th Av. Night quiet	
	2		Day spent by Coys in cleaning up trenches. Advance party proceeded at 10AM to take over camp in X27a area. Guides 1 per platoon & 1 for HQ paraded at Batn HQ. 3.30PM and proceeded via Mametz, Pozières, Contalmaison Villa to be there at 6PM. Relief was complete and Batn moved off by Coys to X27a area. Hot soup was served to the men on arrival.	MAP ALBERT 1/40,000
X27a ALBERT	3		Batn moved off again by platoons at 200 yards distance to ALBERT on arrival Coys were billeted in Rue d'Amiens with Batn HQ 57 Rue de Bapaume.	

Army Form C. 2118.

WAR DIARY
or
INTELLIGENCE SUMMARY.

Vol VII 6/7 Royal Scots Fusiliers

November 1916

Place	Date	Hour	Summary of Events and Information	Remarks and references to Appendices
ALBERT H.	Noon		Fatigue Party of 10 men with spades detailed to Town Major at 9AM for work on roads in town - All officers & o Ranks who remained behind during Battn tour of trenches joined for duty - 2/Lieut Abels, Breslar and 2/Lt Ronald Aeronski Wheatley taken on strength & posted to "B" Coy - Draft of 16 NCO's received from 20th QBR. Orders issued for move to Franvillers following day.	
"	5		Draft of 160 o Ranks received from 20th QBR. The Battn moved off by platoons. A Coy leading at 7.40am & moved by main ALBERT - AMIENS Road to FRANVILLERS arriving there at 10.30am. A & B Coys billetted in KING ST, FRANVILLERS, C & D Coys HIGH ST. HQ 7 KING ST, Orderly Room, HIGH ST.	
"	6		Cleaning up of equipment and clothes by all coys - Debbie named Permanent fatigue parties detailed as follows. 25 o Ranks to work under 8IH AT Coy RE at FRECHENCOURT. 12 o Ranks to work on RE Stores at MERICOURT, and 6 men for work under 281 AT Coy RE at	

T2134. Wt. W708-776. 500000. 4/15. Sir J. C. & S.

WAR DIARY
INTELLIGENCE SUMMARY

Army Form C. 2118.

Vol VII — 1/7 Royal Scots Fusiliers

Month and year: November 1916

Place	Date	Hour	Summary of Events and Information	Remarks and references to Appendices
FRANVILLERS	Nov 6		Point F.2.a.5.8. (Map Fricourt) –	Ref / ALBERT 1/40,000
"	7	9AM	All coys – 10am Cleaning of clothes, equipment etc. Re-equipping – 10 am – Coy inspection by OC Coy – 10.45am – 11.15am Squad Drill 11.15am – 12.30 PM. Handling of ARMS, & Musk. Exercises. Inoculation return received from companies – Batto C Coy 2.30PM D Coy 3.30 PM. Lieut Gape returned from hospital	
"	8		Routine included: Cleaning of equipment, Handling of Arms, Musketry, Musk. Exercises & Reorganising & Section under their respective Signalling Officers. Lewis Gunners Section under their respective Commanders. III Corps School of Instruction for Lewis Gunning, Stokes Mortars & Bombing assembled at MONTIGNY. 2/Lieut Allen Steven 2nd/4 Kings Own Scott. Smith arrived & taken on strength – RC Divine Service Voluntary at 6PM –	
"	9		Routine much the same as previous day with an additional parade for selected men in coy throwing dummy bombs – Draft 5 O.Ranks received from 20th IBD at 3.45 PM. the Battalion was lined up on march	WDT

WAR DIARY or INTELLIGENCE SUMMARY.

November 1916 — Vol VII — of 7 Royal Scots Fusiliers

Place	Date	Hour	Summary of Events and Information	Remarks and references to Appendices
FRANVILLERS	Nov 9.		On ground on NORTH side of village for inspection by General Sir Douglas Haig, Commander-in-Chief, British Army in France. About 4.25 P.M. he came forward taking the General Salute from the Battalion under command of Major J. Smith. The C in C observed having had lightly pleased with the appearance of the men and of the smart way they had given the salute —	
FRANVILLERS	11		The routine included a smart march by Platoons in the early morning (7.15 – 7.35 am), Extended Order drill + Handling of arms, the Battalion formed up in Mass or Battalion drill field at 12 noon. Extended order drill by Companies was held at night from 6 to 6.30 p.m. A Lecture to officers with more than 6 months service as such — on Map Reading — was held. Naval parades were held including Platoon Drill, Handling of Arms, Saluting, Musketry and Muscle exercises. A lecture was given to all officers on points from Brigade Memo on recent tour of the trenches by the	MDT
FRANVILLERS	10			

Army Form C. 2118.

WAR DIARY
or
INTELLIGENCE SUMMARY.
(Erase heading not required.)

Place	Date	Hour	Summary of Events and Information	Remarks and references to Appendices
FRANVILLERS	Nov. 10		Commanding Officer. A draft of 5 other ranks arrived from 20th Infantry Base Depot. Selected bombers carried out bombing. Mild weather prevailed and Church Parades were carried through in comfort — Presbyterians 11.30 a.m on Battalion Parade Ground, C of E in the CINEMA HALL, FRANVILLERS at	
"	12		10.30 a.m, R.C. in FRANVILLERS CHURCH at 9 a.m. A recreation room for the benefit of the NCO's and men in the Battalion has been opened at No 47 Billet, HIGH STREET	
"	13		The routine included a route march for "A" Company in full marching order. The band accompanied this company, whose march occupied from 9 a.m. to 12.30 p.m. The other Companies engaged in Platoon Drill, Extended order drill, and Bayonet fighting. The usual routine inspections were held and selected bombers threw live bombs at Brigade Bombing Ground. The working party at FRECHENCOURT with 214th A.T.Coy was changed. Khaki has issued to men requiring it. Two	(MS)

WAR DIARY
or
INTELLIGENCE SUMMARY.
(Erase heading not required.)

Army Form C. 2118.

Place	Date	Hour	Summary of Events and Information	Remarks and references to Appendices
FRANVILLERS	13		Other ranks were taken on the strength from 20th I.B.D and one from Advanced Horse Transport, ABBEVILLE. Capt Shaw & Capt Clifton RAMC granted 3 days PARIS leave	
"	14		The usual work was carried on. The Range was at the disposal of A Coy, which was exercised in deliberate and rapid firing. One other rank was taken on the strength of the Battalion from 20th I.B.D. The weather was very cold and raw.	
"	15		The routine for the day included Route march for C Coy in full marching order accompanied by band, the range for B Coy, and Extended order drill, company drill, and Bayonet fighting. The latter was visited by C.S.M ROBBINS A.G.S. who suggested improvements. 2/Capt Watson and two other ranks proceeded to LE TOUQUET to attend a Lewis Gun Course there	
"	16		The weather still continued to be cold, but was suitable for training purposes. Training similar to that of preceding days was carried on. May reading lecture under 2/Lieut Pope who held for Junior Officers. 2/Lt J.P. Seward and five	

Army Form C. 2118.

WAR DIARY
or
INTELLIGENCE SUMMARY.
(Erase heading not required.)

Instructions regarding War Diaries and Intelligence Summaries are contained in F.S. Regs., Part II. and the Staff Manual respectively. Title pages will be prepared in manuscript.

Place	Date	Hour	Summary of Events and Information	Remarks and references to Appendices
FRANVILLERS	Nov. 16		Other ranks were taken on the strength from 20th I.B.D. Leave for 3 days to PARIS was granted to Capt. J Gardner, B Coy.	
"	17		2/Lt McMutrie assumed duty as TOWN MAJOR of MIRVAUX. Battalion Drill was carried out under Major Smith, commanding the Batt.n A lecture on the part played by Units in the present war was given under Coy arrangements.	
"	18		A Batt.n route march in full marching order took place between 8am and 11 am. Route — FRANVILLERS — BAIZIEUX — BEHENCOURT — FRANVILLERS. The day was very wet and the men were wet and muddy when they returned. Brigadier-General Allgood inspected the billets of the men at 11.45 am and expressed himself as pleased with their cleanliness etc. 105 other ranks were paraded for inoculation by M.O between 2 & 3pm. 40% of the men refused inoculation. (T.A.B) Colonel Byrne returned from leave to England.	
"	19		Divine Services were held as follows:— Presbyterians in Courtyard of No 20 billet at 11.45 am; Church of England	C.M.S.

T2134. Wt. W708—776. 500000. 4/15. Sir J.C. & S.

WAR DIARY
or
INTELLIGENCE SUMMARY.
(Erase heading not required.)

Army Form C. 2118.

Place	Date	Hour	Summary of Events and Information	Remarks and references to Appendices
FRANVILLERS	Nov. 19		In CINEMA HALL, FRANVILLERS at 10 a.m. and Roman Catholics in FRANVILLERS CHURCH at 9 a.m. One Officer and four other ranks were detailed to attend the Divisional Bombing School at FRANVILLERS, and 1 Officer and 1 Sergeant to attend Divisional Infantry School for a General Course	
FRANVILLERS	20		The day's training was carried out in accordance with scheme submitted to Brigade. A Coy.- Route march in full marching order, B Coy.- Digging trench in accordance with plans submitted to Companies. C Coy.- Range, D Coy.- Musketry, digging strong point & wiring. All officers attended tactical exercise under the Brigadier, after the Corps Commander had inspected the Brigade on football field just outside FRANVILLERS. The Corps Commander expressed himself as well pleased with the "turn out" of the Brigade, and also expressed his satisfaction with the work of the Brigade during its strenuous time on the Somme. 2 men were injured in an accident at the Brigade Bombing Ground.	

WAR DIARY
or
INTELLIGENCE SUMMARY.
(Erase heading not required.)

Army Form C. 2118.

Place	Date	Hour	Summary of Events and Information	Remarks and references to Appendices
	Nov.			
FRANVILLERS	21		The Battalion carried out the usual training. The C.O. lectured all NCOs in CINEMA HALL on discipline duties etc. 2/Lt Jope took over command of "D" Coy from Capt. A.W. Ferguson who proceeded to be attached to Headquarters, 46th Infantry Brigade. 2/Lt Miller was transferred from D to B Coy.	
FRANVILLERS	22		A draft of six other ranks arrived from the base and was taken on the strength of the Battalion. Battalion training continued and selected bombers threw live bombs under Brigade Bombing Officer Capt Gardner, proceeded to Le Jour Major of CONTAY	
FRANVILLERS	23		The weather continued to be cold, but training was not interfered with. Practice in firing the Lewis Guns was afforded the officers at the Range. At night one company was practised in leading out for digging and in filing into a trench in readiness for attack. Major Smith was granted leave of absence to England	
FRANVILLERS	24		Besides the usual parades the Commanding Officer gave	

WAR DIARY or INTELLIGENCE SUMMARY

Army Form C. 2118.

Place	Date	Hour	Summary of Events and Information	Remarks and references to Appendices
FRANVILLERS	Mar 24		A lecture to all Companies (A & B Coys 2pm; C & D Coys 11am) on :- "The Causes of the War; its beginning; the gradual development of the British Army; events in all theatres of war up to date." Lewis gun instruction for officers was carried out, and also practice in filing into a trench in the dark, and in leading out to digging (in the dark) 15 other ranks were sent on a Lewis Gun Course, 9 on a Stokes Gun Course, and 2 on a Bombing Course. Lt. & QM Carpenter was granted leave to England. 2/Lt P. Simpson reported for duty with Battn.	
FRANVILLERS	25		2 Companies at a time had use of the Divisional Course under the supervision of C.S.M. Rothero A.G.S. Baths at BAIZIEUX were available for all Coys. Usual routine work was carried on.	
FRANVILLERS	26		The Battalion moved to BAIZIEUX, D Camp, at 10 a.m. The morning was cold & very wet, but fortunately the weather cleared up immediately before the Battn moved off	A.15

Army Form C. 2118.

WAR DIARY
or
INTELLIGENCE SUMMARY.
(Erase heading not required.)

Instructions regarding War Diaries and Intelligence Summaries are contained in F.S. Regs., Part II. and the Staff Manual respectively. Title pages will be prepared in manuscript.

Hour, Date, Place		Summary of Events and Information	Remarks and references to Appendices
FRANVILLERS	26 Nov.	The usual distance of 200 yds between Batt'ns & 100 yds between Platoons was preserved. The Brigadier watched the march past on the FRANVILLERS — BAIZIEUX road. A draft of 7 other ranks arrived from 20th I.B.D. and was taken on the strength. Lt Miller went on leave to UK.	
FRANVILLERS	27 Nov.	The day, which was very raw & cold, was spent in routine inspections & cleaning up. Baths were available for the various Coys between 1 & 5pm. The following Officers have been sent by M.O. to hospital — Capt Shaw, Lt Hodge, 2/Lt J.B. Scott, 2/Lt Williams.	
"	28 "	The Battn paraded on ground adjacent to camp at 8.10am for inspection by G.O.C. 15th Division. — A Coy was in drill order & did Coy drill & handling of arms. B Coy was in Battle order and did attack and sortees. C Coy "full marching order" — Bayonet fighting and musketry — D "full marching order", Musketry & Bombing.	

WAR DIARY
INTELLIGENCE SUMMARY

Army Form C. 2118.

VOL VII 6/7 Royal Scots Fus.

November 1916

Hour, Date, Place	Summary of Events and Information	Remarks and references to Appendices
FRANVILLERS. Nov 28.	The G.O.C. Div. expressed himself as on the whole well pleased with the turn out. The Divisional Band played selections. Coys. to cant. between 2PM & 4PM.	
" 29	All coys - 9AM-10AM - Coy drill. A & B coys 10AM-12.30PM Route march. C coy digging against time. D coy musketry. 2PM. Officers firing Revolver Exercise under 2/Lt J.R. Cooper. Revd. Seward and Clark were admitted to Hospital sick - orders issued for move next day.	
" 30	The Battn. moved off accompanied by Transport at 10AM. for MAMETZ WOOD Camp. arriving X23a6.4. Advance party 2/Lt H Cooper & 25 O.Rank proceeding advanced 6.30 am - The Battn. rested an hour for dinner close to BECOURT. The roads was not heavy & blocks in traffic frequent & cant. was not reached until 5.30PM. The night was cold and a heavy mist prevailed.	

R.I.S. Jordan
Lieut. Col.
Comdg. 6/7th Royal Scots Fus.

Index

SUBJECT.

6/7th Royal Scots Fusiliers

No.	Contents.	Date.
	December 1916	

CONFIDENTIAL.

War Diary Vol 18

45/15

OF

6/7th (SERVICE) BATTn ROYAL SCOTS FUSILIERS.

From 1st Dec. 1916 To 31st Dec., 1916.

Volume VIII

WAR DIARY or INTELLIGENCE SUMMARY

Army Form C. 2118.

9/7 Royal Scots Fusiliers

December 1916 Vol VIII

Place	Date	Hour	Summary of Events and Information	Remarks and references to Appendices
MAMETZ WOOD	1		Fatigue parties found as follows:- Work at CONTALMAISON - LONGUEVAL ROAD at 1 mill trot X.15.a.3.it at 9.00am. 2 Officers 975 ORanks fm A 9 Camp - sent men on roads under supervision of 2nd Labour Battn. R.E. 25 to be at BAZENTIN Road point S.13.b.2.5 at 9.30am. 2 Officers 975 ORanks fm C & D Coys - next was on roads under 2/Lt South Midland Field Coy R.E. Showerset rations	
	2		Men carried 2 bto served on returns but one of parties 1000/1am. Working parties 200 on previous day - 4 men fm C Coy were trained in construction of dug-outs under Lieut. J Cameron - 4 men were for instruction in rifle grenades under Sgt. Knight - Court of Enquiry held to enquire into the injury of No 13654 Pte. M Shannon A Coy. President Lieut. W Pope - Members 2/Lts. Jm Roh & DeBrown -	
	3		Working parties as on previous day - 2 rendezvous 7am - Divine Service - Presbyterian joint service with 13 Royal Scots in Divisional Recreation tent at 11am. Church of England. In the regimental Recreation tent at 10am. Roman Catholics - In the Divisional Recreation tent at 9.30am. 4 men Coy instruction dug outs under	

WAR DIARY
or
INTELLIGENCE SUMMARY.

Army Form C. 2118.

6/7 Royal Scots Fusiliers.

Vol. VIII   December 1916

Place	Date	Hour	Summary of Events and Information	Remarks and references to Appendices
MAMETZ WOOD	Dec 3		Maj. & Cairncross relieve 2 PM – 4 PM – Believes, Cars & hrs instruction rifle. Parade 4 men wrong under Sgt Wright. Observers Parade 2 PM under 2/Lieut F.K. Cooper. Capt A & M/Gunner Shaw resumed Command "C" Coy having returned from Hospital. Day raw & cold.	
"	4		Fatigue parties as for previous day – other parade of specialists resumed commencing 9 AM –	
"	5		Routine as for previous day – Lewis Gunners with handcarts & equipment inspected by the Adjutant – Draft of 8 O. Ranks received from 2nd & 9th Battns. Major Smith returned from leave.	
"	6		Routine as for previous day – Day wet and camp in a bad state work mud – fatigue parties in charge of camp & making of drains throughout the times. Orders issued for move next day	
"ALBERT"	7		Battn moved to ALBERT going by train from BOTTOM WOOD JUNCTION to MEAULTE. Marched from MEAULTE to ALBERT, reaching the latter place about 7.30 PM – HQ and C Battn in Rue Carnot. Coys spent this day in cleaning equipment, clothes etc – From H Coy, 1 officer	Ex J.

WAR DIARY
INTELLIGENCE SUMMARY

Army Form C. 2118.

(Erase heading not required.) Vol VIII 1/7 Royal Scots Fusiliers

December 1916

Place	Date	Hour	Summary of Events and Information	Remarks and references to Appendices
ALBERT	Dec. 8		4.50 o'clock commencing work at 8am under orders of OC Day Labour Battn. 34 Bn at MARAIS. Also 1 officer & 40 o'ranks for work on Prisoners Cage at Esa.	Refer Map ALBERT
"	9		Routine as for previous day with regard to working parties with the exception that the officer & 40 o'ranks at Prisoners Cage was reduced to 1 Sgt 1 Cpl & 15 men. It men for coy in construction of dug outs under Lt Carnan - 6 men for coy in rifle grenade work by 1/1-99 M. Gun - Baths for each coy - Staff of 5 o' ranks from 70th ? S.G. Capt A.D. McHenry Shaw to Hospital.	
"	10		Divine Service Presbyterian at 11am in Expeditionary Force Canteen in Esa Divisional Band attached - Church of England Service at 9.30am in the S.C.A. Rooms behind West Yorkshire - Roman Catholics service in Cinema Hall at 9am - Parade for dug out construction left Parade at Empires & Observers at 2PM - Fatigue Party as usual.	
"	11		Allotted each coy - Arrival of Lieut Col W.H. Northey - Full General Court Martial held at HQ.	
"	12		Fatigue party arrival & stewards parade - Short route march by	

WAR DIARY
or
INTELLIGENCE SUMMARY

Army Form C. 2118.

Title pages: December 1916. Vol VIII 6/7 Royal Scots Fusiliers

Place	Date	Hour	Summary of Events and Information	Remarks and references to Appendices
ALBERT	1916 Dec 12		Coys delivered 10am - 12.30PM. Draft of 3 ranks from 20th K.O.B Depot. Lieut. N. MacCartney left to join 1st RSF. Capt Taylor RAMC joined for duty vice Capt Ruffton on leave.	
"	13		The day utilised by Coys in complete inspection of all equipment for trenches, and lectures to the men. Draft of 5 ranks posted to Coys. Draft of 103 ranks received from 20th KOB Depot and classified into trained men to trained 9 men of own corps arrived, and the whole posted to coys.	
			Moved to Hut 4 Camp by way of Labosselle. Draft 200 men from 6th R. Scots E. Orders expected to move into front line next day. Major T Smith and Lieut T Meller left at Reinforcement Camp.	
"	14	9.35am	Moved forward from ALBERT to VILLA CAMP, first platoon leaving off at Route Salvarelli - Contalmaison - arrived at camp 11.20 AM	Pt. Mar/ ALBERT 10.900
			Col Al. Skie & Lieut Q/M Cooper proceeded front line for particulars of disposition of Coys &c. Heavy rain.	
"	15		Conference of officers & all arrangements made for relief - moved up to relieve 5th Gloucesters in frontline, first platoon moving at 3.45 AM	G.O.S.

WAR DIARY or INTELLIGENCE SUMMARY

Army Form C. 2118.

December 1916 — **9/7 Royal Scots Fusiliers** — Vol VIII

Place	Date	Hour	Summary of Events and Information	Remarks and references to Appendices
LE SARS SECTOR	Dec. 16		Relief completed by 9.15 PM. – Distribution: A Coy approx. M.15.8 to M.16.2.8. B Coy M.15.6.0.9 to M.15.6.6.8. C Coy in support to A Coy in OG.2 & OG.1. D Coy in support to B Coy in OG.1 & OG.2 (left). Batn. H.Q. 26.2 AVENUE. – Night quiet with exception of occasional sniping from enemy – Patrols went out but encountered no enemy – a buried enemy rifle found at far end of CHALK PIT. Trenches very very bad – non existent in places & the line in parts a series of detached posts.	LE SARS Div Mak admuda 1.
	16		Day normal – at 4 pm one of our snipers claimed a hit on enemy sniper on ridge about LITTLE WOOD – small party of enemy seen to left of LITTLE WOOD about 3 pm – our Lewis Guns fired causing it in Mortier land. Casualties – orderly returned to Batn. our front line closed to the Rifle. WALENCOURT ALLEY exclusive now our Northern right – roughly M.16.C.0.8.	
	17		Night normal – at 5.50 am an enemy party of from 12-14 strong seen seen to be advancing out artillery front in front of CHALK PIT. On being fired at all at a distance of about 40 yds they went over to chop and were lost in the thick mist which prevailed – 10 minutes afterwards between a party	

SDJ

WAR DIARY
or
INTELLIGENCE SUMMARY

Army Form C. 2118.

December 1916 Vol VIII 1/7 Royal Scots Fusiliers

Hour, Date, Place	Summary of Events and Information	Remarks and references to Appendices
December 17 Le Sars Sector	Were again seen to approach this post - our party fired but the enemy ran - on of attaining distance three bombs - One landed in the centre of the post wounding 6 men - our party retired with bombs and rifle fire, the enemy broke & fled - 2/Lt McCook. whereas wounded this time went forward immediately with 12 men in skirmishing order - No trace however could be found of the enemy - the enemy was too faint to start a attack must prevail - the day was normal with intermittent shelling of DESTREMONT FARM. Orders received for relief by 11th A.&S.H. - relief accomplished by 9 P.M. and Battn moved to Support position - B & D Coys in MARTINPUICH and A & C Coys in 26th Av. 9. 70. Trench - Battn HQ remained as before.	
18 —	Day normal - Weather much clearer - orders received for relief next day by 8th Seaforth Highrs - 2/Lt R.A. Clarke reports back from Hospital 2/Lt A.J. British accompanied 2/Lt. (sick).	
19 —	Advance party of 1 NCO & 2 men per Coy & the Adjutant for the left under 2/Lt A. Buchan to take over camp at SHELTER WOODS, from 8th SEAFORTHS, Guide to the Cookhouse 9/1 (nts under 2/Lt F.K. Clark wound at	

EWJ

WAR DIARY or INTELLIGENCE SUMMARY

Army Form C. 2118.

December 1916 b/7 Royal Scots Fusiliers Vol (III)

Hour, Date, Place	Summary of Events and Information	Remarks and references to Appendices
19/12/16 SHELTER WOOD S.	CONTALMAISON VILLA at 4:30 P.M. Relief was completed by 7.45 P.M. Batt. moved to Camp in SHELTER WOOD S and horses was subject to an on return –	
20"	The day was devoted to the men cleaning themselves & baths were allotted to Coys between 2 P.M & 5 P.M. Scheme was drawn up to improve drainage of camp.	
21"	Physical Exercise between 9 A.M – 10 A.M – all companies – Remainder of day spent in digging & improving drainage throughout the camp – Camp nets issued – Tents, Re Stockstown and A Munro reported from 20th EDClrSt Army wet draft of 16 ORanks. Capt A.J. Munro Shaw returned from Hospital. Working parties found as follows:- To work to 5th Sussex (Pioneers) at LANCLANDS Circus, S.14.G1.8 at 8:30 a.m	
22"	3 Officers 4 NCOs and 160 men – To return at Attachment No.7 Field Co. R.E. at CONTALMAISON DONP at 9 A.M 1 Officer 40 men – Order issued for move tomorrow holdley draft of 5 ORanks from Base.	
23"	Untrained personnel left for HAZEBROUCK – Batt. Cam – Baik. moved up First Nation locally at 4:15 P.M.	

Army Form C. 2118.

WAR DIARY
or
INTELLIGENCE SUMMARY.
(Erase heading not required.)

6/7 Royal Scots Fusiliers

Vol VIII December 1916

Hour, Date, Place	Summary of Events and Information	Remarks and references to Appendices
23 Martinpuich	Relief was completed with 7/8 KOSB's in support at 8.15 PM. Distributors: A Coy. STARFISH TRENCH, B & D Coys PRUE TRENCH, C Coy & Headquarters SEVEN ELMS. Night normal.	
24 —	Day hazy — at 10.50am 2 hostile aeroplanes flew over area about M28C — they met & attacked an British aircraft which were forced to descend somewhere about POZIERES — Our artillery fire increased towards evening — night a lull about normal in artillery fire — Wet.	
25 —	Orders received for relief of 6th Cameron Highrs. in the left front same day — 2/Lieut Al Macintosh Kiloh — Relieved 6 Camerons in front line. Distribution D on right C on left B in support & A in Reserve — Battn HQ 6C2. Night quiet but patrols out but encountered none of the enemy.	
26 —	Day normal — Batt HQ & vicinity shelled at frequent intervals — our snipers claim two hits — work continued	

J.V.J.

WAR DIARY or INTELLIGENCE SUMMARY

(Erase heading not required.) Vol VIII w/7 Royal Scots Fus[?]

December 1916

Army Form C. 2118.

Hour, Date, Place	Summary of Events and Information	Remarks and references to Appendices
Mon 26 LE SARS Section	On Flers Line (Reserve) accommodation completed for 180 men — 1 officer & 6 other ranks (at returning) sent by #4 Coy whilst in reserve — Orders issued for relief next day by 6th Camerons —	
27	Day normal except for heavy shelling of Batt HQ — this dug-out seemed to be marked by the enemy on account of runners using the open approaches into the newly-cut actual front. Relieved by 6th Camerons — 7 PM — Moved to reserve position — Pioneer Camp.	
28 Pioneer Camp	Wet day but men fairly comfortable — 40 O Ranks for working party — used divisional personnel — Draft 30 O Ranks from 20th R.S. Bn — on a persons under sentence — orders issued for move next night to front line —	
29	Wet day & cold — HQ moved off first at 6.20 PM proceeded via VILLA Wood camp Eaucourt in order ABDC. Relieved 6th Cameron division being B on right A on left D in support C in reserve — HQ new location on WARLENCOURT RD 10 yds N of shrine O.1 c.a.8. 1 — Heavy rain throughout the night — Patrols were out but saw nothing of the enemy —	
30 LE SARS Section	Work consisted in draining up trenches & endeavouring to drain the night 31st/1st Jany 1917. Day normal — orders issued for relief by 7th Camerons on	

R.G.S.

Army Form C. 2118.

WAR DIARY
or
INTELLIGENCE SUMMARY

(Erase heading not required.)

December 1916 — Vol VIII 6/7 Royal Scots Fusiliers.

Hour, Date, Place	Summary of Events and Information	Remarks and references to Appendices
Dec 31st LE JOHNS SECTOR.	Night of 30/31st - the enemy was very active with artillery fire - Heavy barrages seen from time to time put on 86 Line - Batn. HQ was intermittently shelled between 11PM & 1AM - Day was normal - Batn. was relieved by 7th Cameron Highrs. 91 moved to SHELTER WOOD S. Camp.	

F. S. Jordan
Lieut. Col.
Commanding 6/7th Battn. Royal Scots Fusiliers.

ORDERLY ROOM
1 JAN 1917
6/7 BN. ROYAL SCOTS FUSILIERS

6/7th Batt'n,
The Royal Scots Fusiliers
January, 1917.

Army Form W.3091.

Cover for Documents.

Nature of Enclosures.

G.R. XI

W Dickson

19

Notes, or Letters written.

Operation Order
File
27/7/15

WAR DIARY or INTELLIGENCE SUMMARY

Army Form C. 2118.

Vol I / Army Form 45/15

1/7 Royal Scots Fusiliers Vol IX

January 1917

Place	Date	Hour	Summary of Events and Information	Remarks and references to Appendices
SHELTER WOOD S	1.		Day was spent by Battn in cleaning clothes & equipment –	
"	2.		Evolution of clothes & equipment by OC Coy – laying of Duck boards throughout the Camp – cleaning out of & completing drains and paths. Draft of 26 o'ranks received from 20th G.B.D.	
"	3.		Working parties found totalling in all 7 officers & 360 o'ranks. Orders received for relief of 10th East Riffles in Right front of Reptiles Sector (LE SARS) I/Kent Edgar Saunders reported for duty & posted to D Coy.	
"	4.		Coy completed with bombs, S.A.A. & Sandbags – Rum turnout inspected, HENENCOURT and ACID DROP CAMP – Battn moved off at 8.30 P.M. by Platoons in the following order C.D. HQ, A. B – Guides at Bde HQ in MARTINPUICH at 5 PM – Relief was completed by 7.30 PM – night was normal – Corps worked on posts in front, cleaning out & draining – weak wire in front of left posts was corrected & "fair" – DESTREMONT FARM was shelled at frequent intervals – Orders issued for relief next day by 13th R.Scots –	
"	5.			
"	6.		150 yards of wire was put out on left front, diagonals were made & the Posts all were good – New Post commenced on night also on our left – 25 yards been dug to an average depth of 3'- New Coy HQ commenced at M.15. a.8.6. Posts all deepened & improved – Day normal – Relief commenced at 9 PM –	

237
8/3
POST.

WAR DIARY or INTELLIGENCE SUMMARY

Army Form C. 2118.

6/7 Royal Scots Fusiliers VOL IX January 1917

Place	Date	Hour	Summary of Events and Information	Remarks and references to Appendices
VILLA CAMP	6		Relief completed 9 P.M. Batt. moved K VILLA CAMP – Hot tea served on arrival –	
	7		Day quiet – 50 trench boards received & laid through the Camp – orders received for relief next day of 13th R.Scots in front line –	
	8		An additional 70 trench boards received and partly laid – balance handed over to advance party of 13th RS. Batt. paraded 7.35 P.M & moved off in the following order A.B. HQ. C.D. Guides met at Red Ch at 9 P.M relief completed 11.5 P.M. Disposition A on right B on left C in Support D in Reserve – Night normal.	
	9		Front line were all worked on during the night – a new support trench dug in left front – 40 yds were put on on right front – Shelling of DESTREMONT FARM & 26th AV. fairly continuous by enemy – Day normal – reserve coy worked on shelters. Night fairly quiet – much work done in front – new post made on Right front – dug in 25 yds to a depth of 4' – 2 holes penetrated and revetted – Left front support trench completed – new a depth of 5' 6". Left front was covered from FAIR to GOOD – Releived by 13th R.Scots at DESTREMONT FARM, 26th AV. & MARTINPUICH.	2H
	10		Day usual shelling of LE SARS, DESTREMONT FARM, 26th AV. & MARTINPUICH. Releived Moved to ACID DROP SOOTH CAMP CONTALMAISON.	
	11		Day quiet and devoted to men cleaning themselves. 2/Lewis R Young, Wm Indie and A.D Munro reported & joined for duty – orders received for move next day to SHELTER WOOD N Camp.	
	12		8/10 Gordons took over ACID DROP CAMP – Batt. moved off at 3.15 PM for SHELTER WOOD	R.I.D.F.

WAR DIARY or INTELLIGENCE SUMMARY

Army Form C. 2118.

Place: SHELTER WOOD
6/7 Royal Scots Fusiliers
Vol IX — January 1917

239

Date	Hour	Summary of Events and Information	Remarks
12		Camp. All huts with armstrong huts as Mess. Camp in a muddy state —	
13		Working parties found to the extent of 8 officers & 340 ORanks — 80% of the men all day parties with haversack rations — Hard frost —	
14		Divine Service Presbyterian at 10.30am in SCOTS REDOUBT S — C of England at 10.30am. Roman Catholic nil — Draft of 68 in THCA that Scots REDOUBT at 10.30am — 2/Lieuts W.S. HAMILTON and inspected by Major T Said & attached to Coys. 2/Lieuts W.S. HAMILTON and W. KERR reported from 20 & 9 B.D. & posted to A & B Coys respectively — Gen W. KERR reported from 20 & 9 B.D. & posted to A & B Coys respectively — Gen'l Clothing Inspection — Moth eating of area adjacent Camp during the night — No casualties or damage —	
15		Recce patrol under ?/Lieut G.B. Bogie proceeded to HENENCOURT — Coy inspections in afternoon of trench equipment completed — Orders issued for relief of 7/8 K.O.S.B. on the line next day — 8th shelling of area of Camp area but no casualties.	
16		Blankets, valises, blanket kits etc moved to new huts in Pioneer Camp — Lieuts Marie Carnan, J.S. Smith & Gas Sect proceeded to HENENCOURT — Recce Recce proceeded Lewis Gunners etc moved at 3 A.M. to Pioneer Camp — Batt'n moved off at 4.15 PM in order H.Q. A, B, C & D Coys — relieved 7/8 K.O.S.B. in support in Right Sector — Battalion: H.Q. & D Coy in SEVEN ELMS, B & C Coys in FREE TR. R.O.T. A Coy in STARFISH TR: Night Quiet.	R.O.T.

WAR DIARY or INTELLIGENCE SUMMARY

Army Form C. 2118.

Month and Year: January 1917
Unit: IX Corps Royal Scots Fusiliers

Place	Date	Hour	Summary of Events and Information	Remarks and references to Appendices
SUPPORT RIGHT SECTOR LE SARS	17		Heavy snowfall throughout the night - Coys devoted the day to cleaning & clearing of the trenches of snow - Shelters were improved and Salvage collected - Orders received for relief of 6th Cameron in Left sub-section of Red from the next day - Capt Robinson RAMC joined for duty on 15th inst in lieu of Capt G. F. Clifton transferred to 70 Bde RFA - night quiet -	
LEFT FRONT	18		Day normal enemies Artillery fire but heavy snow fell and Coy was little - Battn moved off by Coys commencing "C" Coy at 8.20AM a relieving 6th Cameron in Left Front - Relief was completed by 1AM - Shelling of Battn HQ intermittent throughout night. Disposition C on Left, D Coy on Right, B in Support, A in Reserve - Most casualties in cleaning of arts & thawing them - a listening post was out in the Left intermittent snow & rain - day normal.	
	19		Intermittent Shelling of Front Line (O.19.a.) and Battn HQ throughout the day - In the evening men for raid made advance M.16.b.2.5½ - Beamont Rd at S end of Cutting M.16.b.3.3. - Two wounded & 9 ordinary individual - others sent into night & duck-boards - 60 yds of wire put in at night Coy front - night normal.	
PIONEER CAMP	20		Day quiet - Batt was relieved in evening by 6th Camerons & moved to Pioneer Camp (Reserve)	
	21		Batt rested during forenoon - in afternoon SD trench boards were laid in Camp - Mass seen Chies herves to haunt holiday.	
	22		Batt moved up at 4 PM to relief of 6th Cameron - Relief completed 8 PM - A raid was	R.I.F.T.

WAR DIARY or INTELLIGENCE SUMMARY

Army Form C. 2118.

(Erase heading not required.) Vol IX 6/7 Royal Scots Fusiliers

Instructions regarding War Diaries and Intelligence Summaries are contained in F.S. Regs., Part II. and the Staff Manual respectively. Title pages will be prepared in manuscript.

Month and year: January 1917

Place	Date	Hour	Summary of Events and Information	Remarks and references to Appendices
LE SARS	22		Capt Nisbet & Quarry on Pola in front (avalanche) 9 in preparation Capt Steel & Lieut Simpson with Henry proceeded with patrols. They reached & examined tank that stathra M16 b 8.7 - they found it to be 20 yards wide, 30 feet deep - sides steep & uncrossed. They then turned right & lay about 10 mins & heard tanks crunching snow & many lights were shown - machine gun & rifle fire was opened on them - they located a lost shattra M16 b 75.7 - patrol returned having been out 2 hours - that Stewart & Lieut Latham M16 b 75.7 - patrol returned having been out 2 hours - that Stewart twenty-strong patrol on right & examined enemy wire - they reported same like story of dark - Night was normal and enemy wire very alert - 2/Lieuts A.J. JOHNSTON & J McGHEE reported for duty - Posts were improved & latrines dug in them - tail-post	Appendices
	23		Day normal - The raid intended was cancelled owing to weather conditions - Posts were worked. Three being made each shift - constructor as protector against aerial dark - Post in FIRST LINE extended and deepened - 2/Lieut R.A. Clark and Major T. SMITH proceeded up to front line for examination of posts etc. ———————— this duty & T/Lt Clark was wounded - ———————— bombs bursts practically on him - Orders were issued for relief next day by 7th Cameron High - Capt A.P. Steel came to H.Q. pending the arrival of Major Mitchell 13th RScots who was coming next day - Night normal. Next post.	
	24		Major Mitchell assumed command 11AM - Wire strengthened between posts 16 and 17 - The continuance of these being carried on - Relief out on left from post 19 proceeded to tank	

WAR DIARY or INTELLIGENCE SUMMARY

Army Form C. 2118.

97 Royal Scots Fusiliers Vol IX

January 1917

Place	Date	Hour	Summary of Events and Information	Remarks and references to Appendices
HE SARS	24		Hot & providing half Bhn for support Coy. – Post located previous night approx M15 a 7½.7 was verified – Enemy was active with Very lights – Relief was commenced 5.30 PM and completed 9 PM – Batt. moved to BAZENTIN Camp arrived 11.30 PM –	
BAZENTIN CAMP	25		Day spent in usual cleaning equipment clothes etc – Conference of Commanding Officers at 15thDiv HQ at 3 PM – Staff of 9 officers received from 50th Bn D (Generals) Major Mitchell returned to 13th R.Scots. Lieut's B & Graham reporting from rest camp.	
–	26		2 Officers 6 N.C.Os and 150 men found for various working parties – Baths were cancelled owing to lack of water through frost – Cold severe with hard hoar frost –	
–	27		Inspections till 10 am – from 10 am – 12.30 PM Batt. march – Staff had training Orders received for relief of 10th Seaforth Rifles in RW front of Eaucourt Devancourt front the next day – Hard frost	
–	28		Reveille Reserve moved to Acid Drop Camp – 2/Lieut Rushan returned from course – Units A.J. Johnston and 10 m/Ghee proceeded to Divisional School – Batt. moved off at 4.15 PM route – BAZENTIN – MARTINPUICH Road, duck board track to W of MARTINPUICH – CHALK WALK – Destination C.Coy R.M.D. – Relief completed 7.30 PM – Left A Support B Reserve – Heavy shelling of October 1 Scars and Destrement Farm between 10 PM & 11 PM and 12 midnight and 3 AM – 2/Lieut T.R. Steenson attached 115th Trench Battery, Killed (AE) with Stringtown on front and holes obtained – Hard frost	142 S.I.D.

Army Form C. 2118.

WAR DIARY
or
INTELLIGENCE SUMMARY.
(Erase heading not required.) Vol IX

January 1917   b/7 Royal Scots Fusiliers

Place	Date	Hour	Summary of Events and Information	Remarks and references to Appendices
RE SARS (left sector)	29		Patrols sent report all quiet — Day normal with intermittent shelling of Right B&B in 26th AV. Work continued on posts. Support and Reserve trenches — Orders issued for Co-operation & demonstration to assist in attack on QUARRY and BUTTE immediately RIGHT. North front	
~	30		Zero Hour for raid by 9/10 Gordons on our Right was 1.45 am — What our front our Artillery commenced an intense barrage — Its 18 Pdrs on our Right and its 3 Heavy Artillery Groups on our front — They bombarded LITTLE WOOD and CALLWITZ Line 4 cm front Search for a period of 30 mins — Our front coys gave rapid rifle fire and machine gun sweep front a near approaches of the enemy — The enemy barrage was slow in opening but between 2.5 am and 2.20 am an intense barrage was opened on 6 lines of KE SARS — We had several very few casualties — Situation was normal by 3 am — Abbotts line coys "STOOD DOWN". Placed double sentries and manned work — Our Right coy C coy Relieved later with a view of possibly gassing hostile look out at M10 c 8.2½ — Patrol found the enemy on the alert and active & having no direct orders to attack, withdrew how — our lines — White night shirts were used on latest to harrass with the enemy which D coy between 8.45 PM and 11 PM & again at 2 AM by the enemy. A machine C coy on Right front B coy D coy in left front C coy K Support & D coy in Reserve — Snow fell — Had post-Work was continued on posts. Recon scouting parties made for SAA & bombs — Rations was constructed in front posts and wire strengthening in front — Patrols went out	243
~	31		but reported all quiet — Rel. of Bath. by 13th Royal Scots commenced	

Army Form C. 2118.

WAR DIARY
or
INTELLIGENCE SUMMARY.
(Erase heading not required.)

VOL IX 6/7 Royal Scots Fusiliers

January 1917

Place	Date	Hour	Summary of Events and Information	Remarks and references to Appendices
LE SARS Left Section VILLA CAMP Lt	31		At 7 PM, guides, 1 Lewis gun team & platoon guides at junction of trench – board walk (CHALK WALK) and GUN PIT RD at 7 PM. 'On relief' instructions of Batt were as follows. M.O. and C & D coy VILLA CAMP, B coy GUN PITS in M21f and A coy in GUN PIT RD. Orders were issued for relief by 25th AUSTRALIAN Batt on night 2/3rd Feby 1917. Hard frost.	

1-2-17

L.V.B.Jordan
Lieut: Col.
Commanding 6/7th Batt: Royal Scots Fusiliers.

244

6/7th (S.) Batt'n,
The Royal Scots Fusiliers

February, 1917.

G.S.
10 sheets

CONFIDENTIAL Vol 19

War Diary

From 1/2/17   To 28/2/17

(Volume xx)

CONFIDENTIAL

Vol 20

245
8B

WAR DIARY

OF 6/7th (SERVICE) BATTⁿ ROYAL SCOTS FUSILIERS.

FROM 1st February 1917 TO 28th February 1917

VOL. X

WAR DIARY / INTELLIGENCE SUMMARY

Army Form C. 2118.

VOL X 6/7 Royal Scots Fusiliers

February 1917

Place	Date	Hour	Summary of Events and Information	Remarks and references to Appendices
VILLA CAMP	1	—	Distribution Bath HQ & Co D Coys VILLA CAMP, A & B Coys GUNPITS Rd & C Coys GUNPITS MARTINPUICH — Officers of 25th Australian Batt. visited the Coys & took particulars of position — Orders issued for relief next day by 25th Australian Batt. —	
	2		Arrangements completed & stores handed over — Batt relieved by 25th Aust. Batt. Batt. moved to C. Camp Friourt arriving about 4.30 PM — A & B Coys from MARTINPUICH reached camp about 8.15 PM — Frosty weather, 9 nights still cold — Poor issue of fuel —	
Friourt Camp.	3		Men spent the day in cleaning up — Equipment etc inspected — Return of small detached parties from dumps etc. Orders issued for more next day ⇒ FRANVILLERS	
	4		Unfortunate accident about 11 AM — bomb exploded in front of men whilst on parade — 1 Killed 2/Lieut P Simpson Wounded (slightly) 10 O.Ranks wounded but recovered — Batt marched off 1 PM & passed starting point F.9.a.5.6. at 1.30 PM — Reached FRANVILLERS 4.30 PM — An advance party under 2/Lt McManus had preceded advance to take over billets — The whole Bde were accommodated where 2 Batts usually were & the relief was overcrowding of billets — Capt. Ferguson who had returned from Div. took Command of C. Coy. —	

Army Form C. 2118.

WAR DIARY
or
INTELLIGENCE SUMMARY.

(Erase heading not required.)

February 1917 Vol X 9/7 Royal Scots Fusiliers

Place	Date	Hour	Summary of Events and Information	Remarks and references to Appendices
FRANVILLERS	5	—	Inspections & cleaning of clothes, equipment etc — Re-sorting of billets — Slightly more accommodation but still overcrowded — Draft of 33 arrived from 2nd Bn. — Weather frosty.	
"	6		Refitting of clothes. Myries received. Reorganisation of sections, Platoon drill. Capt. J. Gardner appointed temporary 2nd Major FRANVILLERS —	
"	7		Reorganisation — new formation commenced. Signallers class commenced for beginners under Coy — Lewis Gunners visit this Coy — Major T.L. de Havilland joined this Batn as 2nd in Command.	
"	8		Short doubli in the morning by Platoons — Reorganisation new formation — Routine inspections by Platoon Commanders — In the afternoon Recreational Training — Football running etc — Football tournament commenced — Weather good.	
"	9		Short "doubli" before breakfast — Reorganisation. Platoon & Coy drill — Inoculation Officers & Ranks — 2/Lieuts W. DUNCAN and K.S. DICK joined Battn. posted to "A" Coy. Recreational training	
"	10		Short doubli — Reorganisation. Musketry & Bayonet fighting — Inspection of Lewis Gun by Armt Sgt Thomson — Rifle Grenadiers lecture QM — A Coy on fire posts — 2/Lieut P.O.G Wetherton joined the Battn.	

A5834 Wt: W4973/M687 750,000 8/16 D. D. & L. Ltd. Forms/C.2118/13.

Army Form C. 2118.

WAR DIARY
or
INTELLIGENCE SUMMARY.
(Erase heading not required.)

February 1917 Vol X 97 Royal Scots Fusiliers

Place	Date	Hour	Summary of Events and Information	Remarks and references to Appendices
GRANVILLERS	11		Divine Service Presbyterians 11 AM. Voluntary Evening Service 6 PM - Church of England 9.30 am Voluntary Evn Service 6 PM. Roman Catholics service 9 AM Lecture by Revd Holmes at 2 PM on "Communication with Aeroplanes" - Lecture 5 PM by Major T.L. de Haviland on the Campaign in German East Africa - this Lecture was most interesting - Capt H. Ritchie taken on strength 9-2-17	
"	12		Lt Leward reported back from hospital. Short double Organisation of Platoons in new formation - Training of Bombers - Platoon & Coy drill Musketry firing at H. range - 2 PM Rifle Grenadiers parady - Recreational training. Lecture by Revd Holmes at 4 PM subject "Pigeon Work" Consent at 6 PM - Divisional band attended & the concert was much enjoyed. Others were not engaged.	
"	13		Short double Instruction of Platoons in marching order - Training of Bombers - Reorganisation - Musketry (Range) 11.30 am Lecture by CO to men of draft Joining since 1st Dec 1916. Lecture was listened & given next day - A school contact Aeroplanes was attended by the Commanding Officer, 2nd in Command Capt H. Ritchie & 2 Officers pr Coy - 2/Lt Wilkinson & 2/Lt Schaler - not very successful - 2 Ranks taken on strength	

A5834 Wt.W4973/M687. 750,000. 8/16 D.D.&L.Ltd. Forms/C.2118/13.

WAR DIARY
INTELLIGENCE SUMMARY

Army Form C. 2118.

February 1917 1/7 Royal Scots Fusiliers

Hour, Date, Place	Summary of Events and Information	Remarks and references to Appendices
14. Itancourt	Short "drill". Reorganisation – training of bombers, rifle grenadiers – Musketry (Range) Recreational evening. Heads of Indentor & Seward & 2 NCOs here. Attended instruction Class beyond Hyttley under Sgt. Stewart. Army Gymnastic Staff. Orders issued for move.	
15.	The Batt. marched to TERRAMESNIL via CONTAY TOUTENCOURT PUCHEVILLERS & BOSQUESNE. Billets comfortable & clean. Mr Williams attended Div. Claims Officer. 29 men fell out but came in well rearguard. On the whole the Batt. marched well. Orders received re. move.	LENS MAP 1/100,000
16. TERRAMESNIL	Coy takes parties out/find – (a) Parts 1 officer 200 o.r. 150 Officers to MULLY for work on Railway. (b) 30 other ranks to BRETMONT for work on roads. Batt. moved off at 9.15 for NONCQ via DOULLENS – The men marched much better 2 only falling out. Needless to say a bit Coy. easy. Orders received re. move next day to NONCQ.	LENS MAP 1/100,000
17. NONCQ	Batt. moved to NONCQ via FREVENT. The men fell out. Billets comfortable & clean. Orders at in. Orders issued for move to GOUY-en-TERNOIS.	

WAR DIARY or INTELLIGENCE SUMMARY

Vol X. 6/7 1 - Royal Scots Fusiliers

January 1917

Place	Date	Hour	Summary of Events and Information	Remarks and references to Appendices
NUNCQ	18.		The Battn. moved off at 8 a.m. and marches to GOUY-EN-TERNOIS via HAUTE-COTE. - Lieut-Col. E.H.D. GORDON proceeds on leave to U.K. and MAJOR T. L. de HAVILLAND assumed command of Battalion. Capt. A. W. FERGUSON Acts as 2ND in Command and CAPT. Q.L. RITCHIE takes over command of "C" Cy as from 18th February. 1917.	LENS MAP 1/100,000
GOUY-EN-TERNOIS	19.		Short doubts by platoons. - Thorough inspections - fitting of equipment. Physical exercises. - Reorganisation. A draft of twelve other ranks reports to-day and were taken on the strength of the Battalion.	
"	20.		Reorganisation - Battalion parade under Commanding Officer. Two other ranks (one under 18 years of age and one returns to front on mining) proceeded to base this day and are struck off strength of Battalion.	
"	21.		Monthly Sartorius - Arms mounting - Bayonet fighting. Battalion parade under Commanding Officer. 2nd Lieut. C. B. OSBOURNE-SMITH is reported to this Battalion from R.S. Pl. attached to Border Regiment and taken on strength of the Battalion from this date.	
"	22.		Early morning exercise - 3/4 h.m. digging new Trench. - Bombing. Bayonet fighting. Gun mounting - musketry and Reorganisation. Nine other ranks reported this day from 20th I.B.D. and are taken on strength of the Battalion. Two other ranks rejoins to-day from Hospital. - Extract London Gazette: - 9-2-17 2/Lieut (A/Capt.) T. WATSON - to be Temp. Capt. 13.8.16. Lieut. H. JOPE - to be Temp. Capt. 15-11-16. 2/Lieut. M.S. HAMILTON and 2/Lieut. W. KERR transfers to Service Battalion with seniority 22-11-16.	

WAR DIARY
or
INTELLIGENCE SUMMARY.

VOL X C/7 & Royal Scots Fusiliers

February 1917

Place	Date	Hour	Summary of Events and Information	Remarks and references to Appendices
GOUY-EN-TERNOIS	23		Morning Exercises - Trench digging - Inspection of Smoke Helmets - Throwing of Bombs. Musketry & Bayonet Exercises.	
"	24		Morning Exercises - Bombing - Extended Order Drill - Company in the Assault. One private (under age) proceeded to Base this day & is struck off the strength of the Battalion.	
"	25		Divine Services were held. An hour and a half in afternoon was devoted to Bombing and Extended Order Drill. Three other ranks proceeded this day to Base for transfer to R.E. (Railway Construction Companies) and are accordingly struck off the strength of the Battalion.	
"	26		Company inspections - Battalion and Companies in morning exercises. - Company inspection of Shipping and Clothing & Equipment. 2nd Lieut. J. CARNAN reports this day from 20th I.B.D. and is taken on strength of Battalion. Forty two other ranks also report from 20th I.B.D. and are taken on strength of Battalion. 2nd Lieut. J. CARNAN is appointed Battalion Lewis Gun Officer.	
"	27		Battalion moves this morning to DIVISANS via AMBRINES - IZEL-LES-HAMEAU - and HERMAVILLE, arriving at 3 p.m. Accommodates in N.O.1. Camp & in huts. 2nd Lieut. A.D. CAMERON reports this day from G.H.Q. (Cadet School and is taken on strength of the Battalion. Extract from London Gazette. Temp 2nd Lt (act) Capt., whilst Comndg. a Coy.) A.P. SKEIL, M.C., to be Temp. Captain. (JAN. 3.) To be Temp. 2nd Lieut. J.B. COOPER Temp. 2nd Lt. A.E. BUCHAN. Temp 2nd Lt. R.A. CLARK 2nd Lieut. J. CARNAN (T.F) (JAN. 3.)	LENS MAP. 1/100,000

Army Form C. 2118.

WAR DIARY
or
INTELLIGENCE SUMMARY.

(Erase heading not required.) Vol. X. 6/7th Royal Scots Fusiliers

February 1917

Place	Date	Hour	Summary of Events and Information	Remarks and references to Appendices
DUISANS	28.		Routine Inspections by Platoons. Drill with Box Respirators & tube helmets. Testing of Box Respirators. - Handling of arms - dismantling practice.	

T.K. Attwull
Major.
Commanding 6/7th Batt. Royal Scots Fusiliers.

Confidential S.A. 21

WAR DIARY

OF

4/7 ROYAL SCOTS FUSILIERS

FROM 1ST MARCH 1917 TO 31ST MARCH 1917

VOL XI

10 G
7 sheets

Army Form C. 2118.

WAR DIARY or INTELLIGENCE SUMMARY.
(Erase heading not required.)

Vol X 6/7 Royal Scots Fusiliers

March 1917

Place	Date	Hour	Summary of Events and Information	Remarks and references to Appendices
DUISANS	1	—	The whole Battalion practically out on working party. — 17 Officers & 600 Other Ranks were employed on Railway construction at WARLUS. — The Ravens of a number of huts were completed. — This was done in A hut in Camp. —	
"	2		The completion of alliances and the Ravens of the remainder of the huts for reinforcements in foremoon through the gas test was carried out. — Movement orders for relief of 7/8 KOSB's in Reserve positions in ARRAS were received. — Major T.L.M Haviland accompanied by the Adjutant (Lieut W Pettigrew) proceeded to ARRAS to reconnoitre the positions. — Coy Commanders went to ARRAS in the foremoon to reconnoitre front line positions. They were the occupied following day. — Orders issued for relief of 10/11th HLI in Right Sub sector T3 Sector. — The Battalion moved off at 11.45 pm for ARRAS arriving & completing relief by 7.30 pm. — Bath HQ were in Rue de Jerusalem. — The men were in GRANDE PLACE. —	
ARRAS	3		The Battalion moved up to Front line relief commencing at 6 PM. Guides were supplied by 10/11th HLI. — Relief was complete at 7.45 am. — Dispositions. — ⓒ coy Front line ½ D coy Support ½ D coy permanent fatigue accommodated in cellars in ARRAS. A & B coys in Reserve in ARRAS. — Night normal Bath HQ Rue St Michel.	
"	4		Occasional shelling of Front & Support trenches but the shelling was for the most part fairly short. — Instructions were issued to deferential Gas discharge. — This was cancelled & postponed. — Working parties were found for new trenches being dug. — The work was under supervision of an officer from 8/10 Gordons & 9th Black Watch. Orders	Appendix I

OC

WAR DIARY
INTELLIGENCE SUMMARY

Vol XI 6/7 Royal Scots Fusiliers.

March 1917

Place	Date	Hour	Summary of Events and Information	Remarks and references to Appendices
ARRAS.	4.		were issued for inter-coy. relief. "A" relieving "C" and "B" relieving "D". Night was quiet.	Appendix 2.
-	5		Relief of "A" & "D" Coys. was completed at 6.30 am. Almost the usual working parties went on and an additional 200 men were found by 6th Cameron Highrs. 2/Lieuts W.C. Austin, Q.G. Blair and S.J. Moore joined for duty. Information was received that the 2 mo divisions would probably, tonight - but this was not definite - be relieving us and at night - Orders were received that the 2 mo divisions would probably, to tonight - but this was again postponed -	
-	6		The day was quiet and went again proceeded with at night. Orders were issued for relief of Batt., following day by 6th Cameron Highrs. Officers from that Batt. reconnoitred the line - Night quiet but about 5.30 am a heavy trench mortar fire was opened on our immediate left. This did not spread to our front -	
-	7		The Battn relief was complete by 12 noon and moved to Reserve position and Coys. in LARANDÉ ROE & Bath. HQ Rue de JERUSALEM. Defence Scheme was issued and 4 officers 200 O.Ranks supplied for work in line at night - Batts were allotted the Batt., latterly 2 Coys managed to avoid themselves of them own to lack of water	
-	8 →		The remainder of Batt. with the exception of HQ were bathed - Platoons were exercised in drills in the rapid adjustment of Box Respirator, rapid loading etc - Usual working parties of 200 ORanks at night.	

WAR DIARY

Army Form C. 2118.

INTELLIGENCE SUMMARY 6/7 Royal Scots Fusiliers

Title pages March 1917 Vol XI

Place	Date	Hour	Summary of Events and Information	Remarks and references to Appendices
ARRAS	9		Day quiet - usual working parties in the line at night - Staff of 19 officers posted to coys - Orders issued for relief of B coy by D coy - & B coy were situated in the Cemetery Defences. Lieut Col C.J.D. Gordon returned from leave & resumed Command.	
"	10		Day quiet. A lecture at GEVENEY le NOBLE on "Employment of tanks" was attended by 2/Lieuts. 23M°Quedor & W.H. Phimister. Orders were issued & relief took place of working parties supplied by the 10th Scottish Rifles - 1½ Coys worked with B (15th Div RE) Signals Rendez-vous Bell all Rue des Augustins at 6.30 PM - ½ Coy with Div Trench Mortar Officer, Rendez-vous Station at 6 PM. 1 Coy with 9th Gordons. in 4 reliefs 6 AM 12 noon 6 PM & 12 midnight. Rendez-vous NE corner of GRANDE PLACE - 1 Coy. with 73rd Field Coy RE Rendez-vous Station 6.30 PM.	
"	11		Work as laid down on previous day - An additional party of 1 NCO & 15 men was supplied Lieut Buchan for work on new trench -	
"	12		Work as for previous day - Signallers were taken in Busses took by Signal Officer.	
"	13		Work as for previous day - Conference of all Coy commanders with Commanding Officer after Orderly Room at 10 am -	

Army Form C. 2118.

WAR DIARY
or
INTELLIGENCE SUMMARY.
(Erase heading not required.)

March 1917 Vol XI 6/7 Royal Scots Fusiliers

Place	Date	Hour	Summary of Events and Information	Remarks and references to Appendices
ARRAS	14		Work as for previous day – Lecture to all officers not on duty, by the Commanding Officer at 10.30 a.m. A lecture on "Listening Sets" by Staff Officer at 2.0 p.m. attended by Capt M? Skill H.C.O & 1 O.Rank – Draft of 20 O.Ranks arrived – Taken on strength as from 11.8.	
"	15		Work & instruction of Signallers as for previous day –	2/Lieut A. Griffiths taken on strength.
"	16		Work & instruction of Signallers as for previous day –	2/Lieut S. J. Moore
"	17		Work & instruction of Signallers as for previous day – Orders issued for move next day to DUISANS –	
DUISANS	18		Work as usual during the day – Shift after 6 P.M. only, worked half and proceeded to DUISANS after. Balance of Coys moved out at 9.30 P.M. – Whole Battalion arrived facility by 11 P.M. – Orders came received for move of Battn. next day, IZEL LE HAMEAU – 2/Lieut S.J.Moore died of wounds –	
IZEL LE HAMEAU	19		Batn. paraded at 1 P.M. & moved off in order "A" D A B C Coys – Batn. arrived in Cellule by 5 P.M. – Platoon Commanders instructed their platoons in "Battle Order" –	
"	20		Completing of defences in the forenoon & Tools drawn – At 2.30 P.M. B & C coys marched to trenches at AMBRINES for manoeuvres – At 1.30 P.M. A & D Coys marched Nelson, moved to Cadet School, BLENDECQUES – At 1.30 P.M. A & D Coys returns – No 9958 Sgt.	
"	21		The Battalion paraded at 9.20 a.m & marched to trenches at AMBRINES. 2/Lieut R.Lee & 2 N.C.O's & party attended Bayonet Training class under Sgt Instructor Leay at AMBRINES.	

WAR DIARY or INTELLIGENCE SUMMARY

Army Form C. 2118.

Vol XI 6/7 Royal Scots Fusiliers — March 1917

Place	Date	Hour	Summary of Events and Information	Remarks
TREL. Re MAREAU	22		Battn. paraded at 9.10 am & proceeded to trenches at AMBRINES. Manoeuvre & attack was carried. The assault was practised this time under orders of Coy Cdrs. — Firing on range by Lewis Gunteams — Inspection of all rifles by Armourer Sgt. — Practice in the firing of No. 23 Rifle Grenade was commenced. 2/Lt Ross was attached to the Battn. for instructional duties in the demolition of dug-outs with Stokes bombs. Two Sqnads of 'A' coy instructed in this.	
"	23			
"	24		Battn. paraded at 8.45 am & proceeded to trenches at AMBRINES. The assault has again practised there under G.O.C. Bde. The throwing of live bomb, firing of No. 23 Rifle Grenade & practice demolition of dug-outs was continued during the afternoon.	
"	25		Battn. paraded at 8.45 am & continued the practice of assault as in previous day. The afternoon was devoted to practice in throwing live bombs and the instruction under 2/Lt Ross was continued in demolition of dug-outs. 2/Lt. W.G. Skeen reports this day on his return to charge the Battalion.	
"	26		Parades under Coy arrangements. Instruction was carried on in firing of No. 20 & No. 23 Rifle Grenades; also No. 5. mills. The subordinate commands was instructed in various orders. Lewis Gunner parties under Lewis Gun Officer for training and firing at Range.	

Army Form C. 2118.

WAR DIARY
or
INTELLIGENCE SUMMARY.

Vol. XI 6/7th Royal Scots Fusiliers

MARCH 1917

Place	Date	Hour	Summary of Events and Information	Remarks and references to Appendices
IZEL-LES HAMEAU	27.		Under Coy. Arrangements. Routine inclusive - efficiency inspection. Uniformity in Battle Order - wire cutting - Bayonet training - firsting - Antimechanical Communism. the giving of fire order. Swing of firearm. The Bayonet fighting Course was continued by Sgt. Instructor Keay when to following attendas - seven officers and 30 n.c.os. A draft of 16 ord.ranks reports this day and were taken on the strength of the Battalion. Several of these has already been with the Battalion and are all here fully trained.	
	28.		Forenoon was spent in completing Battle Order and in organising platoons. In the afternoon the Corps Commander inspected the Battalion on parade with Brigade.	
	29.		Under Coy. arrangements. Bombing was carried out by all Coys during phenomenos afternoon. The Rifle Range was also within aim, to come fairs. Drill was carried out in the adjusting of Base Respirators in reducing time. Bayonet fighting out instructing and indication of targets filled the remainder of days programme. Bayonet sighting class under Sgt. Instructor Keay was continued.	
	30.		As for the 29. L.L. and Range practice for the Companies who did not fire on the 29 th.	
	31.		Under Coy. Arrangements. Rifle Range was used by A and B Coys. in firing Snemann. and all Coys. use instructed & practised in throwing Nos. Mills Grenades. Routine includes - Box Respirator Drill. Bayonet Sighting - Instruction of targets - wire cutting.	

K.C.S. Jordan
Lt.Col.
Comdg. 6/7 R.S.F.

Vol 22

Confidential

WAR DIARY

OF

6/7th Royal Scots Fusiliers

FROM 1st April 1917 TO 30th April 1917.

VOL XI

WAR DIARY

Army Form C. 2118.

Instructions regarding War Diaries and Intelligence Summaries are contained in F. S. Regs., Part II. and the Staff Manual respectively. Title pages will be prepared in manuscript.

INTELLIGENCE SUMMARY (Erase heading not required.)

April 1917   Vol XII   6/7 Royal Scots Fusiliers

Place	Date	Hour	Summary of Events and Information	Remarks and references to Appendices
IZEL-LE-HAMEAU	1		Routine included Rifle Range, Bombing, Bayonet Training and Box Respirator drill - orders were issued for move to ARRAS on the following day.	
" & ARRAS	2		Battn. moved off about 11½ in a blinding snowstorm, to ARRAS marching via HERMAVILLE. I.TRAIN, new road running along R. SCARPE to ROND POINT. Advance Party 2/Lt. J.W. WHITELAW & 1 NCO per coy. met the Battn. at ROND Pt. Disposition Coys. Rue MOULENS & RUE des trois VISAGES and HQ along with B&e in RUE des AUGUSTINES	
ARRAS	3		Conference of Coy Commanders at HQ. Munitions to complete new dress from Ad Store, RUE de CRINCHON. Battn. moved up to bombardment position about 7·45 PM "A" in position "A" in Disposition "A" coy on left Day on Right Left of Battn. about CROWS NEST. Pt. between Saps 66A & 66B. 2/B dug-out 11 in support line between INCOME TAX & GARDE of COURT. Night normal with intermittent shelling of INNS of COURT. Heavy enemy barrage on about 11·30PM lasting about 12·30PM on our front - 2/Lieut A.D. MUNRO wounded. Relieved by 2/Lieut A.H. Phimister.	
front line	4		Day normal - Enemy T.M. activity on SUPPORT LINE near Battn. HQ. Aerial clash in Suffort & new Suffort. Our guns active - work at night was on CT's, Front & Support lui - Patrols report enemy wire badly torn up & in heaps in places. No suspected in enemy front line -	
"	5		Day normal - Raid by TL on our left at 12 noon - 7 prisoners taken & 1 killed T.Marks about 10·45PM 2 heavy barrage upon our general dark activity continued on our front line. Ortro' returned to mere back Batt	R.S.F.

Army Form C. 2118.

WAR DIARY
or
INTELLIGENCE SUMMARY.

(Erase heading not required.) Vol XII 6/7 Royal Scots Fusiliers

April 1917

Place	Date	Hour	Summary of Events and Information	Remarks and references to Appendices
ARRAS FRONT LINE	5		our front & support lines lasting 20 mins; nothing however was attempted by the enemy - 2/Lieut. A.J. Johnstone killed - 2/Lt W.G. Austin replaced him.	
	6		Work overnight was continued but much hampered by shell fire. Orders received to move back HQ to dug-out 13 on BLANGY RD, off IRON ST. Night normal & work continued on lines.	
	7		Enemy artillery very active - INCOME TAX, BLANGY RD & INGLE ST being heavily shelled periodically. Patrol under 2/Lt Duncan entered enemy trench, moved down it for 30yds & returned to our lines - Patrol reported trench badly damaged & unoccupied at that pt - Work continued on trenches & our own wire cut -	
	8		Enemy continue active - Orders issued for operations next day - Officials W.C. Austin and J P Seward wounded. Final arrangements made & Zero hour for attack given out as 5 30 am on 9th. At 11 PM B & C coys. moved from ARRAS into assembly position - HQ & Lewis position dug-out 11 at 1.15am 9th.	
	9		2/Lieut P Simpson replaced 2/Lt W G Austin wounded - Coy. Commanders at HQ at 3 30am - Watches synchronised at 3 50am. Bath on position 3.15 am. At 5 am after Zero (5.30am) a mine was exploded at G 24 a 5.4.; our Artillery opened an intense creeping barrage & the attack commenced see appendix.	
	10		See appendix.	
	11		See appendix.	

Army Form C. 2118.

WAR DIARY
or
INTELLIGENCE SUMMARY.
(Erase heading not required.) Vol XII 6/7 Royal Scots Fusiliers

April 1917

Instructions regarding War Diaries and Intelligence Summaries are contained in F. S. Regs., Part II. and the Staff Manual respectively. Title pages will be prepared in manuscript.

Place	Date	Hour	Summary of Events and Information	Remarks and references to Appendices
ARRAS	12		Batt. was relieved in front of MONCHY by part of 17th Division – On relief moved to BLANGY area – Batt. moved at 2PM to PLACE de LA CITÉ, ARRAS. HQ 13, 89 JUILLET. Personnel (Reserve) returning from DUISANS.	
"	13		Parades for Battle order & completing of deficiencies – Arrival of personnel from FRÉVENT.	
"	14		Batt. order parade – Draft of 61 O Ranks arrived –	
"	15		Divine Service. Presbyterian 11.30 AM in Concert Hall, behind theatre – Coy. E. in R.C. l'école normale at 11AM. R.C. in Catholic Club at 10 AM.	
"	16		Short route march – moved H.Q. to 26, Rue des Agaches with coys in same area – Two drafts of 26 & 70 received –	
"	17		Batt. order continued – Inspection of B Coy by Brigadier –	
"	18		Completing of coys in munitions, sandbags etc. & warning order issued to move into line next day.	
"	19		Batt. moved off leaving Sh x Rds 6.30 PM – Major T.K. de Haviland went up in Command of Batt. – Batt. relieved 1st Border Regiment Ref. Vis en front A coy support C & D BROWN LINE (Reserve) Disposition on relief B coy front enemy holding STRONG ARTOIS Pt. N.12.d.2.1 approx. Deepening & improving trenches.	Ref. Vis en ARTOIS
MONCHY SOUTH	20		Day normal but enemy artillery active on BROWN LINE area, FEUCHY CHAPPELLE Cross Rds, & CAMBRAI RD 9PM – 9.30 PM 2 Stokes guns bombarded point N.12.d.2.1 & at 10 PM Artill. went out to ascertain damage – Patrol was heavily fired on by enemy machine R.O.T.	

WAR DIARY or INTELLIGENCE SUMMARY

Army Form C. 2118.

April 1917   Vol. XII   6/7 Royal Scots Fusiliers

Place	Date	Hour	Summary of Events and Information	Remarks and references to Appendices
MONCHY SOUTH	20		Gen. of Kent W. KERR wounded - Improving trenches continued - C coy. moved up into Close supports into new trench dug by C & Gordons. 2 platoons of D coy moved forward to new supports -	
"	21		Enemy artillery active throughout the night - About 1 PM enemy ammunition dump blown up by no. in approx. O.C. Orders issued for relief by 11th A.S.H.	Ref Vis En ARTOIS
"	22		Batt. relieved by 11th A.S.H & moved to BROWN LINE with HQ at "82". Throughout the day enemy artillery had been active on LA FOSSE FARM & LA BERGERE FARM.	
"	23		Shrapnells employed by enemy on BROWN LINE in the early morning - Attack to be proceeded with Zero hour. 4.45 AM. Batt. relief positor 3.15 am. See appendix	Appendix 2.
"	24 25 26 27 28		See Appendix II	Appendix II
AALMS	29		Batt. moved to BERNEVILLE marching off at 1.15 P.M. Advm billets 8 PM - Batt. HQ. No 4. Rue de WALRUS. -	
BERNEVILLE	30		Cleaning up of billets & cleaning of equipment routine for companies - Draft of Post	

Army Form C. 2118.

WAR DIARY
or
INTELLIGENCE SUMMARY. Vol XII 6/7 Royal Scots Fusiliers

April 1917

(Erase heading not required.)

Army Form C. 2118.

Instructions regarding War Diaries and Intelligence Summaries are contained in F. S. Regs., Part II. and the Staff Manual respectively. Title pages will be prepared in manuscript.

Place	Date	Hour	Summary of Events and Information	Remarks and references to Appendices
BERNEVILLE	30		4 Officers & 51 Ranks received Officers, 2/Lieuts J.O. DEANS, E.C. Cunningham, J.J. Kilpatrick, and E.W.N. Ironson.	

L.I.D. Jordan
Lieut: Col.
Commanding 6/7th Batt. Royal Scots Fusiliers.

6/7TH BATTALION,
THE ROYAL
SCOTS FUSILIERS.
No. ASF 209
Date 1.5.17

Operations of April 9, 10 & 11, 1917.

Mon. April 9, 1917.

At Zero, 5.30 a.m., my Battn. was formed up in 8 waves (each wave of 2 platoons in line in this formation:—

```
A Coy. { ≡ ≡ } D Coy.
B Coy. { ≡ ≡ } C Coy.
```

and disposed as follows:—

    1st & 2nd waves in the front trench
    3rd & 4th waves "   " control "
    5th & 6th   "   "   " new Support "
    7th & 8th   "   "   " old   "   "

The bombing squads of the 8th wave accompanied the 1st wave with the object of remaining in O.G.1 (after the 1st wave passed on), bombing dug-outs & garrisoning the trench continuously until the 8th wave came up to occupy it. The bombing squads of the 5th, 6th & 7th waves accompanied the 2nd wave in order to occupy O.G.2 GLOUCESTER TERRACE & GOSFORD TERRACE in the same way. The bombing squads were provided with "P" bombs & Stokes Mortar shells made up for bombing dug-outs, in addition to Mills bombs. In accordance with the orders of the Brigadier the 1st & 2nd waves got out of the front trench at Zero, the 1st wave advancing about 50ˣ into "No Man's Land" & lying down there, & the 2nd wave advancing about 15ˣ.

On the day before the attack I ordered my Coy. Commanders to close up all their waves one trench at Zero, i.e., the 3rd & 4th waves in the control trench to advance into the front trench, the 5th & 6th from the new Support trench into the the control trench, & the 7th & 8th from the old Support into the new Support. As a matter of fact the 3rd & 4th waves did not really stop in the front trench but began at once to get out of it on to the parapet, while the waves behind pushed on towards the front trench.

I am quite certain that had I not ordered all the waves to close up at zero, the 7th & 8th waves would have lost many casualties for about 1 or 1½ minutes after zero the enemy opened an extremely heavy barrage on our old support line. The speed with which this barrage was opened was due, I think, to the fact that a great many signals were sent up by the Germans a few minutes before zero. It appeared to me that this alarm came down the German line from the North.

The advance began at Zero + 3'. Our barrage was extremely good in consequence our casualties were very small during the advance to the BLACK LINE.

During the advance, in accordance with orders given by me, the Lewis guns were fired from the hip from time to time, on several occasions this was most beneficial in dealing with Germans who shewed fight in the O.G. lines, though very little opposition was encountered there owing to our barrage & the heavy bombardment to which these trenches had been subjected previously.

A minenwerfer in concrete emplacement between O.G.2 & Gloucester Terrace was captured together with the officer in charge (wounded) & all the detachment, who were in a dug-out near by.

At 5.55 a.m. (zero + 25') the BLACK LINE was reached by the 2 front Coys. D Coy. on the right (in touch with the 9th Black Watch on the right) & A Coy.

on the left, in touch with the 11th A. & S. Highrs.
Both Coys. at once commenced digging in about
50ˣ or 60ˣ in front (East) of FRED'S WOOD,
each Coy. also making 2 strong points (each containing
a Lewis gun) about 70ˣ in front of the trench.
At this time (6 a.m.) the 4 O.G. Lines were
occupied by C & B. Coys.

At 8.30 a.m. I received a message from the O.C.
A Coy. (on the BLACK LINE) stating that the 2 rear
Coys. B & C had passed through his line at 7.50 a.m.
going well, & that the barrage was very good.
I retained in my hands at the beginning of the
attack 4 Lewis guns (1 from each Coy.) & the
2 Vickers Guns & one Stokes gun which had
been attached to me. Soon after 8 a.m. having
received a verbal message that the 13th Royal Scots
were being held up in Blangy by a German post
of bombers & snipers & that a Stokes gun was
much needed, I sent my Stokes gun to assist
there & then proceed to the S. end of FRED'S WOOD
& thence to the Triangle if required. At about 8 a.m.
I sent Lt. Lipscomb & 5th M.G. Coy. with his
2 Vickers Guns to the BLACK LINE to strengthen
that line, assist the advance to the BLUE LINE
if held up, & to assist in the consolidation of
the Railway Triangle after its occupation.

At 10.50 a.m. I received a message (timed 9.25 a.m.)
from O.C. A Coy on BLACK LINE stating that
the Coy. Sgt. Major of B Coy, who had come in
wounded reported that B & C Coys. were held up
by machine gun & rifle fire from the railway
embankment, & were lying about 30ˣ in front of
(i.e. East of) HAC TRENCH suffering casualties

& that the 9th Black Watch & 11th H. & S. H. were also held up. What actually happened was that some of our men were hit by our own shells with the result that the line stopped, while the barrage went on as arranged, & so the men were not close enough to the embankment when the barrage lifted off it.

At 11:35 a.m. (10:35 a.m.) I received a report with map (time from Lt. Lipscomb 45th M. G. Coy., stating that he had his 2 guns in action at the point where HALF TRENCH meets the Western side of the Triangle, & showing on the map where the hostile machine guns were, behind the E. side of the Triangle. I reported this to Bde. H.Q. & was informed at 11.40 a.m. that it had been decided to bombard the E. side of the Triangle again from 11.55 a.m. to 12.5 p.m. I at once sent runners with a memo. to O.C. B Coy notifying him of this bombardment but owing to the distance they did not reach 2/Lt. McCosh (the O.C. B Coy) who had been wounded & was lying in HALF TRENCH until just after 12.5 p.m. as the bombardment was finishing, & too late to arrange for an advance under cover of the barrage.

At 12:10 p.m. I got a further message from O.C. A Coy (in writing) confirming his previous message & stating that B. & C. Coys were suffering heavy casualties & that a wounded Corpl. reported that the barrage lifted from the railway embankment too soon before B Coy. got near it & the Germans came out & lined the embankment

At 12.15 p.m. I received a report on map (timed 10.50 p.m.) from 2/Lt. McIndoe (now O.C. C Coy.) stating the same as the above 2 messages from O.C. A Coy.

A Stokes gun was brought up into the Triangle by the 9th Black Watch & fired several rounds at the E. embankment, also a Tank came up & B & C Coy with the A. & S. H. on the left advanced, the Germans retiring hastily down FEUCHY LANE, some of them throwing away their equipment.

At 12.50 p.m. I received a verbal message from my L. G. officer whom I had sent forward to get information, that the Triangle had been taken, & at 1.45 p.m. I received a report on map (timed 12.55 p.m.) from O.C. B Coy. informing me that the 2 Coys. were digging in E. of the E. side of the Triangle, exactly in the same position as was done on the practice trenches, with two strong points (each with Lewis gun) out in front of each Coy, & that a patrol had gone forward into WATERY WOOD but had not yet returned, but no sign of enemy visible.

I then moved my H.Q. to a dug-out in O.G. 2 & after waiting there a little went forward to FRED'S WOOD & the Triangle & then on to the slope between the railways

WATERY WOOD as the Brigadier had told me that I was to take over the line there from the 9th Black Watch. On returning to Battn H.Q. I found that new orders had been received to occupy FEUCHY REDOUBT & I accordingly moved my Battn there arriving about 8 p.m.

Tues. April 10 During the morning the Coys. were completed in S.A.A. & bombs.
About 2 p.m. orders were received for the Battn to proceed to consolidate a position along the spur running N.N.E. in Sq. H 36 d & b. Marched off about 2.30 p.m., got on to the railway line at the level crossing at H.21c central, & proceeded along it as far as the cutting in H 23 c. Just as the head of the Battn reached this cutting the enemy began shelling the slopes to the S. of it & as some shells dropped almost on the top of the cutting, I made my Battn lie down on the S. bank of the railway cutting with the head of the Battn about 150x W. of the level crossing at H.23 b 2½ 1½. I went forward to that level crossing & found Lt. Col. Hannay & Lt. Col. Russell, the 13th R. Scots being disposed along the railway & along the sunken road running S.E. from the level crossing, while the 6 Cameron Highrs. were on their way from FEUCHY. We found that the situation was widely different from what

had been understood to be the case; & that it was impossible for me to carry out my instructions as the 37th Division had not yet taken MONCHY-LE-PREUX.

I also found that I was not more than 700 x at most from our front line, & that there was certainly one German machine gun in or near the chemical works in I.13.d., which partially enfiladed the railway cutting, but apparently could not see the South bank of the cutting. The enemy now began to shell the cutting (probably owing to a German aeroplane having passed over a little time before, & as I had 3 men killed & 9 wounded & the cutting would have become a death-trap if the machine gun or guns had completely enfiladed it & there was no suitable position S. or W. of the railway, I decided to move back to the E. end of FEUCHY village, thereby anticipating orders which were at that time being sent to me from Bde. H.Q. A heavy snow-storm coming on at this time very opportunely covered our movement back along the railway line.

On arriving in FEUCHY I distributed the men in various cellars & got cover of some sort for all of them, the snow still falling heavily. The 6th Cameron Highrs. had already returned to FEUCHY.

~~Wed. April~~ 11.

Wed. April 11

At 2.30 a.m. I received orders to attack, on the left of the 6th Cameron Highrs., the German position on the spur running N.N.E. from MONCHY-LE-PREUX through H.36.d.&b. & then push on till my Battn. reached the spur running N.E. through I.31.c.&b. & I.26.c, the centre of my Battn. to be directed on PELVES MILL. The 46th Infy. Bde. were attacking on the right of the 45th Bde. The position of assembly was to be the sunken road running N.E. from H.29.b.4.1 & the attack to commence at 5 a.m.

Owing to the fact that a number of men had shifted to other cellars etc than those they were first put into, having found better accommodation for themselves, that the cellars were very difficult to find (for rousing the men) in the darkness & snow, & that in 2 Cos. the rations had not yet been issued, there was considerable delay in getting out of the village. I led the Battn. out of the village & across the railway by the level crossing at H.29.b.9.9, just beyond which I met an officer, Lieut. Wood, who was taking up the Divisional observers to about the same place as my position of assembly & who told me that he knew the route so I got him to guide me as I had never seen the ground before.

We proceeded in a S.E. direction until we struck the E. & W. road in H.29.c, about H.29.c.8.7, where we found battalions of the 46th Bde. forming up. On reaching what was the road junction (it was impossible to see any road there) at H.29.d.1½.8, Lieut. Wood was of opinion that that was not the sunken road & we proceeded on.

On arriving at a cross-roads which I found, soon after the attack had started, it was light enough to see, was H.29.d.8.9, I found the 6th Cameron Highrs.

forming up & I at once ordered my Coy. Commanders to form up on their left. I had already before leaving FEUCHY told the Coy. Comdrs. that the Battn. was to form up in exactly the same formation as ~~in the morning of April 9th~~ for the attack on the BLACK LINE on the morning of April 9 v.3", 8 waves, D & A Coys. in front, C & B behind, with 100x between waves in this case. It was about 5.3 or 5.4 a.m. when the head of my Battn. reached the cross-roads, the 6th Camerons began to move forward at about 5.6 a.m., I think, & it was about 5.8 a.m. when my front Coys. began to advance. The men came up extraordinarily quickly, doubling into their places, & as far as I could see in the dim light my front Cos. were in line with the 6th Cameron Highrs.

As my rear 2 Coys. were passing the cross-roads to form up a Coy. of the 6th Cameron Highrs. ("C" Coy. I think) passed through them, also coming up in rear of their front Coys.

There was no barrage by our artillery when the advance began.

Directly the ~~Battalions~~ passed the crest of the ridge German machine guns began firing very heavily (from ~~the~~ the North side of the River SCARPE & also from the South side of the river below the ridges ~~along which~~ & spurs along & across which we were passing, (I think) & enfiladed the line & this seems to have pushed the whole line over to the right.

From this point onwards it ~~becomes~~ is extremely difficult to give any connected description of what happened, especially as I had no reports from any one during the day.

One of my Coy. Comdrs. sent ~~me~~ 2 reports but in one case the runner was wounded & in the other case he is missing. Another of my Coy. Comdrs. also sent me a report but in that case also the runner was wounded

At 6.20 a.m. a wounded man of my Battn. who was shot through the arm & was quite collected & cool assured me most definitely that "our men were entering the village" when he was wounded & came away, & a wounded officer, whom I did not see, also told my Medical Officer the same. At first I thought that the village referred to might be PELVES but I soon came to the conclusion that it must be MONCHY.

From the information I have been able to obtain from the 4 surviving officers & from various N.C.O.'s it appears that the advance was held up about 200x or 300x North of MONCHY by Germans in a trench in front on the left flank. A good many casualties were suffered here but the trench was taken & some prisoners captured, a Lewis gun being sent to protect the left flank. Some men worked round the flanks of the village & others advanced straight into the village driving such Germans as remained out at the other side (S.E.)

By this time all battalions were mixed up & officers & N.C.O.'s generally collected such men as were near them & "carried on" with them. 2nd Lieut. W. McIndoe showed great initiative in collecting Lewis gunners & riflemen & forming posts outside the S.E. of the village, which were re-inforced by 2 Vickers & machine guns of the 8th Cavalry Brigade. 2nd Lieut. McIndoe, who had about 150 men of 8 or 9 battalions manning 7 posts, worked under the orders of the O.C. one of the Cavalry regts. (I think it was the O.C. Essex Yeomanry) who took charge of all the posts. At night orders were received for the Battalion to be relieved by a battalion of the 17th Division & a battalion of the Dorset Regt. took up its position from the railway Southwards through H.29.d.8.9 where were my Battn. Hdqrs. & some men whom I had collected.

The men in & round MONCHY withdrew as they could be collected, & marched back to dug-outs & cellars in the Support & Reserve Lines E. of ARRAS.

The casualties of the Battalion were as follows:—

	April 9		April 10		April 11		Total	
	Officers	N.C.O.'s & men	Off.	N.C.O.'s & men	Off.	N.C.O.'s & men	Off.	N.C.O.'s & men
Killed	2	15	—	3	1	8*	3	26
Wounded	6	85	—	9	5	144	11	238
Missing	—	—	—	—	1	32	1	32
	8	100	—	12	7	184	15	296

* The number given as killed on April 11 only includes those of whose death there is no doubt.

16.4.17

E.I.D. Gordon
Lt. Col.
Comdg. 1/7th R. Scots Fus.

I

Report on Operations 19th April - 25th April 1917

On the evening of the 19th April the Battalion marched from ARRAS to the BROWN LINE where guides from the 1st BORDER REGT. led the four companies up to the trenches in the front line - S. of LA BERGERE FARM on the CAMBRAI ROAD. Immediately in front of our position about 100 yds due E the enemy had established a small "strong point" which was surrounded by a barbed wire entanglement. It was also believed to contain a machine gun emplacement. On the evening of the 20th a patrol under command of Lieut Kerr was sent out but was not successful, the Officer being wounded & four casualties amongst the party. The next night, April 21st another attempt was made, and a patrol under Sergt. NIBLOCK remained out for half an hour and obtained good information. It was discovered that about 120 of the enemy were seen moving towards this post which established the fact that the position was occupied by night and not by day. There were no casualties. That night the Batt moved back to the BROWN LINE being relieved by the 11th A+S.H. From 9.30 to 11.15 several Tear Shells & Gas Shells were put over the line. During Sunday 22nd April the Batt remained in the BROWN LINE trenches making final preparations for the attack which was to take place the next morning. Later in the day orders were received to the effect that the Batt would act as support to the 13th Royal Scots & 11th A+S.H who would advance from the front line trenches at Zero hour.

At 3.45 am on the 23rd the four companies were in position in the following order C+D in the O.S.2 Lines & A+B in the O.S.1 Line. At 4.15 a.m. the O.C & Adjutant reported at Adv. H.Q. in accordance with verbal instructions previously given. Zero hour had been fixed at 4.45 a.m. and an intense bombardment took place.

At 6.20 p.m. C Company was ordered forward in "diamond" formation and to occupy trench in N.12.c (Old German Gun Pits). Shortly afterwards at 6.30 p.m. D Co moved out 500 yds in rear of C Coy & A + B Coys. & Headquarters followed at a somewhat equivalent distance in similar formation.

It was not known how the advance was progressing but as a measure of precaution C & D Coys. were moved forward & occupied the front and supervision trench - C Coy being in the front assembly trench previously occupied by the 13th Royal Scots. D Coy in trench in immediate support. Battn H.Q being established with A + B Coys. who were in the Communication Trench.

The Brigadier had previously instructed me to establish Battn H.Q at LA BERGERE FARM on the CAMBRAI ROAD and as soon as the Companies were in position I moved across the valley accompanied by the Adjt. At this time the farm was subjected to a good deal of attention from the enemies artillery. Shells were falling all round but a hope was entertained that a cellar might be found which would be sufficient for H.Q so as to link up by wire to Bde. H.Q. I had previously met 2/Lt Boag of the Bde. Staff who conveyed a message from the Brigadier that I was to send one Co to support the 11th A & S.H. on the right and one Co to get in touch with the 13th Royal Scots on the left. C & D Coys were detailed & the position explained to the two Coy. Commanders - 2nd Lt Lee & Lieut. J.B Rooper respectively. I then moved to LA BERGERE FARM. On my arrival there I found that there was a small cellar, but it was over full with officers & men of other units endeavouring to find temporary refuge from the storm of shells & that it was not possible to connect up with Bde. H.Q. the wires being cut almost immediately after they were mended.

While there I heard the advance was not going too well. I remained at LA BERGERE FARM for an hour or so. hoping the bombardment would lessen down

3.

but it seemed to increase in density. I decided to get out and try and pick up a telephone to speak with Bde HQ. I eventually managed to get to the Bde Report Centre. While at the FARM I received a report that 2/Lt. Lee had been wounded. It was not known where the 13th Royal Scots actually were except that they were somewhere N. of CAMBRAI ROAD.

My instructions from the Brigadier were that I was to get in touch & press with the "utmost vigour". I was now in a position of considerable difficulty as I had no spare officers & I was not willing to send a Company in command of an N.C.O. to undertake a movement that undoubtedly required firm & deliberate handling. I instructed Lieut Carman the Lewis Gun Officer who was attached to Batt. HQ to at once take over command. From information I had previously received I learnt that the position on the Left — that is the part of the ground where our Co. had to support the 13th R.S. — was very obscure. It was known that the enemy occupied STRING TRENCH & SHOVEL TR & with part of the CAMBRAI ROAD formed a triangle of defence of considerable strength. C. Coy had by this time proved across from the South side but when Lieut Carman arrived only 27 men & 2 Lewis Guns could be found. They were occupying shell holes on N. side of the ROAD about 200 yds. E. of LA BERGERE FARM. but they were scattered & disorganised.

11-15 AM Report now received from that D. Coy had found the 11th A. & S. H. to be in BULLET TR & as it was narrow & well held a trench immediately in rear of SPEAR LANE was occupied.

On receipt of a message from OC C Coy that he could only number 50 pill ranks I immediately ordered A Co to pass across at once & act as reinforcements.

12.30 PM Report received from OC C Co. that STRING TR & PICK TR were in our possession & also part of SHOVEL TR and that he was sending out a patrol to find out the situation lower down in SHOVEL TR and also that 20 prisoners had been sent to the rear + one machine gun & plenty of ammunition captured. The machine gun was being used against the enemy. At this time shells from our own Artillery were falling short

1-10 pm. After speaking with Bde HQ I instructed O C Coy that his Right Flank was to rest on the CAMBRAI RD & that he was not to go to the South side. Also that a barrage of 18 pdrs had been asked for 300 yds E of SHOVEL TR. N of the ROAD. Furthermore, two Stokes Guns would be sent to him & he was to commence clearing SHOVEL TR. SOUTH & to occupy it as soon after as possible

2-20 PM I instructed B. Coy to move into STRIVE TR & to support C Coy

The disposition of the Batt at 3.30 was as follows. C Coy in STRIVE TR. 2 Platoons of A Co in SHOVEL TR. B Coy had 1 Platoon in PICK TR & D Co supporting the 11th A & SH.

At 3-45pm a determined counter attack was made by the enemy from N of CAMBRAI RD due E of our position but it was repulsed by our artillery & MG fire from two guns in SHOVEL TR. At 4.45 PM the attack was over and conditions were normal. At 5pm the 29th Div advanced their line 300 yds occupying SHRAPNEL TR. Shortly afterwards a message was received from Bde that the 46th Bde would pass through & take the BLUE LINE.

At about 6 PM a second counter attack was attempted but without special Artillery preparation. Our Artillery were immediately active and destroyed the attack carrying the barrage into the enemies lines under cover of which the 46th Bde passed through us

OC C Coy who was now in command of A + B Coys as well consolidated his position & threw out posts for the night. Rations & water were sent up to the Coys under cover of darkness together with ammunition bombs, flares and Lewis Gun ammunition. Every man was completed as far as possible to Batt. Order.

24.4.17   The morning was quiet except for intermittent shelling. D Co which was in a trench behind SPEAR LANE was brought back to occupy a trench running E & W through N.11.D close to Batt. H2.
4 PM   Intensive barrage and the 46th Bde supported by the 6th Camerons & 8/10th Gordons attacked.
6.45 PM Orders were received to move A B & C Coy. from the triangle - at dusk - to the BROWN LINE. D Co was to dig and occupy strong Points 200 yds E of Bde. H2 on spur of slope. Three of these were completed and occupied.
11 PM. The Batt. less D Co. was in position in BROWN LINE Night was normal.

25.4.17   Orders were issued at 8 PM for Batt to move up & occupy SHOVEL TR. & STRING TR. with 1 Co in rear in a trench to be dug. C Co dug a trench 50 yds behind the sunken road. Move commenced at 11 PM.
Disposition. D Co in SHOVEL TR. A & B Co in STRING TR. C Co in new trench dug from a point 200" E of LA BERGERE FARM for 100" northwards.
3 PM   Orders were received that 6th Camerons would assault trench immediately in rear of CAVALRY FARM at 10-35 PM.

26.4.17. Remained in trenches. SHOVEL TR. was subjected to a heavy bombardment throughout the night - Casualties 4 killed. 10 wounded

27-4-17. Day normal. New Trench was dug by C. Co 150 yds in front of SHOVEL TR. D Co moved back to trench occupied by C. Co. It was originally intended that D Co should dig this trench but the were considerably shaken by the persistent bombardment & C. Co was ordered forward to take the work over.

28.4.17 At 8.30 PM the Batt was relieved by D Co of the 1st London Regt. 56th Div.

———

This is a short account of the operations in which the Batt took part from the evening of the 19th April to midnight of the 28th April

From the above account it will be noticed that the work of the Batt was of a very exacting nature. The attack on the 23rd was of the fiercest description & during the time all ranks were in the front line trenches they were subjected to an intense Artillery bombardment especially by night.

I am bringing to your notice under separate cover the very excellent work of Lt Ramon who commanded C. Co on the 23rd. By the judicious & careful handling of his men he was instrumental in taking STRING TR & so thereby materially assisting in the forward advance. He went forward himself with a few men & bombed the enemy out of S. STRING TR and by his personal example steadied them under heavy fire. A list of N.C.Os & men deserving special recognition will also be submitted for consideration

The total casualties for the period under review were
4 Officers wounded
Other ranks K. 23 W. 99 M. 23 M BW. 3
Total 148.

In the field
April 29th 1917

T. Lawhurst
Major
C/Y R. S. Fusiliers

13.

1.10 p m.   After speaking with Bde H Q. I instructed O C
C Coy that his right Flank was to rest on the CAMBRAI RD.
& that he was not to go to the South side. Also that a
barrage of 18 pdrs had been asked for 300 yds E of
SHOVEL TR. N of the ROAD. Furthermore two Stokes Guns
would be sent to him & he was to commence clearing SHOVEL
TR. SOUTH & to occupy it as soon after as possible.

2.20 P M   I instructed B. Coy to move into STRING TR & to
support C Coy.

　　　　　The disposition of the Battn at 3.30 was as
follows. C. Coy in STRING TR. 2 Platoons of A Co in
SHOVEL TR. B Coy had 1 Platoon in PICK TR & D Co
supporting the 11th A & S H.

　　　　　At 3.45 p m a determined Counter Attack was
made by the enemy from N. of CAMBRAI RD due E of our
position but it was repulsed by our artillary & with
M G Fire, from two guns in SHOVEL TR. At 4.45 P M the
attack was over and conditions were normal at 5 p m.
The 29th Div advanced their line 300 yds occupying
SHRAPNEL TR. Shortly afterwards a message was received
from Bde. that the 46th Bde would pass through & take
the BLUE LINE.

　　　　　At about 6 P M a second Counter Attack was
attempted but without special Artillary preparation. Our
Artillary were immediately active and destroyed the
attack continuing the barrage into the enemies lines
under cover of which the 46th Bde passed through us

　　　　　O.C. C Coy. who was now in Command of A & B Coys
as well consolidated his position & threw out posts for
the night. Rations & water were sent up to the Coys
under cover of darkness together with ammunition bombs,
flares and Lewis Gun ammunition. Every man was completed
as far as possible to Batt Order.

24.4.17.   The morning was quiet except for intermittent
shelling D Co which was in a trench behind SPEAR LANE
was brought back to occupy a trench running E & W. through
N.11.D close to Batt H Q.

4 P M.   Intensive barrage and the 46th Bde supported by
the 6th Camerons & 8/10th Gordons attacked.

5.45 P M. Orders were received to move A B & C Coy. from
the triangle - at dusk - to the BROWN LINE & D Co was
to dig and occupy strong Points 200 yds E of Bde. H Q on
spur of slope. Three of these were completed and
occupied

11 P M.   The Batt less D Co. was in position in BROWN LINE
Night was normal.

25.4.17.   Orders were ~~ree~~ issued at 8 P M for Battn to
move up & occupy SHOVEL TR. & STRING TR. with 1 Co in
rear in a trench to be dug C. Co dug a trench 50 yds
behind the sunken road. Move commenced at 11 P M.
Disposition - D Co in SHOVEL TR A & B Co in STRING TR.
C Co in new trench dug from a point 200^x E of LA BERGERE
FARM for 100^x northwards.

13.

1.10 p.m. After speaking with Bde H Q. I instructed O C C Coy that his right Flank was to rest on the CAMBRAI RD. & that he was not to go to the South side. Also that a barrage of 18 pdrs had been asked for 300 yds E of SHOVEL TR. N of the ROAD. Furthermore two Stokes Guns would be sent to him & he was to commence clearing SHOVEL TR. SOUTH & to occupy it as soon after as possible.

2.20 P M I instructed B. Coy to move into STRING TR & to support C Coy.

The disposition of the Battn at 3.30 was as follows. C. Coy in STRING TR. 2 Platoons of A Co in SHOVEL TR. B Coy had 1 Platoon in PICK TR. & D Co supporting the 11th A & S H.

At 3.45 p m a determined Counter Attack was made by the enemy from N. of CAMBRAI RD due E of our position but it was repulsed by our artillery & with M G Fire, from two guns in SHOVEL TR. At 4.45 P M the attack was over and conditions were normal at 5 p m. The 29th Div advanced their line 300 yds occupying SHRAPNEL TR. Shortly afterwards a message was received from Bde. that the 46th Bde would pass through & take the BLUE LINE.

At about 6 P M a second Counter Attack was attempted but without special Artillery preparation. Our Artillery were immediately active and destroyed the attack continuing the barrage into the enemies lines under cover of which the 46th Bde passed through us

O.C. C Coy. who was now in Command of A & B Coys as well consolidated his position & threw out posts for the night. Rations & water were sent up to the Coys under cover of darkness together with ammunition bombs, flares and Lewis Gun ammunition. Every man was completed as far as possible to Batt Order.

24.4.17. The morning was quiet except for intermittent shelling D Co which was in a trench behind SPEAR LANE was brought back to occupy a trench running E & W. through N.11.D close to Batt H Q.

4 P M. Intensive barrage and the 46th Bde supported by the 6th Camerons & 8/10th Gordons attacked.

5.45 P M. Orders were received to move A B & C Coy. from the triangle - at dusk - to the BROWN LINE & D Co was to dig and occupy strong Points 200 yds E of Bde. H Q on spur of slope. Three of these were completed and occupied

11 P M. The Batt less D Co. was in position in BROWN LINE Night was normal.

25.4.17. Orders were ree issued at 8 P M for Battn to move up & occupy SHOVEL TR. & STRING TR. with 1 Co in rear in a trench to be dug C. Co dug a trench 50 yds behind the sunken road. Move commenced at 11 P M. Disposition - D Co in SHOVEL TR A & B Co in STRING TR. C Co in new trench dug from a point 200^x E of LA BERGERE FARM for 100^x northwards.

1.10 p.m. After speaking with Bde H Q. I instructed O C C Coy that his right Flank was to rest on the CAMBRAI RD. & that he was not to go to the South side. Also that a barrage of 18 pdrs had been asked for 300 yds E of SHOVEL TR. N of the ROAD. Furthermore two Stokes Guns would be sent to him & he was to commence clearing SHOVEL TR. SOUTH & to occupy it as soon after as possible.

2.20 P M I instructed B. Coy to move into STRING TR & to support C Coy.

The disposition of the Battn at 3.30 was as follows. C. Coy in STRING TR. 2 Platoons of A Co in SHOVEL TR. B Coy had 1 Platoon in PICK TR & D Co supporting the 11th A & S H.

At 3.45 p m a determined Counter Attack was made by the enemy from N. of CAMBRAI RD due E of our position but it was repulsed by our artillary & with M G Fire, from two guns in SHOVEL TR. At 4.45 P M the attack was over and conditions were normal at 5 p m. The 29th Div advanced their line 300 yds occupying SHRAPNEL TR. Shortly afterwards a message was received from Bde. that the 46th Bde would pass through & take the BLUE LINE.

At about 6 P M a second Counter Attack was attempted but without special Artillary preparation. Our Artillary were immediately active and destroyed the attack continuing the barrage into the enemies lines under cover of which the 46th Bde passed through us

O.C. C Coy. who was now in Command of A & B Coys as well consolidated his position & threw out posts for the night. Rations & water were sent up to the Coys under cover of darkness together with ammunition bombs, flares and Lewis Gun ammunition. Every man was completed as far as possible to Batt Order.

24.4.17. The morning was quiet except for intermittent shelling D Co which was in a trench behind SPEAR LANE was brought back to occupy a trench running E & W. through N.11.D close to Batt H Q.

4 P M. Intensive barrage and the 46th Bde supported by the 6th Camerons & 8/10th Gordons attacked.

5.45 P M. Orders were received to move A B & C Coy. from the triangle - at dusk - to the BROWN LINE & D Co was to dig and occupy strong Points 200 yds E of Bde. H Q on spur of slope. Three of these were completed and occupied

11 P M. The Batt less D Co. was in position in BROWN LINE Night was normal.

25.4.17. Orders were ~~ree~~ issued at 8 P M for Battn to move up & occupy SHOVEL TR. & STRING TR. with 1 Co in rear in a trench to be dug C. Co dug a trench 50 yds behind the sunken road. Move commenced at 11 P M. Disposition - D Co in SHOVEL TR A & B Co in SPRING TR. C Co in new trench dug from a point 200^X E of LA BERGERE FARM for 100^X northwards.

Confidential

War Diary

of

6th/7th Royal Scots Fus.

1st to 31st May, 1917

Vol. 23

Army Form C. 2118.

WAR DIARY
or
INTELLIGENCE SUMMARY.
(Erase heading not required.)

XIII 6/7 Royal Scots Fusiliers

MAY

Instructions regarding War Diaries and Intelligence Summaries are contained in F.S. Regs., Part II. and the Staff Manual respectively. Title pages will be prepared in manuscript.

Place	Date	Hour	Summary of Events and Information	Remarks and references to Appendices
EKMEVILLE	1		Coy routine including Coy. Drill, musketry, rapid aiming, Physical training. Bayonet fighting & Box Respirator Drill. A Draft of 7 Officers and 109 Other ranks received. Officers Major T.A. McEwan, Capt N.S. Rose ?, to command 'B' Coy. 2/Lts. E.F. Salmon, Allan Henry, J Simons, F.S. Forrest, M. Oliphant, Capt N.S. Rose, M. Oliphant & No. 15273 Capt. Commands. Two awards of Military Medal for 2nd Lts gazetted, to No. 16/36 A/Cpl. T. Mulholland, Cpl Pollock H, No. 45236 & Cpl N. Wilson.	
Berneville	2		Coy routine including Coy. Drill musketry. Physical training. Bayonet fighting. Box Respirator Drill. Two Coys were on Large practices.	
BERNEVILLE	3.		Route March by Coys. Later Coy Drill, exercises Order Drill. Bayonet fighting. Physical training. The other two Coys were firing on range in afternoon. Capt A.D. McShane? shared reports the day for duty & was posted to command 'A' Coy. Rifle aiming. Physical training.	
BERNEVILLE	4/5		Coy Routine including Coy. Drill. Musketry. 'B' + 'C' Coy reorganising in the evenings. Church Services from 9 – 9.45 pm. – 6 – 6.45 pm.	
BERNEVILLE	6		The Battn. marched for BERNEVILLE & WANQUETIN, marching off at 10.25 am.	
WANQUETIN	7.		The Battn. must k-day... Drill. No orders of any kind were taken in. A draft of 90 O.R.s shorts. Coy ??? arrives at 3 pm.	
IVERGNY	8.		The Battn. moved to-day to IVERGNY, moving off at 9 AM, arrival at 3 pm. All the Battalion in Billets.	
"	9		'B' O/C Coy on Range. A'O'D' Coy. Drill, Bayonet fighting, Physical training. 3 pm – ?pm – Games. Capt GARDNER transfers command. Capt. A.O. McShane ? who commands Coy. to 'A' Coy and assumes the... to 'B' Coy as noted ? for duty.	

Army Form C. 2118.

WAR DIARY
or
INTELLIGENCE SUMMARY.
(Erase heading not required.)

XIII 6/7.th Battn. Royal Scots Fusiliers

MAY.

Place	Date	Hour	Summary of Events and Information	Remarks and references to Appendices
IVERGNY	10	–	The Battn. moves off at 7.55 a.m. for this day's end ~ Belle arrangements. arrived back at 3 p.m.	
"	11	–	"A" & "D" Coys on Range – "B" & "C" Coys worked out in small retorts in LUCHEUX WOOD. 5-6 p.m. Games. A draft of 5 other ranks joined to-day.	
"	12	–	"B" & "C" Coys on Range – "A" & "D" Coys – a scheme in LUCHEUX WOOD.	
"	13	–	Church Services.	
"	14	–	The Battalion paraded at 9.30 a.m. for this day under Bde. arrangements in LE CAUROY	LE CAUROY
"			training grounds	
"	15	–	"B" & "D" Coys on Range – 1 platoon of each Coy. doing platoon scheme in turn – Remainder of Coys doing MUSKETRY – A rifle Gun & team was available for practice with platoon. "A" & "C" Coys in LUCHEUX WOOD. 5-6 p.m. Games. Lieut. N.C. FRASER reported for duty this day to "B" Coy. A draft of 9 o.r. also arrived.	
"	16	–	"A" & "C" Coys – Platoon scheme to LUCHEUX WOOD Gun & team. "B" & "D" Coys in small retorts in LUCHEUX WOOD. The Field Marshal Commanding in chief has under authority granted by His Majesty the King awarded the Military Cross to 2/Lt. (A/Capt) W. McINDOE. arrangements in LE CAUROY	
"	17	–	The Battn. paraded at 7.30 a.m. for this day under Bde. arrangements in LE CAUROY. training grounds. arriving back in billets about 2.30 p.m.	
"	18	–	"B" & "C" Coys on Range – "A" Coy. Musketry – "D" Coy. Platoon scheme – "A" & "D" Coys. open Games. 5 p.m. Wind shifting in LUCHEUX WOOD worked out scheme in LUCHEUX WOOD	

WAR DIARY or INTELLIGENCE SUMMARY

Army Form C. 2118.

6/7th Battn. Royal Scots Fusiliers

Month: MAY

Place	Date	Hour	Summary of Events and Information	Remarks and references to Appendices
IVERGNY	18		The following have been awarded the Military Medal for Gallantry in the field. No 11895 A/Sgt TONNER J., No 13580 Cpl. HOUSTON G, 16365 Pte LENNON J., 1587 Pte McLAUGHLIN, No 34905 Pte N. DUNN, and 39590 Pte G. CAMPBELL J., and Bar to Military medal to 10/3005 A/L.Cpl. C. McLENAGHAN.	
"	19		"A" "D" Coys on Range - Musketry & Physical Exercises. "B" & "C" Coys working against each other taking up position in N.W. portion of LOCHEUX WOOD, and the other Coy attacking from direction of LE SOUICH and BREVILLERS at 2.30pm the Bombers & rifle Bombers of B & C Coys firing & throwing live Grenades. A & D Coys practicing re-organising in advance at 9 pm. A Draft of 12 O.R. reports to day. Church parade.	
"	20		The Battn. moves to day to BONNIERES	
BONNIERES	21		The Battn. moves to day to CHERIENNE parading at 9.15 am all men reporting by 11 pm.	
CHERIENNE	22		The Battn. moved to day to CHERIENNE parading at 10 am all were reporting in by 5 pm. Billets all very good. 3 men fell out on the march.	
"	23		All Coys Bayonet fighting, Physical Training. Platoon & Coy Drill & exercises of the various attainments.	
"	24		The Battalion paraded at 8.45 am and marches to training grounds, for Battalion schemes "B" Coy acting as enemy. A Draft of 6 other ranks reports to day and is taken on Strength.	
"	25		Under Coy arrangements - training included Coy Drill, extending nopsey, Physical Training, Bayonet fighting, Rifle Bombers firing 6 fire School. 5. 6 pm Games the following are struck off strength to day being posted to 1st Battn. P.S.F. Major I. A. M'WAN, Capt. A.D. McFARLANE, Lt. W. ORR, 2/Lt R.L. M'MURTRIE, 2/Lt T. LIMOND, 2/Lt E.F.G. LMOUR and 2/Lt M. McQUISTON.	
"	26		Coys under respective Commanders to Chateau Park FONTAINE L'ETALON. Training re Bayonet fighting, Physical Training re Cup.	

Army Form C. 2118.

WAR DIARY
or
INTELLIGENCE SUMMARY.

(Erase heading not required.)

MAY XIII 6/7th Battn. Royal Scots Fusiliers

Place	Date	Hour	Summary of Events and Information	Remarks and references to Appendices
CHERIENNE	27	-	Church Parades - Parity/Union - Church of England - in Interior -	
"	28	-	Battalion Parades at 7.40 A.M. in Battle Order & shirt sleeves for scheme on Training Ground under Brigade Arrangements. Arms Truck & Pickels at 2.15 p.m. The following draft arrived to Coy and were taken on strength - 16. other Ranks	
"	29	-	8.30 to 12.30 p.m. Coy. under Coy arrangements. Training includes Bayonet Fighting, Physical Training, Musketry for Respirator Drill. Sm Contest & Training of entrenchments Commands) 5 - 6 p.m. Games.	
"	30	-	8.30 A.M. - 12.30 p.m. Under Coy. arrangements - Ceremonial Drill, Coy. Drill - Bayonet Fighting, Physical Training &c. The following Staff arrived today & is taken on strength. - 6 - recruits. The following have been mentioned in Despatches - for bravery and Good work. No 16/131 Pte BELCHER No 129/9 A-Cpl T FANNING, 43203 Pte E. HOUSTON, 14985 L-Cpl LISTER No 13290 Pte QUINN J.7, No 15710 Pte ROLFE, F.E.	
"	31	-	A" & "E" Coys. on Range - Musketry & Physical Training - "A" & "D" Coys. under Company arrangements - Coy. Drill, Physical Training - Bayonet Fighting &c.	

S.V.S. Forbes
Lt. Col.
Commdg. 6/7 R.S.F.

To go with
diary
6/7 RSF

CONFIDENTIAL.

WAR DIARY Vol 24

OF

6/7TH (SERVICE) BATTN. ROYAL SCOTS FUSILIERS.

From 1st June 1917. To 30th June 1917.

Vol. XIII

Army Form C. 2118.

WAR DIARY
or
INTELLIGENCE SUMMARY

(Erase heading not required.)

16/7 Royal Scots Fusiliers
Vol XIII
JUNE 1917

Place	Date	Hour	Summary of Events and Information	Remarks and references to Appendices
CHERIENNE	1		Battalion Scheme on training ground near GARAMETZ. Baths for Transport & Headquarters at CAUMONT. Notice received that the Corps Commander had awarded the Military Cross to Lieut. T CAIRNS and T/Capt F.K KERR, medical officer attached.	
	2		Parade - "A" & "D" Coys on Range. "B" & "C" Coys under Coy's arrangements. Lewis Gunners & Signallers under their respective Commanders. Baths at CAUMONT allotted "C" & "D" Coys. The Military Cross awarded by Corps Commander to 8/Lieut J.D SMITH, Stokes Batt. & attached Trench Mortar Battery.	
	3H		Parade - "A" & "D" Coys. "B" & "C" Coys on Range. "B" & "C" Coys on Range. Lewis Gunners under Lewis Gun officer at Signallers arrest their Coys.	
	23		Divine Service Presbyterian Parade at 11AM. Church of England Parade 9.30AM. Voluntary service in the evening at 6.30PM. Roman Catholic service in the Church, CHERIENNE.	
	5		Parade "A" & "D" Coys on Range. "B" & "C" Coys under Coys arrangements. Lewis Gunners under L.G.O. Night Operations took Place in the wood in the N/W Training area. Batt. returned about 2AM. Draft 2 Ranks received.	
	6		Parade "A" & "D" Coys under Coys arrangements. "B" Coy firing "C" Coy on Range. M/Gunners free these new ???	

Army Form C. 2118.

WAR DIARY
or
INTELLIGENCE SUMMARY
(Erase heading not required.) Vol. XIII

Title: 6/7th Royal Scots Fusiliers
JUNE 1917

Place	Date	Hour	Summary of Events and Information	Remarks and references to Appendices
CHERIENNE	6		Games were indulged in from 5PM to 6PM. The following cases were brought to the notice of the Commanding Officer of confusion but went under extremely heavy & trying conditions when employed with the Brigade mobile dump:- No 16270 Pte J CAMPBELL, No 25149 Pte J SMITH, No 12306 Pte J McGUINNESS, No 13542 Pte J TEMPLETON - Baths at CAVMONT were allotted to "A" Coy. -	
"	7		Parades "A" & "B" Coys on Range - "D" Coy joining "C" Coy General routine - Games from 5PM - 6PM. Baths at CAVMONT. "C" & "D" Coys -	
"	8		Field Firing Exercise near VAULX - 20 Rounds SAA were carried per man & 3 magazines per Lewis Gun. Cooks & Officers were sent round with Battn. Mar'n T/Lt du Haviland was in command in the absence of Lieut Col Gordon on leave. The exercise was favourably commented upon by the Brigadier who was present.	
"	9		A tactical exercise under Battn arrangements took place in WAR TRAINING AREA 2/Lieut R. LEE (wounded 23/4/17) rejoined Battn. 9 taken on strength 2/Lieuts A.F. MORSE, N.W. ROBERTSON taken on strength along with draft of 55 o Ranks -	
"	10		Divine Service Presbyterian Service at 11.15 AM - Church of England Service at 11.30 AM under 2/Lt Dickinson - Roman Catholic Service	Lieut Col R.R.W Gordon RSF OC

WAR DIARY or INTELLIGENCE SUMMARY

JUNE 1917 Vol XIII 6/7th Royal Scots Two

Place	Date	Hour	Summary of Events and Information	Remarks and references to Appendices
CHERIENNE	10		at LE QUESNOY under 2/Lt A.D. Cameron. Draft to O'Ranks received.	
"	11		NAIL Training Area occupied by Batt. A B & D Coys did the attack with C Coy as enemy. Cookers accompanies the Batt.	
"	12		The Battalion was inspected by the G.O.C. Division, Major Tho. Stewart Command. The Batt. was drawn up in column of coys, in line next 20 hours between Coys. After inspection A Coy were detailed to the Range. B Coy to Wiring & Coy drill, C Coy to do a small attack. D Coys too Outposts. A & B Coys saw in Marching order C D 9 HQ in Batt order. The Batt. returned about 6 P.M. The Divisional Ruevue performed in the evening.	
"	13		Routine B & C Coys Range & Physical Exercise. A & D Coys Wiring & Outposts. Night Operations took place in the evening. Baths were allotted all Coys.	
"	14		Routine as for previous day.	
"	15		Practice attack under Batt. arrangements in training ground near GAUNNETZ. This attack on the whole was well carried out.	

Wyttgens
Lieut/Adjt
6/7th R.S.

Army Form C. 2118.

WAR DIARY
or
INTELLIGENCE SUMMARY
(Erase heading not required.)

Vol LXIII 1/7th Royal Scots Fusiliers

Place	Date	Hour	Summary of Events and Information	Remarks and references to Appendices
CHERISY	16		B & C Coys on Range. The Batt. also doing Bombing - A & D Coys Coy drill Wiring Physical Ex. & Outposts - Adjut. & C. Bland & 2 NCOs & nery attended a course at Bde HQ. in "Bullet & Bayonet" a system of Bayonet Training -	
"	17		Divine Service Presbyterian Service at 11AM. Church of England Service at 9.30 AM. Lieut a. 9.30 AM. Roman Catholic Service at L= QUESNOY at 9.30 AM. Lieut a. Dingwall taken in charge as from 15th	
"	18		B Coy on Range. A C & D Coy Coy drill wiring, Artillery formation & extended order drill. A B & D Coys Bombing in the evening. Baths were allotted at CAUMONT.	
"	19		Field Firing Exercise at VAUX. Start was at 5 AM. The practice was well done & the shooting good. The Batt. returned about 2 PM. Bombing in the evening was carried out by B & D Coys.	
"	20		Warning order received that the Batt. would move on 21st. Billets thoroughly cleaned & all bomb, SAA etc cleared. C Coy on at Range for 2 hours - D Coy did bombing for an hour - Field practice took place in the evening but was rather spoilt by the weather conditions - Lieut.Col. Gordon Commanding leaving returned from leave the previous day.	

W Gatasius
Lieut Colt
1/7 R.S.F.

Army Form C. 2118.

WAR DIARY
or
INTELLIGENCE SUMMARY
(Erase heading not required.) Vol XIII 6/7th Royal Scots Fusiliers

JUNE 1917

Place	Date	Hour	Summary of Events and Information	Remarks and references to Appendices
CHERISNE	21		The Battalion moved to BLANGERVAL starting at 4.50 A.M. Route HAUTE MAISNIL - FILLIEVRES - MONCHEL - Area Picard was furnished by 1 Platoon of "D" Coy until 2/Lt ENON THOMSON. Coys were very negligent. Orders were received for move next day. Draft of 20 O'Ranks received.	
BLANGERVAL	22		The Batt. moved to HESTRUS via CROIX WAVRANS. Start was at 2.45 A.M. An advance billeting party under 2nd Lieut J CARNAHAN proceeded at 9 AM. A few men fell out on this march but they went mostly from men of draft of previous night. Batt HQ in the MAIRIE	
	23		The Battn. moved to FEBVIN-PALFART via FIEFS. Start was at 2.10 P.M. An advance billeting party under Lt J Carnahan proceeded at 8.45 AM. No one fell out on this march which was not a long one. B HQ were at Cros Roads. Billets were quite open. Social from London Gazette D 9/6/17 Temp 2nd Lieut N. McINDOE (T.F) to be 2nd Lieut 19/5/17. and 2nd Lieut D.C. Brown to be Temp B. Lieut 10/4/17. Divine Services were held this day at above mentioned place. Strength 5 other Ranks was 2900.	
FEBVIN-PALFART	24.			
FEBVIN-PALFART	25.		The Battn moved to LAMBRES via LINGHEM. Start was at 8.30 A.M. The usual Billeting Party Proceeded in advance. Billets were very good indeed, accommodation being plentiful. B HQ were in Chateau with Orderly Room in School. No one fell out on the march, the battalion arriving at 11.30 A.M.	

W Hutchison
Lieut & Adj
for O.C. 6/7 R.S.F.

WAR DIARY
or
INTELLIGENCE SUMMARY.
(Erase heading not required.)

June 1917. Vol XIII 6/7 ½ Royal Scots Fusiliers

Place	Date	Hour	Summary of Events and Information	Remarks and references to Appendices
LAMBRES	26	-	The Battn. moves to BORRE, area N.E. of HAZEBROUCK at 4 am. The march was made in good time and under good conditions. The billets were very scattered, Companies being accommodated in barns at some distance from Battalion HQ. which were at BORRE.	
BORRE	27	-	The Battn. continues its march, proceeding via STEENVOORDE to an area round RATTEKOT INN, just inside BELGIAN border. Here again billets were very scattered, Companies being about a mile to a mile and a half from Battn. HQ. which was in a farm north of the INN, on road to WOTAV. No one fell out on march.	
WOTAV AREA.	28	-	Parade. 8.30 - 12.30 pm. under Coy arrangements. Routine includes S. Coy Drill, Musketry, Box Respirator Drill, Bayonet Fighting & Physical Training. In the afternoon there was a lecture on Trench Warfare for all Companies.	
do.	29	-	Parade 8.30 am to 12.30 pm under Coy arrangements. Routine as for 28th. The following officers reported for duty and were taken on strength of Battalion. Lieut. G.P. CROCKETT. Lieut. J. COGHILL, and Lieut. E.B. SYKES.	
do.	30	-	The Battn. moves to BROXEELE AREA, via WORMHOUDT. Start was at 3.50 am and the Battn. arrives about 12.30 pm. The billets were very good for men but not for the officers. Companies at considerable distance from Battn. HQ. which is situated in a farm about 1 mile S.E. of BROXEELE Ch.	

W. Whiteside
Lieut Col.
7/2 R.S.F.

CONFIDENTIAL.

WAR DIARY

OF.

6/7th (SERVICE) BATTn. ROYAL SCOTS FUSILIERS.

From 1st July 1917 To 31st July 1917.

VOL XIV

Confidential

War Diary

of

6/7th Royal Scots Fusiliers

1st to 31st July, 1917

Volume 25

Army Form C. 2118.

WAR DIARY
or
INTELLIGENCE SUMMARY.
(Erase heading not required.)

Vol 25 O/7 Royal Scots Fusiliers   July 1917

Place	Date	Hour	Summary of Events and Information	Remarks and references to Appendices
BANTEUX AREA.	1/7/17		Parade. Divine Service for Presbyterians was held in a field near "A" Coy billets. A demonstration for the carrying of Lewis Guns and ammunition on pack ponies was given at same.	
do.	2/7/17		Parade under Coy arrangements. Routine includes Musketry, Physical Training, Bayonet Fighting, Coy, Bttn, Box Respirator Drill, Artillery formation & extrication therefrom. Also the loading & unloading of various ammunitions on pack ponies. Lecture in afternoon on "Gas Attacks & precautions" & various other subjects.	
do.	3/7/17		Parades. Practice in moving in single file & forming up in Artillery formation and extricating therefrom in & out formation for attack. Loading & unloading of Lewis Guns and pack animals. Bayonet training & Box Respirator Drill.	
do.	4/7/17		Battalion parades for Brigade tactical scheme. Training area. Practice an dummy trenches for attack, see appendix I for Operation Order.	Appendix I
do.	5/7/17		Parades under Coy arrangements. Practising moving in single file, forming up in Artillery formation & extricating therefrom. Box Respirator Drill, Physical and Bayonet Training. Loading and unloading of Lewis Guns & ammunition on Pack Ponies. In the afternoon practice with aeroplane in Contact Patrol work. The distinguished services in the field of Sjt. 6/Supp. k. London Gazette of Friday 1.6.17. the distinguished conduct medal is awarded to No. 13540 C.S.M. BURNS. J.	
do.	6/7/17		Parade.- Brigade tactical scheme as for Att. instr. as above.	
do.	7/7/17		Parades for "A","C",& "D" Coys, usual Coy arrangements. Routine to include Artillery formation, extrication therefrom, Physical Drill, one hour Coy Instr, one hour Sergeant Drill Instructor Instruction therefrom. Training area practice on dummy trenches. A draft of 15 other ranks "B" Coy to training area practising, thinning of whom 6.R.S were not Battalion before.	

SLJ.

WAR DIARY
or
INTELLIGENCE SUMMARY
6/7th Royal Scots Fusiliers XIV

Army Form C. 2118.

Place	Date	Hour	Summary of Events and Information	Remarks and references to Appendices
JULY	8		Cleaning up of Billets - Physical Drill - Orders issued for move - The Batt. marched off at 2.50 P.M. to ARNEKE entraining there for ST LAWRENCE CAMP in approx. G 11 C. "B" Coy were left behind to practice road - The arrival in Camp was late -	
	9		Orders issued for move - The Batt. moved to Bayne Junction (On Rly line in the line) to area H16 a. The Batt. marched off at 6.45 P.M. reaching destination at 11.15 P.M. - Night quiet.	Ref map Sheet 28 NW
	10		Various working parties found the Batt. working out at 8 Officers 546 ORs.	
	11		As for previous day - "B" Coy rejoined Batt. from ARNEKE. Shelling of Back Area by the enemy. Several Shells bursting near Batt. billets - several casualties in working parties caused by Gas - The gas was to the troops a difficult to detect -	
	12		Working parties as for previous day - Shelling of back area by the enemy continued - Night working parties experienced difficulty in working owing to shell fire & gas.	
	13		Several officers went round front line - new track (F track) to front line reconnoitred by officers & NCOs at intervals - Night normal -	Capt.

Army Form C. 2118.

WAR DIARY
or
INTELLIGENCE SUMMARY.
(Erase heading not required.)

XIV Corps 6/7th Royal Scots Fusiliers JULY

Place	Date	Hour	Summary of Events and Information	Remarks and references to Appendices
H16a	14		Orders received for move into front line – boys completed in coha S.A.A. Bombs etc. – Night quiet.	Ry Sheet 28 NW
	15		Bath moved up to front line via REIGERSBERG CHATEAU CANAL BANK & MENIN GATE – Relieved 11th A&SH – Relief complete 6 AM. Disposition B coy front line. C coy Support – D coy 2nd Support – A coy Reserve – Day normal except for intermittent shelling of PICADILLY TR and DRAGOON TR and DRAGOON FARM.	
	16		Frequent salvos on HALF MOON TR & DRAGOON FARM. About 9.30 PM a steady Bombardment of HALF MOON TR. took place – BHQ had 6 casualties then quarters & men H ECOLE – About 10.15 PM a heavy gas shell bombardment by the enemy on Reserve Trenches & back area took place – This continued till 4.30 AM – 150 Respirators were worn practically all night – Very few casualties considering density of gas –	
	17		Day normal – Front of Bath or Right both blown in by shell fire by enemy a raid anticipated – Lewis & Machine Guns on flanks warned – Night was normal with usual shelling of back area –	
	18		Day normal – At 10.30 PM through "B" coy lines up in NO MANS LAND, Commenced a raid on enemy trenches ICE TRENCH & ICE SUPPORT, between ICE AV & ICE LANE – Much damage done to enemy Trenches & 1 prisoner taken – Belonged to 75th Regt 17th Div. Raiding party returned about 11 PM – 14 Casualties (slight)	W.S.J. Lieut. report attached

A 3834 Wt. W4973/M687 730,000 8/16 D. D. & L. Ltd. Forms/C.2118/13.

WAR DIARY
or
INTELLIGENCE SUMMARY

Army Form C. 2118.

JULY **XIX** **1/5th Royal Scots Fusiliers**

Place	Date	Hour	Summary of Events and Information	Remarks and references to Appendices
Front line YPRES.	19		Day normal. In the evening Gas bombs for LIVENS Projector were carried up & placed in front line. Patrols went out at 11 P.M. and found the enemy wire to be badly cut and of little resistance. No front line was empty and no movement could be seen in the line.	Sheet 28 NW.
	20		Orders issued for relief by 8th Seaforth Highlanders, also orders re discharge of gas. Guides under Lt Cameron were at BELGIAN BATTERY CORNER at 9.15 P.M.	
	21		Gas discharged at 2 A.M. Heavy retaliation of front Support & Reserve lines by the enemy. Relief complete 6 A.M. Batt. moved to ERIE CAMP. Batt. moved at 3 P.M. to WATOU No 2 Area being in Camp.	
Camp	22		Divine Service. Presbyterian Joint Service with 6th Cameron Hicks at 11 A.M. Communion afterward of Service. Church of England - Service in D coy billets at 9.30 a.m. Brigadier congratulated "B" coy on road - Short route march. Officers & selected NCOs viewed model of ground for future operations at HQ 19th Corps at TEN ELMS CAMP. G.O.C. 2nd MGB from division inspected helmets.	
	23			
	24		Route march by Coys - Practice in Artillery formation	

P.D.J.

WAR DIARY
or
INTELLIGENCE SUMMARY

Army Form C. 2118.

(Erase heading not required.) XIV 6/7th Royal Scots Fusiliers

Month: JULY

Place	Date	Hour	Summary of Events and Information	Remarks and references to Appendices
Camp	25		Inspection in Battle Order - Allocups - Details of forthcoming operations explained to N.C.O.s & men - Plan on ground used - Officers A.I. Milne to Hospital (sick). Orders issued for move -	
St Lawrence Camp	26		The Batt. marched off at 8.50 AM to ST LAWRENCE CAMP. Arrangements in forthcoming operations gone over by Officers -	
	27		Under Coy arrangements routine to include musketry, physical exercise, & Box Respirator Drill. Draft & blanks taken on strength as from 24/7/17.	
	28		Inspection in "Battle Order" each coy being fully equipped. Box Respirators. Also each Platoon inspected with helmets on for ½ hour - The Brigadier General inspected A coy in "Battle Order" -	
~	29		Operation Orders issued for operations on Z day - The Batt. moved off about 11.45 PM for Bivouac Camp in H16.a. Only those for action moved, the reserve personnel being accommodated in area ERIE CAMP - night quiet.	Ref map Sheet 28 NW
~	30		Batt. notified - ZERO HOUR notified as 3.40 AM, 31st JULY 1917.	
~	31		Batt. moved off at 3.30 AM via F Trench - Full account of operations will forwarded with August War Diary.	

R. V. Forder Lieut. Colonel
Comdg. 6/7th R. Scots Fus.

CONFIDENTIAL.

WAR DIARY

OF

6/7TH (SERVICE) BATTN. ROYAL SCOTS FUSILIERS.

FROM 1st August 1917 TO 31st August 1917

VOL XVI

Army Form C. 2118.

WAR DIARY
or INTELLIGENCE SUMMARY

Army Form C. 2118.

Instructions regarding War Diaries and Intelligence Summaries are contained in F.S. Regs., Part II. and the Staff Manual respectively. Title pages will be prepared in manuscript.

August 1917 **6/7th Royal Scots Fusiliers** Vol XV

(Erase heading not required.)

Place	Date	Hour	Summary of Events and Information	Remarks and references to Appendices
FREZENBURG LINE	1		Bath. was relieved at 3 AM. in the front line (see operation report of 31st July, attached XV) by 8/10th Gordon Highrs & moved to CAMBRIDGE TR. - At 5.30 P.M., an order was received from Col. R.	Appendices 1st Red TR. map.
	2		Stand To. Bath. proceeded at 7.25 PM. to BLUE LINE - About 10 P.M. D coy under Capt TATE proceeded to SQUARE FARM - Order received that the Brigade would attack cork 11 7.45 PM on the Right & 6/7 KOSB (B Coy) on the Left - Objective BEEK HOUSE. The Bath. at that time numbering from 130 - 150 Rifles. The attack on troops moved off at 8.30 P.M. - BEEK HOUSE was not taken but part of the BLACK LINE which has been in enemy hands was recaptured and the line consolidated - Enemy attempts at organized counter-attack broke off by Artillery fire. Order received for relief of Bath. by 8/9 RTF & 11 KOSB. Relief completed 12 midnight.	
H16a.	3rd		The Bath. moved into camp at H16a. Order issued for further move from camp. Bath. moved to "C" Camp.	Sheet 28 FRENCH and BELGIUM
NINNEZEELE	4		The Bath. Also details returned from leave embussed and moved to "C" Camp. NINNEZEELE. (J11b)	
	5		Bay spent in cleaning up equipment - distribution of linen, trench puttees etc - Denise Union Church of Scotland	
	6		Camera Comp. (B coy) at 10.45am. - Parade service at cabaret Beugnie held in field adjacent to Bivouacs - at 11 AM. Brigade & Divisional staff attended - Church of England Service in camp at 11 AM. Roman Catholic Service in the village church at 11 AM. Cleaning up continued in the afternoon.	
			Routine includes Reorganization of Coys. Section Commanders appointed Coy Drill. Physical Training ½ hour Bayonet Fighting. - Boots & Clothing further issue - Training of	

[signature]

Army Form C. 2118.

WAR DIARY
or
INTELLIGENCE SUMMARY.
(Erase heading not required.) Vol XV 6/7 Royal Scots Fusiliers

Instructions regarding War Diaries and Intelligence Summaries are contained in F.S. Regs., Part II. and the Staff Manual respectively. Title pages will be prepared in manuscript.

Army Form C. 2118. August 1917

Place	Date	Hour	Summary of Events and Information	Remarks and references to Appendices
WINNEZEELE	6		Specialists commenced Signalling, Lewis Gunners, Snipers, Scouts. 18 o'clock reveille. and later on strength.	
"	7		Routine - practice of Subordinate Command - ½ hour Physical training - Coy drill - Bayonet training under Army Instructor - Training of Specialists continued - Bell tapd Class of new recruits was sent 4 men -	
"	8		Routine as for previous day and the addition of Musketry Practice - 13 o'clock taken on Strength of Batt - Promotions & Appointments made -	
"	9		8.30am. Physical training, Bayonet Fighting & Musketry - 4 hour route - 10.30am - 1PM Bath Route March - 2.30PM - 3.30PM Games (by Coys) Baths continued in the evening -	
"	10		8.30am - 12.30PM. Routine Bayonet Fighting, Physical training, Musketry marching order Box Respirators on, Coy drill & throwing of dummy bombs - Inspections of the Reticulars by Div Gas Officer - Training of Specialists continued - Games (by Coys) in the afternoon. 4 o'clock taken on Strength -	
"	11		6.30am - 10am. Physical Exercise. Bayonet Fighting, Musketry. 10.30am. Batt. Route March. Games by Coys in the afternoon.	
"	12		Divine Service. Church of Scotland Service in field adjoining camp at 11.15 am. - Church of England Service in field adjoining camp at 9.30 am. - Roman Catholic Service in church at WINNEZEELE at 11.15am. - Baths for A & B Coys - Brigade Lewis Gunclass of men sent R/outine -	

A5834 Wt.W4973 M687 750,000 8/16 D.D. & L. Ltd. Forms/C.2118/13.

WAR DIARY or INTELLIGENCE SUMMARY

Army Form C. 2118.

(Erase heading not required.)   Vol XV   6/7th Royal

August 1917

Place	Date	Hour	Summary of Events and Information	Remarks and references to Appendices
Camp WINNEZEELE	13		Routine included Musketry, Naval Training, Bayonet fighting, Physical training, Coy Drill & Marching with Gas Respirators on. Boxing was carried out by A Coy. Afternoon Games by Coy. The following officers joined the Battn and were taken on strength - 2/Lieut P. Simpson, 2/Lt G. Atkinson, 2/Lt J.H. Muir, 2/Lt R. Thomson - 26 O'Ranks taken on strength.	
"	14		Routine - Stripping of arms, Musketry, Bayonet Fighting, Physical Drill and Battalion Drill - Afternoon Games (by Coy)	
"	15		Routine 8.15AM - 10AM. Musketry, Bayonet Fighting & Physical Drill - 10.30AM - 1PM. Battalion route march - Throwing of Live Grenades 1 hour B C & D coys -	
"	16		16 new horses, under 2/Lt A.D. Cannon, proceeded to V Army Rest camp. Warning order received for move next day to forward area - 2/Lt. T. Shanks joined & taken on strength - Lieut Morris took over Stationery Medical charge of unit - He was attached from United States Army.	
"	17		Battn moved to ST LAURENCE camp by march route.	
"	18		Platoon inspections & issue of SAA, bomb, tools etc to complete in battle order - Revolution in Battle order.	
"	19		Divine Service - Voluntary services for those who on duty, to Presbyterians Church of England in YMCA Hut. Class Academy - B de Maestres in field adjacent to Camp - Bath. under Command of Major J.R.R. Robertson moved up area H16 central M10 A SHEET 503 120 beray the balance at Bath HQ	Sheet 28 N.W.

A5834 Wt. W4973/M687. 750,000. 8/16. D.D.& L. Ltd. Forms/C.2118/13.

WAR DIARY
or
INTELLIGENCE SUMMARY.

(Erase heading not required.) 4th XV 6/7 Royal Scots Fus.

Army Form C. 2118.

Title pages August 1917

Place	Date	Hour	Summary of Events and Information	Remarks and references to Appendices
H16.a	20		Slight shelling of area mostly overhead shrapnel from sheels bursting near Observation Balloons. In the evening the Battn moved up into the ECOLE, YPRES.	Sheet 28 NW
YPRES	21		at 9.30 P.M. Battn moved to forward area with HQ at BILL'S COTTAGE. See Operation report attached	Appendix I
"	22		"	
"	23		"	
"	24		"	
"	25		"	
"	26		Battn moved to PRISON YPRES.	
"	27		Battn resting in PRISON. Working parties out in the evening, digging trenches in front line system.	
"	28		As for previous day. About 9 P.M. the Battn moved into CAMBRIDGE TR. and was attached to 46th Inf. Bde. - Warning order to move out next night to PIONEER CAMP, H7C 3.6. under Command of Major T. M. Haydand	Sheet 28 NW
"	29			
"	30		Quiet day. Battn moved out being relieved by 7th Lan. Fus. & a relief proceeded to PIONEER CAMP H7C.	
H7a.	31		Orders issued to move next day by bus to WORMHOOT "A" Area.	

P. Lawson Mar[?] Major[?]
Comdg 6/7 R.S.F

REPORT ON OPERATIONS - YPRES 1917.

(Phase 2. 11.)

6/7th. Royal Scots Fusiliers.

On the evening of Sunday 19th. August the Battalion, composed of 4 Coys. each 120 strong and together with H.Qrs. making a total of 17 Oficers and 501 Other Ranks moved from ST. LAWRENCE CAMP to the BIVOUAC CAMP in H.16. They remained there the night and the next evening marched to the ECOLE. At 9-30p.m. on august 21st. they took up the positi n allotted them in the vicinity of BILL COTTAGE 1.6.b.3.7. about 150 yds. west and behind the FREZENBERG RIDGE, in the following order:-

B.	C.
A.	D.

Here they dug themselves in. During the night a good deal of shelling took place and for three quarters of an hour Gas Shells were put over the lines.

The ordɗrs received for the operations the next day were to the effect that two Battalions of the Brigade - 11th. A&SH on the left and 13th. the Royal Scots on the right would attack and that 6/7th. R.S.F. were to act in close support and be prepared for counter attacks.

In order to make doubly sure, that, after the first wave had passed certain Strong Points, none of the enemy were left in them unattended to, 4 Platoons of the Battalion were detailed to clear these places and then Garrison them as follows:-

EMPLACEMENTS)	2/Lt. Thomson	"C" Coy.)	
Bit Work.)	D.25.d.75.50.	)	Attached to
" ")	D.25.b.35.05.	)	13th. Royal Scots.
VAMPIR FARM)	2/Lt. Shanks	"A" ")	
BORRY FARM	" Cunningham	"B" ")	Attached to
BECK HOUSE	" Muir	"D" ")	11th. A.& S.H.

A separate report dealing with each of these parties is attached. The remainder of the Battalion was to move forward from their position near BILL COTTAGE at about ZERO plus 1 hour and occupy the line of trenches in the BLACK LINE - which had previously been held by the two attacking Battalions.

Though in the written orders I was given definately 1 hour in which to move the Battalion into position I was personally informed by the Brigad Brigadier that I was to act on my own initiative and that the 1 hour was to be considered an "elastic" period. My duty would be to avoid casualties, but at all events the Battalion was to be on the BLACK LINE at not later than ZERO plus 1 hour.

ZERO was fixed at 4-45a.m. 22nd. August 1917.

Our barrage opened exactly to the time and at 5o'clock the enemy commenced an exceptionally heavy fire. It appears from the Intelligence Reports received later that information had been conveyed to the enemy through a prisoner that we would attack about 5a.m. At ZERO and for a considerable time afterwards the enemys artillery kept up a very severe barrage between the BLACK LINE and the FREZENBERG RIDGE, so much so, that I was doubtful whether it would be possible for the 4 coys. to pass through or get round it, and be in position at the time stated. At ZERO plus 35 minutes there seemed to be a slackening off in the intensity of fire and I ordered a move forward. "C" & "D" coys. advanced over the ridge to the right of DOUGLAS VILLA by Platoons, and "A"&"B" moved round to the left to LOW FARM, all in artillery formation. All 4 coys. arrived at their allotted positions in the BLACK LINE at ZERO plus 55 minutes, with few casualties. This is attributed to the careful handling of coys. and platoons, together with close compliance with orders. The route followed had been previously reconnoitered. On arrival at the BLACK LINE "A" coy. dug themselves in behind LOW FARM and "B" coy. went into a trench to the left rear of "A" coy.

"C" COY. moved to the left of DOUGLAS VILLA and between the GUN PITS D.25.d.33. & D'25.d.5.6. taking up a position on the BLACK LINE with its centre resting on D.25.d.4.4. Just before reaching the BLACK LINE in large numbers of men were seen moving back on the left. To counteract the affects of this move which was rapidly becomming infectious,1 platoon of "C" coy. was ordered forward to the GUN PITS at D.25.d.7½.5. This was found to be held by No. 9 platoon of "C" coy. under 2/Lt.

The

Thomson (one of the clearing up parties) The other two platoons remained behind the BLACK LINE until later in the day when the reorganisation of the line took place under Major Mitchell D.S.O. 13th. R.S., and No. 12 platoon under Sgt. Mushett was sent forward to dig in and connect up the GUN PITS with the BLACK LINE. This line was heavily shelled and eventually nearer the BLACK LINE was occupied. The garrison of the GUN PITs remaining in them. The other platoon No. 10 formed a support to the GUN PITS
"D" Coy. under command of 2/Lt. Simpson at first moved off in support of "C" Coy. at a distance of about 100yds. When at the BLACK LINE they moved up on the right which was the right of our Brigade position i.e. the Railway Line. Shortly afterwards 2/Lt. Simpson went forward and was wounded.

"A" Coy. on arrival at the BLACK LINE dug in, on either side of LOW FARM Capt. Gardner the Coy. Commander was wounded early in the morning and 2/Lt. K.S. Dick took over command. The Coy. remained in this position until relieved.

"B" Coy. remained on the BLACK LINE, entrenched, all day until relieved The 2 Officers in the Coy. were wounded and the command divolved on Sgt. Hopwood.

On the afternoon of 22nd. August at 2-10p.m. I received a warning order that the attack would be continued at dusk and that the 6/7th. R.S.F. would be on the left and the 6th. Camerons on the right. I was also instructed to commence concentration in the area marked in red on map sent me, and that this had to be done by by men moving only one at a time and at long intervals. The attack would not take place before 7p.m. I at once sent my Intelligence Officer tom ascertain the situation in the front line. From the various reports I had received in the course of the day I knew that the four coys. occupied a line running more or less along the BRIGADE front. The report I received from this Officer only substantiated what I already knew, and that was, that owing to the activity of the enemy snipers and on account of the severe losses the Battalion had sustained in Officers & N.C.O's. it would be a matter of extreme difficulty to concentrate what remained of the four coys. less 4 Platoons for the purpose of offensive action. "A"&"B" coys. could be concentrated but "C"&"D" being on the right and exposed to Machine Guns and snipers fire the situation was far more difficult. It would be almost impossible to concentrate these two coys. without affecting severe casualties. After very careful consideration I telephoned to Brigade H.Qrs. that if I was ordered to carry out an attack as outlined in this warning order in my opinion it would be a matter not only, frought with grave responsibility but also one which might have far reaching consequences. I communiated verbally with the only Coy. Commanders I could get in touch with, viz., "D" "C" "A" and gave all the instructions I considered necessary for the efficient carrying out of the order under the very difficult circumstances. These orders were eventually conveyed to O.C. "C" Coy. and as he was the only Capt. on the right I placed him in command of "C" & "D". Later in the afternoon the warning order from the Brigade was modified and eventually cancelled and the Battalion was relieved, Batt. H.Qrs. moving to Cambridge Trench and 3 Coys. to BILL COTTAGE area with the fourth resting behind DOUGLAS VILLA. At about 6p.m. 23rd. August 1917 the Brigadier came to Cambridge Trench and communicated further orders with reference to future operations and at 10p.m. Batt. H.Qrs. moved to WILDE WOOD and took over from the 13th. R.S. The coys. remaining in the BILL COTTAGE area still occupying the trenches they had dug. The Batt. remained in this area until the evening of 26th. August. The whole of the period was a very trying one as all ranks were continually subjected to artillery fire, sometimes of considerable severity and also from aeroplanes dropping bombs, and though the casualties were not many I can only attribute this to the fact that the men had dug themselves well in and also that the trench from WILDE WOOD - BILL COTTAGE - BAVARIA HOUSE was a winding one and in a continuous line and not spread out in depth.

On the evening of the 26th. we were relieved by 1 Coy. A.&.S.H. & 2 Coys. 13th. R.S. and marched to YPRES, where the Batt. was billeted - 2 Coys. in the prison and the other 2 close by. From 23rd.-27th. Various working parties were found for work in the front line at night. Casualties for period 22 - 27th. both days inclusive :-

	K.	W.	M.	W. at duty.	Total.
Officers.		6		1.	~~7.~~ 7
Other Ranks	~~15~~ 27	~~157~~ 159	~~65~~ 23		~~242.~~ ~~240~~ 209 216

CLEARING UP PARTIES.

"A" Coy. No. 1 Platoon, Commanded by 2/Lt. T. Shanks chief duty was to clear up and garrison VAMPIR FARM and to be under the orders of the O.C. 13th. The Royal Scots.
The platoon was attached to B. Coy. 13th. R.S. on 20th. August & on 22nd. August followed the second line of the first wave at a distance of 25 yds. They advanced to within 15 - 20 yards of their objective but were held up by Machine Gun fire coming from the direction BORRY FARM. At this time (about ZERO plus 30 minutes.) men were seen coming back on the right and as touch had been lost with 11th. A.&.S.H. the left was exposed. It was impossible to hang on and a withdrawl was absolutely necessary. This was done gradually and finally a position was taken up about 50 yds. in front of the original starting point. It was only then that touche could be got with the troops on the left. What was left of the platoon consolidated the position taken up.

"B" Coy. No. 7 Platoon commanded by 2/Lt. E.C. Cunningham and later by No.29998 L/Cpl. Duncan Chief duty to clear up and garrison BORRY FARM At ZERO hour the platoon moved behind first wave of "C" cOy. 11th.A&S.H. Some men went beyond the farm. Machine Gun fire was opened on them and they tried to work round. The left flank was apparently held held up. The men went beyond the farm and remained for some hours in the open, when they saw that troops on their right flank were withdrawing, and at the same time they noticed some of the enemy in the small wood on their left front. To avoid being cut off they came back to within about 150 yds. of the BLACK LINE. They lay in shell holes all day remaining there until the next day when they were relieved. 2/Lt. Cunningham was wounded early in the day and the command of the Platoon eventually divolved on L/cpl. Duncan.

"C" Coy. No. 9 Platoon Commanded by 2/L^T. Thomson Chief duty to act as clearers and to garrison EMPLACEMENTS at D. 25.d.75.50. and Bit Work at D. 25. b. 35.05. joined the 13th. R.S. at Bivouac Camp on August 10th. and on Monday 20th. August moved into trenches in rear of WILDE WOOD. The right half went with 2/LT. Thomson to the EMPLACEMENT and the other half under Sgt. Fitzsimmons towards Bit Work. The former made straight for the GUN PITS and garrisoned them meeting with no opposition though all day considerable trouble was caused by enemy snipers on the right flank and also from a Machine Gun about half left. The other half platoon was on the left of the 13th. Royal Scots. and linked up with the 11th. A. & S. H. the boundary being the FREZENBERG ROAD. The men only advanced a few yards when the A.& S.H. came bunching in and around. The N.C.O. looked about for his men but could only see 3 left. He took them with with him down the side of the road until he was left with only one. He then reported to an Officer in A.&.S.H. who instructed him to get get some men together any he could,, and advance in the direction of the concrete shelters which were in front of them. They managed to get close up. The enemy threw bombs at them. This N.C.O. & the few men with him got into a shell hole & remained there sniping. This prevented the enemy from erecting a Machine Gun on the roof of the shelter. Eventually owing to casualties, the party had to withdraw They dug in the BLACK LINE and remained there until relieved at night.

"D" Coy. No. 13 Platoon commanded by 2/Lt. H.M. Muir and later by Sgt. Stevenson. Chief duty to clear up and garrison BECK HOUSE. On August 21st. this platoon joined 11th. A.&.S.H. and moved to LOW FARM on the BLACK LINE. At about 1a.m. 22nd. August almost immediately 2/Lt. Muir was wounded. Sgt. Stevenson took command and reported the O.C. 11th. A.&.S.H. who told him to move to a position behind "D" coy. (11th. A.&.S.H.) The platoon advanced at ZERO about 50 yds behind the second line of the first wave. Shortlty afterward they came under heavy Machine Gun and Rifle fire. By creeping forward they managed to get to within about 20 yds. of BECK HOUSE but could get no further. They remained all day in shell holes and at night came back th the BLACK LINE and joined up with the 11th. A.&.S.H.

Confidential

WAR DIARY

OF

6/7TH (SERVICE) BATTⁿ. ROYAL SCOTS FUSILIERS.

FROM 1ˢᵗ Septr 1917 TO 30ᵗʰ Septr 1917

VOL XVII

WAR DIARY or INTELLIGENCE SUMMARY

Army Form C. 2118.

Vol XVI 6/7th Royal Scots Fusiliers

September 1917

Place	Date	Hour	Summary of Events and Information	Remarks and references to Appendices
PIONEER CAMP WORMHOUDT	1		The Batt. moved by Bus to WORMHOUDT "A" Area - Buses were drawn upon road outside H.Q. at 5.55 to A.B.d. 70.35. 1st Batt. marching off at 4 A.M and entraining at 4.50 a.m. Transport moved under Batt. Transport Officer, moving off at 4.30 a.m. via SWITCH ROAD, ST JAN TER BIEZEN - WATOU. Arrived in WORMHOUDT about 8.45 a.m. but had a slight delay in getting into billets owing to them being still occupied by awake unit when we arrived. Orders issued for move next day.	Sheet 28 NW. See Appendix I
WORMHOUDT	2		Through in Divisional Orders that Capt. W JOPE and LIEUT. A. DINGWALL had been awarded the Military Cross for gallantry in the field, also the D.C.M. for No 19951 L/Cpl BARKER. The Batt. moved off at 9.45 a.m. for ESQUELBECQ where they entrained for AUBIGNY. Arrived at AUBIGNY and marched to Y HUTMENTS, ETRUN - Settled down in camp by 9 P.M. Draft of 45 O.R.s allocated to coys -	LENS SHEET.
Y HUTMENTS ETRUN	3		Parades under Company arrangements - Musketeers.	
"	4	8.30 a.m - 12 noon	Routine included Physical Training & Bayonet fighting, Musketry marching order Box Respirators on, Coy drill. Lewis Gunners & Signallers under their respective Commanders - Baths were allotted & made full use of - S.H. OR's taken on strength and posted to Coys - OC Coys & Senior NCOs reconnoitred the trenches - Orders issued for move next day.	
"	5	10.15 a.m	The Batt. paraded ready to march off, at 10.15 a.m. Order of march D A B C Coys HQ marched with D Coy. Batt. proceeded to BALMORAL CAMP Route ARRAS RD, ROND POINT ST NICHOLAS - arrived 2 P.M. Order issued for move into line next day.	G. 18 a. 51 B NW.
"	6		Forenoon Winch under Sgt Instructors - Batt. moved into the line C & D Coys completing their relief by 6 P.M. A & B Coys by 11.30 P.M - Batt took over Right sub-section, Left Divisional	

Army Form C. 2118.

WAR DIARY
or
INTELLIGENCE SUMMARY.   VOL XVI

(Erase heading not required.)

September 1917   6/7th Royal Scots Fusiliers

Place	Date	Hour	Summary of Events and Information	Remarks and references to Appendices
ROEUX	6		Front ROEUX Sect. - Night quiet - Battalion relieved 2nd Seaforth Highlanders, 4th Division, in this front -	5T BNW
"	7		Patrols sent out the previous night on whole front but saw no signs of the enemy - Occasional trench mortar in SCABBARD SUPPORT. Work consisted of improvement of line -	
"	8		Slight shelling of WELFORD RES. and aerial darts on Regtl. coy front - Otherwise quiet - An Officers patrol went out on the left and was to locate enemy post on entrenchment near LAGOON - Nothing was seen - Work revetting of front & support trenches carried on -	
"	9		2/Lt. Dixon with small patrol went out on left - He reached enemy wire & threw 2 Bombs into his trench - This brought out heavy machine gun fire and throwing of Grenades at his wire by the enemy - Party returned safely - Night quiet - Work and corvey continued - Orders issued for relief next day -	
"	10th		Relieved by 13rd. A.& S.H. relief completed. 1 A.M. Day had been quiet - Battn moved to STIRLING CAMP (support) with C & D coys A & B coys remaining in CUTTING near Bde HQ. about H.23 C & d. Many working parties taken over -	
STIRLING CAMP	11st		Coys at camp, & not supplying working parties for the line carried out Physical Training, Coy drill & musketry. 2/Lieut J.T. DAVIES joined Battn. for duty - draft 4 ors.	
"	12		As for previous day -	
"	13th		As for 11th inst.	

WAR DIARY
INTELLIGENCE SUMMARY

Vol. XVI
6/7th Bn. Royal Scots Fusiliers
September 1917

Place	Date	Hour	Summary of Events and Information	Remarks and references to Appendices
STIRLING CAMP	14th		As for previous days. The Battalion moves to day to Barossa Camp as per Operation Orders attached. Appendix II.	575 N.V. See Appendix II
BAROSSA CAMP	15th		All Coys wiring and assault Course training - mist practice on miniature range and Snipers Range. Remainder of Personnel was employed in Coys. Drill, Bayonet fighting, Physical Drill and marching. 4 pt Br. R. Lets Inns. per Reports on - Lt. 863 & Sergt J.D. Prescott to reports to pt Br. R. Lets Inns. from this date.	
	16th		Church Parades. Church of Scotland - joint service not. 8t. Leofort Stepns. C.of E. Service formally mid. 11 A.S.H, and voluntary evening service at 6.30. Roman Catholic Service at 10 a.m. The following officers joined the Battn. to-day and were taken on Strength - 2/Lts. H. Gooding, G.H. Caldwell, W. McMinn, A. Sherriff, T.H. Bryson, E. McQuaid and H. Lambroughton - 25 O. Ranks were also taken on strength	
	17th		Forenoon was spent on Rifle Range, each Coy having an hours or two hours shooting.	
	18th		Ye not q to Ten firing practice were continued on miniature & Snipers Ranges - Continued Range practice to-day. The range being allotted to each Coy for a period of two hours. When not on range the other Coys were employed in wiring, bodymat fighting, extending order drill &c. In the afternoon all Subalterns were instructed in trench construction.	
	19th		As for 18th. All the Subaltern officers were again out with the afternoon a had construction. At 6.30 p.m. A & B Coys. Practiced moving out in darkness, marching on a Compass. They returned and about 9 p.m. C & D Coys did a similar practice. Capt. A.P. Gled M.C. Resigned to Battn. This day & was taken on strength. At again assumes Command of "B" Coy.	
	20th		From 7 a.m. to 9.45 p.m. Rifle Ranges were used by "B" Coy and by "C" Coy from 9.45 a.m. to 12.30 p.m. D & A Coys having amphibious wiring, extended order drill Physical training and practice in Rifle bombing.	

WAR DIARY or INTELLIGENCE SUMMARY

Army Form C. 2118.

6/7th Battn Royal Scots Fusiliers

September 1917

Place	Date	Hour	Summary of Events and Information	Remarks and references to Appendices
BAROODA CAMP	21st	8.45AM - 12.45PM	"A" Coy. morning Extended Order Drill. Bombing by 1 Platoon after 10 am. Physical Training. Bayonet fighting. Snipers Range available from 10.45am - 12.45pm.	
		2.15pm - 10 am	"B", "C" & "D" Coys - wiring. Musketry Order Drill. Physical Training. Coy Drill	
		at 10 am	"B", "C" & "D" Coys formed up for practice in attacking strong points under arrangements of Company Officers. Part of the afternoon all subaltern officers paraded for trench Construction. At 8.30 pm Battalion paraded for night manoeuvres. Lt. J.B. LOGAN reports to-day for duty and is taken on strength of Battalion. 3 recruits are taken on strength to-day.	
"	22"	8.45AM - 12.45pm	All Coys. routine including wiring, Coy. Drill, Bayonet fighting, Physical Training Practice attack by Platoons. Minority line Bomber. The miniature Range was also available for "A" & "B" Coys, and the Snipers Range for "C" & "D" Coys. The Battn rifle team over the Right sub section of the Divisional front to-morrow night.	578 N.Y.
"	23"		Church Services. Church of Scotland at 10 am by Rev. St. Kilman, St. Georges 2nd Church, Edinburgh. C. of E. at 11am and Roman Catholic Service at 10am. Bn. move to line to-night on Operation Orders attached. Appendix III	Appendix III
In the Line	24th		The Battalion relieved the 10th Scottish Rifles in the Right sub-section of the Divisional front. Relief being completed at 1.50A.M. at 4.30A.M. the enemy attempted a raid on our left Coy. "D" Coy. which failed. One of the enemy was shot by our sentry whilst entering the 2nd belt. One casualty 2 killed and 1 OR wounded slight. 4.30 to 12 holding out from 10th D.Rifles was continued the closing of various sunk formation of 2 firing in front and support trenches. Trenches in good state of repair. Being constructed. 51	B.N.V.
"	25th		Battn. still at junction CURB SWITCH SOUTH and ORANGE AVENUE trenches. Shelling at time of Working parties went forward to support Junction as for world Table attackers - Appendix IV. Raid was going to and to capture shelling of CHAIN SUPPORT - a few aerial darts were just took up for that. Occasional shelling of left Coy. front. Front line was closest where it has been taken in - two fistages were completely sandbagged. Duckboards in parts of front trench effects & cleaner. No constructed in listening posts from Front line near LINK ALLEY - 30.0 of. dug. Trench	Appx IV

WAR DIARY / INTELLIGENCE SUMMARY

Vol. XV.
O/C 1 Bn. Royal Scots Fusiliers
September 1917

Army Form C. 2118.

Place	Date	Hour	Summary of Events and Information	Remarks and references to Appendices
In the Line	25th (contd)		Wiring – 30 yds. Got wire put up in front of No 2 Sap. 40 yds. strengthened by night of wire BEDDOOR LANE needs front line. Patrols found touch over often with BEDDOOR LANE on night. Patrol which went out in front found enemy repairing a gap which our Arty had cut in his wire – L/Gun was trained on this spot and fired on it intermittently. Another patrol found dead German in front of our wire as result of yesterdays raid. Area around TWIN COPSE. Heavily dusk mortared. CHAIN SUPPORT got a few 77mm shells. Casualties nil.	
"	26th		Work. 2 Airtraps No 1 Stand completely rivetted – Berm made + back slopes k. requires angle-Iron. Islands No 5, 3 A. frames laid and 3 firetraps rivetted. 4 amm: pits dug. 1600 sandbags in left front used in rivetting. Wires 30 yds. in front of Sap K. 12 onto a 3 drum + wires put up in front of Pats. M3 + P.H. About 7 p.m. enemy fired rifle grenades on front line + CHAIN SUPPORT. Some 77mm shells primarily on CHAIN SUPPORT. No other shelling of note. Casualties from rifle grenades 1 Br. Killed 4 wounded – None of these remained at duty.	
"	27th		Work continued – rivetting trenches and making the walls to required slope. News approx. 37 yds. long. Ave aff. apex 4½ feet. Wiring 30 yds. apron in front of No.1 Pat. in M + 20 yds by 3 yds broad completed. Odd wire strengthened O gap fires – 25 yds put up in front of Pat. H. Gaps cut in wire in front of CHAIN SUPPORT, to allow of supports moving our to front line if necessary. Patrol forms fire + explosive attached to new wire – Very little shelling, except for a few rifle grenades on front + support trenches – Casualties – 1 OR wounded –	
"	28th		Enemy fires several T.M's about 12.30 am. on right front. Three direct hits in LINK ALLEY E. of CHAIN SUPPORT. Also active on night Coy front. 6 Arnd shorts fell near it. Coy. HQ. ORANGE RESERVE and area around Battn. HQ. Shelled by enemy field guns during morning.	

Army Form C. 2118.

WAR DIARY
or
INTELLIGENCE SUMMARY.

Vol. XVI.

(Erase heading not required.) 6/7 Bn Royal Scots Fusiliers

September 1917

Place	Date	Hour	Summary of Events and Information	Remarks and references to Appendices
In the Line	28th (Contd.)		Work.- Approx. 17m sandbags filled in Battn. front, emptied in parapet to thicken same and used in revetting. Stopping of sides continued between BRIDOON ALLEY and LINK ALLEY. Two bay recesses in CHAIN SUPPORT. Anti-aircraft Lewis Gun emplacement dug between BRIDOON ALLEY and LINK ALLEY. Two CAT Lengthened another 20yds. to depth of 2 feet. 30yds. apron wire put out in front of "Stack" at C6.b. Concertina wire pieces in front of posts 4 and 5. Casualties. 2 O.R. wounded (one accidental).	
"	29th		Hostile T.M. fire in INN COPSE about 2 A.M. Casualties 2 O.R. wounded (Shrapnel) in front trench J. Work 8 continued - sloping walls of trenches Bern to retest of 250 feet made. 1100 sandbags filled during the night & used in revetting & strengthening parapet. Two CAT continued over top of ridge. No wiring done owing to moonlight. Patrol moved out to about 60 yds. in front, listened for ½ an hour - nothing unusual seen or heard.	
"	30th		Situation fairly quiet all day. About 6 p.m. enemy shelled CHAIN SUPPORT with a few 5.9. One direct hit. Casualties 1 killed and 1 wounded. Later a few H.E. shells fell in MUSKET TRENCH. Trench now 70 yds. long, average depth 6 feet, width at top 3½ feet. Left Coy. front line - dugouts started and made reverse slope, amount done 14.8 yds. 700 sandbags used in revetting. One shell completes on M. Coy front line. From 21st of the month Lieut. Col. F.J.D. Gordon took over temporary Command of the Bn. Major T.L. du Havilland comdg. the Battn. in his absence.	

T.L. du Havilland
Major
Comd. 6/7 Royal Scots Fusiliers

ROUTINE ORDERS:
Issued by
Lt. Col. R.I.D. Gordon, Comdg. 6/7th. Royal Scots Fusiliers.

Orderly Officer.   Under Coy. arrangements.
Reveille   7a.m.
Breakfast   7-30 a.m.
Tea.   On arrival in Camp.

Appendix I

6/7th. R.S.F.   OPERATION ORDERS NO. 7.

(1) The Battalion will move to the XVII Corps Area to-morrow 2nd. inst.

(2) The Battalion will rendezvous in the square at 9-45a.m. order H.Qrs. C.D.& B. Coys. and will march to ESQUELBECQ Station where they will entrain. Haversack rations will be carried on the Man and waterbottles will be carried FULL.

(3) Train Orders.
a. No personnel will be allowed in the brake vans at each end of the train, or on the roof of the trucks, and no covered trucks will be used for baggage as it restricts space available for personnel.
b. The strictest discipline must be maintained in the train. Men will not be allowed to leave it unless under orders of the Commanding Officer. There will be a definite halt on the journey when men may leave the train, and this will be notified later.
c. All doors of covered trucks and carriages on the RIGHT side of the train, when on the main line, should be kept closed.

(4) The transport will proceed in advance of the Battalion under
a. 2/Lt. R. Lee and will move off at 8a.m. to reach the entraining station at 9a.m.
b. Supply and baggage waggns will proceed with transport.
c. Breast ropes for horse trucks will be taken by transport but those for lashing vehicles on the flat trucks will be provided by the railway.
d. All water carts will entrain FULL.

(5) Ration and refilling arrangements have already been communicated to Quartermaster.

(6) Two Motor Lorries will meet train on arrival at AUBIGNY to transport surplus stores.

(5) a. It is understood that 2 lorries will also be available for transport of stores from here to ESQUELBECQ STATION. O.C. B. Coy will detail one officer and 20 men to unload lorries on to train at ESQUELBECQ and to unload from train at AUBIGNY. This party should proceed to ESQUELBECQ STATION at 8-30a.m.
b. Mess Cart will be loaded this evening commencing with Batt.H.Q. at 8-30 p.m. 1 Mess Box per Coy. will be retained for Breakfast purposes and will be collected by Motor lorry commencing with Batt. H. Qrs. at 8-30a.m.
c. Valises will be collected by G.S. Wagon commencing with Batt. H Q. at 7-35a.m. This wagon must on no account be delayed as minimum time to collect and arrive at station has been given.

Issued to all recipients
of Batt. Routine Orders.
1st September 1917.

Lieut.&Adjt.
6/7th. R.S.F.

appendix II

SECRET.   OPERATION ORDERS NO. 9.   6/7th. R.S.F.

Ref. 51B. N.W.   In the Field 13th. Sept. 17

1. The 45th. Inf. Bde. will be relieved to-morrow 14th. inst. by the 44th. Inf. Bde.
   6/7th. R.S.F. will be relieved by the 9th. Black Watch relief to be completed by 12 noon.

2. (a) "A" Coy. R.S.F. will be relieved by "D" Coy. 9th. B.W.
   "B" Coy. R.S.F. will be relieved by "B" COY. 9th. B.W.
   O.C. "C" Coy. will detail 4 guides (1 per platoon) to be at Bridge over road, approx. H.14.a.00 35. at 8-30a.m. to guide "A" Coy. 9th. B.W. to "A" Coy. R.S.F. quarters.
   O.C. "D" Coy. will detail 4 guides (1 per platoon) to guide "B" Coy 9th. B.W. to be at same rendezvous at 8-45a.m.
   These guides will return with "A" & "B" coys. R.S.F. respectively. To obviate any trouble in case of change since "C" & "D" Coys. R.S.F. occupied these quarters O.C. "A" & "B" Coys. R.S.F. will have guides (1 per platoon) to take over their respective reliefs at point approx. H. 32 d. 35.25. at 10a.m.
   (b) "C" Coy. R.S.F. will be relieved by "C" Coy. 9th. B.W.
   "D" " " " " " " "A" " " "
   No guides are required. Advance parties of 9th. B.W. will report here at 8-45a.m. and will be shown over the quarters to be occupied by incoming Coys.

3. On relief, the Batt. will move to BAROSSA CAMP. All movement will be by platoons at 200yds. interval and steel helmets will be worn in the case of "A" & "B" Coys.
   H. Qrs. "C" & "D" Coys. will be formed up ready to move off at 10a.m. H. Qrs. will lead off at 10-5 a.m., the others following in sequence.

4. All trench stores, tools, maps, defence schemes, aeroplane photos, position calls, A.A. mountings, anti-gas appliances etc. will be handed over and receipts obtained. These lists will be handed in to Orderly Room in duplicate by 6p.m. 14th. inst.

5. An advance party consisting of 2/Lt. A.D. Cameron and 1 N.C.O. per "C" & "D" Coys. with Sgt. McVeigh for H. Qrs. will parade at Orderly Room at 8a.m. and proceed to BAROSSA CAMP to take over Camp R.S.M. will detail 2 N.C.Os. from H.Qrs. to parade at same time and place to take over the accommadation for "A" & "B" Coys. The advance party will meet incoming platoons and conduct to quarters 2/Lt. Cameron will forward list of stores etc. taken over, in duplicate, to Orderly Room by 2p.m.

6. Transport Officer will detail the following:-
   (a) 1 Limber to be at "A" Coy. H. Qrs. at 9a.m. to collect Mess Kit and Lewis Guns of "A" & "B" Coys. These will be brought to BAROSSA CAMP.
   (b) Necessary transport for transfer of Officers Valises to BAROSSA CAMP, Mess Kit, Canteen Stock & Orderly Room. These will be ready for collecting at 9a.m.
   (c) Horses for cookers, Water cart, and Medical Cart.

7. All quarters will be left thoroughly clean.

8. Relief complete will be reported in the case of "A" & "B" Coys. by sending AOK BOK over the phone.

9. Attention is drawn to the relief of working parties issued under separate cover.

Lt. & Adjt.
6/7th. R.S.F.

Issued to all recipients
of Batt. Routine Orders.
1 Copy to O.C. 9th. Black Watch.
1 "   War Diary.
1 "   File.

Secret.   6/7th. Royal Scots Fusiliers.   *appendix III*   In the Field.

OPERATION ORDERS NO. 10.   22/9/17.

Ref. 51B.N.W.
PELVES & MONCHY 1/10,000.

1. The Battalion will relieve the 10th. Scottish Rifles in the right sub-section of the Right Divisional Front to-morrow evening.

2. "B" Coy. will take over Right Front.
   "D" "   "   "   "   Left   "
   "C" "   Support "in MUSKET RESERVE.

3. Guides will be at FAMPOUX STATION H.23 a 8.9. at 8p.m. 2/Lt. G.A. Massie will be at STATION and have guides told off so that each Platoon can move off immediately after detraining.

4. The Battalion will proceed to FAMPOUX STATION by train from BLANGY LOCK G.24.a.7.9.
   "B" Coy. will entrain at 7-20p.m. (4 Trucks.)
   "D" "   "   "   " 7-25p.m. (4   "   )
   H. Qrs.&"C"Coy." "   " 7-30p.m. (6   "   )
   Parade at 6-55p.m. marching off in above order.

5. Advance parties will proceed as follows:-
   (a) 1 N.C.O. per Coy. and 1 for H. Qrs. to take over trench stores to parade at Orderly Room at 1p.m.
   1 Cook per Coy. to parade at Orderly Room at 1 p.m. They will take over cooking arrangements in HAPPY VALLEY.
   (b) To facilitate relief the three posts supplied by "B" Coy. will proceed under an officer in advance and will commence relief as soon as darkness sets in. They will parade outside Orderly Room at 1p.m. prompt and will get barge at BLANGY LOCK at 1-40p.m.

6. All trench stores, A.A. Mountings, Maps, Defence Schemes, Position Calls, Aeroplane Photographs, etc., will be taken over and receipts forwarded to Batt. H. Qrs. by 8am 24th. Inst. The number of rattles, for use in the event of gas shelling, taken over will be reported by same hour.

7. Completion of relief will be reported by phone by the word "APPLE"

8. Working parties will be found as per separate memo.

9. (a) Valises will be stacked outside Guard Room at 5-30p.m.
   (b) Blankets "   "   "   "   "   "   " 2p.m.
   (c) Mess Kit and Lewis Guns will proceed with Coys.
   (d) Mess Cart for balance of kit remaining at stores will be forward at 6pm.
   (e) The camp will be left thoroughly clean.

10. (a) "A" Coy. will be detached during forthcoming tour for course in Musketry. Detailed orders for this course will be issued later. "A" Coy. less working party will parade at 5p.m. and march to billets in ARRAS. Transport Officer will detail a limber to be at Guard Room at 2pm for transport of Mess Kit etc. etc.
    (b) 1 Platoon of "C" Coy. under 2/Lt. Thomson will also be detached for Musketry Course. Separate Orders have been issued 2/Lt. Thomson. This platoon will parade at 5p.m. and move to billets near Q.M. Stores O.C. "B" Coy. will detail one cook to parade with this party. He will cook lately for whole Brigade Party. This platoon will take their own Camp Kettles with them. This platoon will be struck off ration strength from 26th. inst. inclusive to 1st. October inclusive.

11. All work in progression in the line will be taken over.

12. Amendments to timings for reports due Batt. H. Qrs. will be issued to-morrow.

Capt.& Adjt.
6/7th.R.S.F.

Appendix 14.

Table of Working Parties.

Serial No.	Work.	Strength.	Report.	Found By.	Remarks.
2.	Carrying Party.	1 Officer 2 N.C.Os. 30 Men.	3 p.m. on 23rd.	"A" Coy.	Party accommodated in Happy Valley. Rationed by 93rd. Field Coy. R.E's. Party will take over by 3 p.m. on 23/9/14.
3.	Work till 1 p.m. 20 Shovels & 10 Picks to be taken.	1 Officer 40 Other Ranks.	7 a.m. on 24th.	"C" Coy.	To be at Junction of Bridoon & Snaffle Trenches at 7 a.m. daily commencing 24th. Inst.
12.	Bridoon Trench. Slope Sides & Trench Board Trench.	1 Officer 20 Other Ranks.	8.30 p.m.	"C" Coy.	To be at Junction Chain Support & Harness at 8.30 p.m. daily commencing 24th Inst.

Confidential

WAR DIARY
OF
6/7TH (SERVICE) BATTN. ROYAL SCOTS FUSILIERS.

FROM 1st Oct 1917 TO 31st Oct 1917

VOL XXVII

17G.
8 sheets

6/7 R Scot Fus
Vol 28

WAR DIARY
or
INTELLIGENCE SUMMARY.
(Erase heading not required.)

Army Form C. 2113.

VOL. XVII 6/7 Royal Scots Fusiliers

October 1917

Place	Date	Hour	Summary of Events and Information	Remarks and references to Appendices
In the Line	1st		Situation all day very quiet. Work of resetting front and support lines continued. Other two shelters completed on Lt. Col. Trenches. The Battn. was relieved by and moved to Support in WILDERNESS CAMP.	
WILDERNESS CAMP	2nd		Battalion supplied working parties at night for work in forward area. Those not on working parties carried out unit training which comprised practise in wiring by Squads, Physical Drill and Bayonet fighting, under instructors. A draft of 4-8 O.Ranks reported for duty and taken on strength b. day - mostly casuals from Stopbase re. as for 2nd.	
"	3rd and 4th		as for 2nd.	
"	5th		The Battalion was relieves in Support by the 6th (Cameron Highlanders, moving to RESERVE as per Operation Order No.16., attached.	Appendix 1
"	6th		Parade 8.30 A.M. to 12.30 p.m. under Coy arrangements. The Sergt. Instructor in WIRING continued work with all Coys, as did also the Sergt. Instructor in Physical training - at 2 p.m. all N.C.O.s & Battalion paraded for drill and instruction under 2/Lieut J.T. DAVIS. One Officer & Battalion proceeded for instruction in ARTILLERY WORK in conjunction with INFANTRY to the 71st Battery R.F.A., spending one day at the guns and one day at the O.P. Church Services:- Church of Scotland held in spare hour at 11 am - joint service 6th Cameron Highlanders and C. of E. at same hour in Camp area. The under have been awarded decorations for acts of gallantry in the field - 7/2 Lieut. T.SHARKS, Military Cross, and No. 16229 Pte (L.Cpl.) A.M.CUTCHEON. Military Medal - a draft of 25 O.Ranks reported for duty and were taken on strength yesterday.	
"	7th		Parade 8.30 A.M. - 12.30 p.m. under Coy arrangements - Rifle Range at disposal of Coy for 1 hour each - training to include wiring - Physical Drill & Bayonet fighting. Regimental Drill - Bvt. Paul VC. The following officers reported for duty and came posted - Lieut. W.R. HUTCHISON. 6/10/17 to "C" Coy. and 2/Lieut. T. SMILIE 7/10/17 to "A" Coy.	
"	8th			

Army Form C. 2118.

WAR DIARY
or
INTELLIGENCE SUMMARY.
(Erase heading not required.) Vol XVII. 6/7th Royal Scots Fusiliers

October 1917.

Place	Date	Hour	Summary of Events and Information	Remarks and references to Appendices
Wilderness Camp	9th		Parade 8.30am - 12.30pm. Under Coy. arrangements on disposal of Coys. for one hour etc. The Battalion was relieved by the 9th Bn. the Black Watch, and moves on relief to Bivouis in ARRAS at Oil Factory - relief complete by 3.30 pm.	
Oil Factory ARRAS.	10th		Parades. 9am - 12.30pm. Under Company Commanders. Training area at MOAT, ARRAS. A working party of 2 officers and 180 men were employed on CAMP CONSTRUCTION at BLANGY, and one Officer and 60 men were lent to the New Zealand Tunnelling Co. Carrying material for dug-outs. These parties found by "B" Coy. Parade 8.30am - 4pm. The Rifle Range at MOAT was allotted to Battalion and one Coy. had 2 hours practice, with the exception of "A" Coy. which Coy. found working parties as above (10th).	
"	11th			
"	12th		Parade. 8.30am - 4pm. Under Coy. commander. Training to include wiring. Physical training. Rifle Range at HQ. was allotted to Coys. as follows:- 1pm - 2pm "A" Coy. 2pm - 3pm "B" Coy. 3pm to 4pm "C" Coy. Whilst "D" Coy. found above mentioned working parties. Baths were also allotted to all Companies - from 9am - 2pm.	
"	13th		Parade 8.30am - 3.30pm. Under Coy. arrangements - to include wiring, Physical Drill, Bayonet Fighting, Coy. Drill - under instructors - The Range at Rifle Camp was allotted in the afternoon to "A" & "B" Coys. "C" Coys. found alone working parties.	
"	14th		Church Services. 11.30am. Church of Scotland in ST. ANDREWS SOLDIERS CLUB. 11.0am C. of E. in Y.M.C.A. Hut and at 11.15am Roman Catholic in CATHOLIC CLUB. ARRAS.	
"	15th		Parades. 8.30am to 12.30pm "B" & "D" Coys. at MOAT, Training in WIRING, Physical Drill &c. "A" "C" Coys. on Rifle Camp. RANGE. When not shooting, training in WIRING was carried on. The following Officers with reports to 1st Battn. R.S.F., and accordingly struck off strength. 2/Lieuts. W. McMINN, D. McCOLL YOUNG, H. LAMBROUGHTON, and J.F. LOGAN.	

[signature]

Army Form C. 2118.

WAR DIARY or INTELLIGENCE SUMMARY

(Erase heading not required.)

Vol XVII. 6/17. Royal Scots Fusiliers

October 1917

Place	Date	Hour	Summary of Events and Information	Remarks and references to Appendices
ARRAS	16th		Batt. at Rifle Range allotted to Coy. from 8.30 am – 4 pm. When not firing – training in wiring – carried on. Shooting practice met. Park Respirators one carried out.	
"	17th		Forenoon spent in cleaning up billets, preparation to move. The Battalion relieved the 12th H.L.I. in the Right FRONT of the LEFT SECTION of the CENTRE SECTOR of CORPS FRONT (ROEUX AREA). "A" Coy. were on left and "C" Coy. on right of Battalion front – B and D Coy. in SUPPORT and RESERVE in LANCER LANE, occupying "K", "L", "M" Posts there.	
In the Line	18th		Trenches were in a very heavy condition and entails much work on the garrison. Small blocks in front and support trenches cleared and sandbag revetment of ELBOW ALLEY was carried on. Patrols were out and found no signs of enemy. Gaps in enemy wire kept open by Lewis gun fire.	
"	19th		Work on Trenches continued under supervision of R.E. Company. Enemy 2in/2 active on SCABBARD SUPPORT in the forenoon and again in the afternoon about 4 pm. Our artillery retaliation in each case was effective in stopping fire.	
"	20th		Patrols went out this one on the left Coy. front meeting with M.G. fire from a point approx I.25.d.45.75. 1 N.C.O. was wounded. This Lewis gun was covering a work party which Patrol got L.G. fire on returning to trench. Night was otherwise normal. Orders were issued for work as for previous day. Enemy artillery activity below normal. No sign of enemy.	
"	21st		Relief next day – Night normal – Patrols (Fri-Clip?) Bright's + Foreades to the Battalion was relieved tonight by the 11th Argyll's + Sutherland's Highrs. + Foreades to MIDDLESEX CAMP. on relief. Relief complete by 8.30 pm.	
MIDDLESEX CAMP	22nd		Under Coy. arrangements – cleaning of equipment, clothes, rifles etc. and Inspection of Respirators by Platoon Officers.	
"	23rd		Parade. 8.45 a.m – 12.45 pm. Under Coy. arrangements – training to include WIRING, marching and Port Respirators on drill in rapid adjustment of Box respirators, Physical Training, Coy. Drill. Extended Order Drill. Parade at 4"17 allotted to "D" + "B" Coys. from 9 a.m – 1 pm.	

WAR DIARY
or
INTELLIGENCE SUMMARY

Army Form C. 2118.

October 1917. Vol XIV. 6/7: Royal Scots Fusiliers.

Place	Date	Hour	Summary of Events and Information	Remarks and references to Appendices
MIDDLESEX CAMP.	24th	8.45 AM & 12.45 pm	Parades 8.45 AM & 12.45 pm. Under Coy. arrangements as for 23rd except Range not available. A short course in Trench Instruction was held by an R.E. Officer for officers and N.C.Os. of Battalion. Also a class of 1 N.C.O. and 9 men attended at Camp of 9th GORDON H'dshrs. (Pioneers) for instruction in wiring.	
"	25th	8.45 AM & 12.45 pm	Parades 8.45 AM & 12.45 pm. Under Coy. arrangements as for 24th.	
RT SUB-SECTOR ROEUX.	26th		Battn. relieves the 11th A.& S.H. in front line. Right Sub. Section ROEUX Sector. Today as per Operation Orders attached — 10/17. A working party for work in RIFLE CAMP. was from Battalion being left out of line — they paraded at 7.30 am working with 73rd FIELD Coy. R.E. Night normal.	Appendix. 11.
"	27th		Day quiet except for occasional shelling of SCABBARD ALLEY and SCABBARD SUPPORT by enemy Trench Mortars — All detached or very precise with Stokes & Artillery — Night fairly quiet owing to moonlight — C, D & E Saps worked on front. Heavy enemy sniping — 3 Casualties in wiring party — 50 yds wire put out between B & E Saps.	
"	28th		At 12 noon Heavy Trench Mortar bombarded Y & Y½ trenches — very effective. Enemy seen to run from shell holes & trenches & run back — Casualty and Lewis gun fire — 5 dead counted — 4 other hits claimed — Night quiet. Saps in enemy wire reply opened by machine gun fire — Major D. REITZ joined Battn. and taken on strength. Enemy Artillery & Trench Mortars much more active — Front & Support lines went shelled intermittently by 77mm. Work parties as on 27th & 28th — Under R.E. supervision — Orders issued for relief next day — Night quiet — Bright moonlight.	
"	29th			
"	30th		Day quiet — Battn. was relieved by 11th A & S.H. — Relief completed 7.30 pm — Work Parties provided — Moved in relief to SUPPORT Position — Disposition 1 Coy LANCER LANE 2 Coys 9.B. HQ in H23C and 1 Coy in STIRLING CAMP.	

Army Form C. 2118.

WAR DIARY
or
INTELLIGENCE SUMMARY.

6/7th Royal Scots Fusiliers
October 1917

Place	Date	Hour	Summary of Events and Information	Remarks and references to Appendices
SUPPORT ROEUX SECTOR	31		Day quiet - Baths - working parties under Batt Orders Details 9 Officers 525 O Ranks - Major D REITZ whilst riding to attend Court Martial, was injured by his horse bolting & throwing him down whilst turning across Corner - Admitted to Hospital. On 30th inst the Divisional Commander made a tour of the trenches & expressed his satisfaction at the way the men had worked and generally improved the trenches occupied by this battalion.	

T.K. Howlenew
Major
Comdg 6/7 R.S.F.

Secret.   6/7th. R.S.F. OPERATION ORDERS No. 171   25th. Oct. 1917.

Ref. Map:- (a) 51 B. NW. 1/20,000. (b) Trench Map.

1. The Batt. will relieve the 11th. A.& S.H. in the Right Sub Section, ROEUX Sector, tomorrow 26th. inst.

2. DISPOSITION.
"D" Coy. 6/7th. R.S.F. will occupy Right Coy. Front.
"B" "   "   "   "   "   "   Left   "   "
"A" "   "   "   "   "   "   Support in WELFORD RES.
"C" "   "   "   "   "   "   Reserve in LANCER LANE including K, L, & M Posts.

3. GUIDES.   The only guides required are for "B" Coy on Left Front ---- 1 per platoon---. To be at Batt. H.Q. JOHNSON AVENUE at 5-30 p.m.

4. (a)   "A" & "C" Coys' R"S"F" will have their relief over by 3-45 p.m.. This is to allow the 11th. A.& S.H. Coys' to be clear of LANCER LANE by 4-45 p.m., so as to leave trench clear for "D" & "B" Coys'.
Leading platoon of "A" Coy. will march off at 1-15 p.m. the succeeding platoons and those of "C" Coy. following at 200 yards interval.   2 limbers to convey Mess Kit, Lewis Guns and dixies will be at Guard Room at 1-0 p.m.. This limber will proceed to junction of road and camouflage screen near LANCER LANE where Coys' will arrange to collect------ 1 man per Coy. will proceed with limber as guard.

(b)   "D","B" & H.Q. Coys' will march off by platoons in that order. Leading platoon of "D" Coy. will march off at 2-30 p.m.   Cookers will proceed with their Coys', tea to be served between ATHIES LOCK & FEUCHY.   ½ H.Q. Coy. will feed with "D", and ½ with "B" Coy.
O.C. Coys' will so time themselves to march off so as "D" Coy. enters LANCER LANE at ~~RNRT~~ p.m. 4*45 p.m.
1 Limber for Mess Kit and Dixies for these Coys' will be at Guard Room at 2-0 p.m. Limber will proceed as in para (a), 1 man per Coy. & H.Q. proceeding as guard.

5. (a)   The observers will proceed in advance and take over by 10-0 a.m.   They will parade outside Orderly Room at 8-0 a.m. and proceed under L/Cpl. Fairbrother. Guides will be obtained at Batt. H.Q., at JOHNSON AVENUE.

(b)   1 N.C.O. per Coy. and one for H.Q. will proceed in advance to take over Trench Stores.   These will be carefully checked.   They will parade outside Orderly Room at 9-15 a.m. and catch 9-40 a.m. barge at BLANGY for FAMPOUX.

(c)   20 men per Coy. will be left out in details.   O.C. "C" Coy. will detail 2 Officers to remain with this party and supervise training.   These details will parade outside Orderly Room at 1-30 p.m..   Billets are in RUE ST. MAURICE, No.49 for the men and No. 66 for the Officers.

(d)   New table of Working Parties will be issued later.

(e) Blankets will be stacked in bundles of 10, and each Coy. will use a tent for this purpose, Company fatigues standing by ready to load on arrival of waggons.

(f) Officers' Valises will be loaded at 1-0 p.m.

(g) Mess Cart will be forward to take surplus Mess Kit to Q.M. Stores at 1-45 p.m.

OPERATION ORDERS No.17 (contd).

6. Lewis Guns and teams of "B" & "D" Coys' will proceed in advance.
   Whether the relief takes place in daylight will be at the discretion of O.C. Coys' to whom they report. O.C. "A" Coy. will also send 1 gun and team with this party to relieve A.A. gun on Left Coy. Front. 1 Limber will be at Guard Room for theseguns and S.A.A. at 12-20 p.m. Teams will parade at Guard Room at 12-30 p.m. and march off under Sgt. Tonner. Guides, 1 per gun will meet party at junction of LANCER LANE at 1-45 p.m.
   Each gun and team will move up at 3 minutes intervals.

7. The camp in all probability will be disbanded after our exit, but this in no way alters Standing Orders for cleanliness. All rubbish will be cleared and taken to incinerator. 1 Officer per Coy. will report to the Adjutant ¼ of an hour before his Coy. moves off that his Coy. lines are clean and sanitary.
   The Orderly Officer will report at 1-30 p.m. that the camp is clean.

8. Completion of all reliefs will be reported by the word-- ZINC.

Issued to:-
```
        1 copy.  O.C. Coys'.(each)
        1  "     O.C. 11th.A&S.H.
        1  "     T.O. & Q.M.
        1  "     R.S.M.
        1  "     War Diary.
        1  "     File.
```

25th. October. 1917.

Capt.
Adjt, 6/7th. Royal Scots Fusiliers.

Secret.   6/7th. R.S.F. OPERATION ORDERS No. 16.   4th. Oct. 1917.

Ref. SHEET.

1.   The Battalion will be relieved by the 6th. Cameron Hgrs. to-morrow 5th.inst. moving to camp at present occupied by them, relief to be completed by 3 p.m. The Battalion will then be Reserve Battalion.

2.   "A" Coy. will take over Billets at present occupied by "A" Coy. 6th. Cameron Hgrs. the other Coys. taking over in like manner. An advance party of 1 N.C.O. per coy. and 1 for H. Qrs. will proceed to camp immediately after breakfast taking over their respective areas.

3.   H. Qrs. will move off from present position about 10.30a.m. the coys. following in sequence at 5 minutes interval. "D" Coy. will move to new camp on relief, likewise party Serial 4 ("A" Coy.)
     Garrison of "G" post will be relieved by 8p.m. to-night by
4.19th. The Royal Scots ~~and battalion relief be completed~~.

4.   Serial 4 will be taken over by 6th. Camerons on night of 5th./6th. and serials 14,15,16,&17. will continue to be supplied by "B" & "C" Coys.
     These latter parties move to forward billets at 4p.m. to-day under command of Lieut. D.S. Brown.

5.   All work in progress will be handed over on relief and any details of parties explained to relieving units. All trench stores will be handed over on relief and receipts obtained. These latter to be handed in to Orderly Room by 4p.m. on 6th. inst.

6.   Transport Officer will arrange with Q.M.S. Paton to bring on to new camp valises of all "D" Coy. officers, together with mens blankets. Mess-Kit and Cooker will also be brought forward. These to be at
[Collected] new area by 10.30a.m. Valises will be collected at 9a.m. commencing with "D" Coy., then H. Qrs. "B" & "A" coys. Mens Kit will be collected by Mess Cart at same hour, commencing with "D" Coy. Mens blankets will be stacked under Coy. arrangements and collected by limber, commencing with "D" Coy. at 9.30a.m. Horses for Cooker, Maxims, Medical Cart, and Water Carts to be forward by 10a.m. and a limber for Orderly Room Stores and Canteen at same hour.
     Dinners will be served on arrival in new camp.

                                                    G. Albt. Massie
Issued to all recipients
of Batt. Routine Orders
  1 Copy to 6th. Cameron Hgrs.   Lt.
  1 "   War Diary.   Adjt.
  1 "   File.   6/7th. R.S.F.

Confidential 9/1029

WAR DIARY

OF

1/7th (SERVICE) BATT. ROYAL SCOTS FUSILIERS.

From 1st Novr 1917 To 30th Novr 1917

Vol. XVIII

18 G
17 sheets

Army Form C. 2118.

WAR DIARY
or
INTELLIGENCE SUMMARY.
(Erase heading not required.)

Vol. XVIII 6/7th Royal Scots Fusiliers

November 1917.

Place	Date	Hour	Summary of Events and Information	Remarks and references to Appendices
Support Roet Sector.	1st		Day quiet. One Coy. was in forward trenches with two companies near Roeux H.Q. in the Railway Cutting, Fampoux, and one Coy, in Reserve at STIRLING CAMP. All employed on working parties. 9 Officers and 525 other ranks. Orders issued to-day for move tomorrow to OIL FACTORY, ARRAS, au operation Order No. 20.	Ref. Map 51.B.N.W. Appendix 1.
ARRAS	2nd		Battn. was relieved by the 8th Bn. Seaforths, moving to ARRAS, with H.Q. at OIL FACTORY. Relief complete by 6.30 p.m.	
"	3rd		Common Garrison in clearing up, and inspection of kits. 1.30 pm - 4 pm All Coys Routine includes Physical Training, Coy. Drill - Bose Respirator Drill o Coy Drill - Bullet o Bayonet Course in neighbourhood of Butte de Tir at disposal of Corp. A/Sgnal, N.C.O. and 9 men from "A" Coy. attended a course in wiring with 9th Gordon Highlanders (Pioneers.) One Platoon from "D" Coy. on Musketry Course at Camp while Battalion in ARRAS. A working party of 10 off. - 50 other ranks was to day found by "A" Coy. carrying bombs to forward dumps. Major J.C. HIGHAM, M.C. from 9th Battn. joins 3/11/17 and was taken in charge of Unit.	
"	4th		Church Services Presbyterian at 11 am, in Salle du Concert, C. of E. in Church Army Hut at 11 am and Roman Catholic in Chapel of R.C. Club at 10.30 am. Above working party was taken over by "B" Coy. The wiring squad o musketry course continued. Also 5 officers attended a Course in the placing of "V" frames in trench building.	
"	5th		Parade 8.30 am - 10 pm under Coy. arrangements. Routine to includes Box Respirator Drill. Marching with Box Respirator on. Physical Training Coy. Drill and Standing 9.3. Arms. The Assault Course was allotted to "A.B. & C" Coys. for one and a quarter hour each. "D" Coy the most Rifle Range was also alloted to these Coys. Batch for two hours. "D" Coy who employed one platoon Musketry Course and remainder on working parties -	W.O.T

Army Form C. 2118.

WAR DIARY or INTELLIGENCE SUMMARY

(Erase heading not required.)

Vol. XVIII 9/7 - Royal Scots Fusiliers

Month and year: November 1917

Place	Date	Hour	Summary of Events and Information	Remarks and references to Appendices
ARRAS	6th		Parades 8.30 A.M - 1.0 P.M Routine included Physical training, Box Respirator Drill, Rapid adjustment of Box Respirator. Coy. & extended Order Drill. The Assault Course was allotted to "A", "B", "C" Coys. "D" Coy. practised in neighbourhood of RIFLE CAMP. One platoon of each Company trained as for previous days. Major J.C. WHIGHAM admitted to Hosp. One Platoon of musketry as for previous days.	
"	7th		Parades 8.30 A.M - 1.0 P.M as for 6th. 2 P.M - 3 P.M. BUTTE de TI R Rifle Range instruction of Led shots.	
"	8th		Parades 8.30 A.M - 1.0 P.M Assault Course was at disposal of Battn. 6 day Rifle Grenadiers Ref. Prog. The Battn. Lewis Gunners had the 5/13 M.M. Fire Line bombs in neighbourhood of BAROCA CAMP. One platoon of H.Q. at the Rifle Range in H.Q.A.	
"	9th		Parade. Route march by Companies. Training of Rifle Grenadiers as for yesterday.	
"	10th		Orders came to day for move into line tomorrow, relieving the 10th Scottish Rifles in the Right Sub section Gavrouval front, as per O.Orders. no 21.	Appendix II.
Right Sub Sector MONCHY	11th		Relieved 10th Scottish Rifles on Right Sub. section. MONCHY sector. Weather approaching winter which made in a very bad condition, especially night Coy. front, where it was necessary to use sand bags. At 2 A.M. Enemy attempted to raid our trenches on our front. Heavy bombardment in reaching our parapet, but was immediately shot by sentry.	
"	12th		Continues repair of trenches, which were falling in in many places owing to heavy rain. Good progress made in pumping out water. Artillery quiet, though several Trench mortars were fired on front and support trenches. No casualties.	

WAR DIARY
INTELLIGENCE SUMMARY.

(Erase heading not required.)

Vol. XVII. 1/4th Royal Scots Fusiliers.

November 1917.

Place	Date	Hour	Summary of Events and Information	Remarks and references to Appendices
Right Sub Sector.	13th		Enemy artillery more active. Casualties 1 O.R. killed and 3 wounded. Work of repairing trench continued and parties were employed under R.E. supervision. Patrols went out from no contact with enemy. Enemy quiet during night.	
MONCHY.	14th		Day quieter. Enemy shelling of MONCHY TRENCH. There were some T.M's fell on Left Coy. Front line. Orders were issued for move to support position but no direct hits were obtained - no casualties.	
"			Bn. H.Q. moved to STIRLING CAMP, and "A" & "D" Coy. "B" Coy occupied JOHNSON AVENUE and "C" Coy was in HAPPY VALLEY. The relieving unit was the 13th Battn. The Royal Scots.	
STIRLING CAMP.	15th		Battalion was largely occupied in working parties and the Coy. and Company were occupied in maintenance of trenches other than R.E's. Major J.C. WHIGHAM, evacuated to U.K.	
"	16th		as for 15th.	
"	17th		as for 15th, except that "B" & "C" Coys relieved "A" & "D" Coys in forward positions. Church Services for "A" & "D" Coys. - Camp. Orders issued to day for move into Rear Areas tomorrow.	Operation Order No 23 appendix III.
"	18th			
Right Sub Sector.	19th		The Battalion relieved the 13th Battn. The Royal Scots in the Right Sub. Section of the Divisional Front, with Battn. H.Q. at junction of CURB SWITCH and ORCHARD RESERVE. 9. To "D" Coys were front line. Right Coy front: "B" Coy in support and "C" Coy in Reserve. See Operation Order No 91. on Left & Right Coy front.	Appendix IV.
MONCHY.	20th		Working parties were employed improving trenches under R.E. Supervision. Garrisons repaired front trenches where shown in. Enemy artillery much more active than when we were last front Casualties 1 O.R. wounded. Enemy aeroplane flew low between 10 and 10:30 A.M. in this sector. Casualties 1 O.R. wounded. Our Sent Sec. but were driven off by A.A. in vicinity of MONCHY TRENCH. Enemy aeroplane on our front lines attempts to raise the enemy fire and send Smoke. 2/Lt M.B. F.E. and 12.0 Ranks of "D" Coy. attempted to raid the parky rockets. Winds. fire and found Smoke. 2/Lt M.B. D. WHIGHAM and trench mortar barrage at Zero, the party reached the enemy wire but found him on exploding that part of the enemy machine gun fire.	

G.O.S.

WAR DIARY or INTELLIGENCE SUMMARY

Army Form C. 2118.

Nov. 1917 — 6/7 th Royal Scots Fusiliers

Place	Date	Hour	Summary of Events and Information	Remarks and references to Appendices
Right Sub-Sector MONCHY.	20th		After waiting five minutes for an opportunity to meet in Mt N.15. The watcher, the party in Roy de Object had been gained viz: that the enemy was holding his hind- and to endeavour to obtain a prisoner, which was the other half of the object, seemed only fraught by a negative return, and the possibility of heavy casualties. Casualties on 20th nil. Slightly wounded.	
"	21st		Work on new line MONCHY TRENCH, continued also repair of front line. Enemy artillery less active though his T.M.s did considerable damage to front line on left Coy sector, and on HIGHLAND SUPPORT. CUBA SWITCH SOUTH near fork. G.G. also needed a good deal of attention.	
"	22nd		Enemy activity normal, and intermittent shelling of MONCHY, HIGHLAND SUPPORT and BRIGADE ALLEY. Work was continued in improving trenches. (At midnight 2/L. A.W. MCKENZIE with 10 Scouts went out on patrol with a Lewis Gun and team to endeavour to get into enemy trenches. The covering party of 6 O.R.s and the Lewis Gun were posted to cover the party, in return and Mt MCKenzie & the balance went forward but found the enemy wire contained no gap or even chance to roll at, and was unable, therefore, to reach the enemy trench. Party withdrew without casualty.	
"	23rd		Day generally quiet. Work on trenches continues. Orders issued for relief of Battalion by 1st Bn. the Royal Scots. Our relief Battalion moved to WILDERNESS CAMP.	
WILDERNESS CAMP.	24th		Parades were mostly Coy: arrangements - cleaning of equipment and clothes re - making up of deficiencies. 20 officers and 165 others on permanent working parties, working in forward area. On night of 24/25th 2 Lts and MCKenzie and a party of 100 O.R.s proceeded to front line for the purpose of entering the enemy trenches at some point, as were attempts on night of 22nd. The 587 party left the trenches at a point I.31.d.75.90 and got to enemy wire. They found the enemy alert and owing to enemy machine gun fire from flanks playing on the	Appx No. 9 5/A.W.N.

Army Form C. 2118.

WAR DIARY
or
INTELLIGENCE SUMMARY.

(Erase heading not required.) Vol. XVIII 6/7th Royal Scots Fusiliers.

June 1917

Place	Date	Hour	Summary of Events and Information	Remarks and references to Appendices
WILDERNESS CAMP.	24th		Owing to the enemy wire, the party was unable to proceed. They waited however to see if their wounds had any opportunity of reaching the gap, but as none shewed, withdrew after reaching our lines in safety.	
"	25th		Church Service - Church of Scotland at 11 a.m. in Scottish Chruches Tent, and Church of England same place at 9.30 a.m. - Roman Catholics in Marquee at Tilloy at 9 a.m.	
"	26th		Orders issued for move to-day to ARRAS. Battalion being relieved in Reserve Position by the 4th Bn. Cameron Highlanders. as per Operation Orders No 30.	Appendix V.
ARRAS	27th		Battalion were billeted in Oil Factory. Paraded from 8.30 a.m. to 10 a.m. under Coy. arrangements. There were to have been a Battalion Route March but this was cancelled owing to heavy rain. Companies Carried on training in Oil Factory. Orders issued late for move into line, owing to redistribution of troops.	
GREENLAND HILL SECTOR	28th		The Battalion relieved the 2/1st and 2/8th Worcestr Regiment in the Central Section of the Bde. Front in the GREENLAND HILL SECTOR. Trenches generally in good condition. Enemy artillery very active, many direct hits being obtained on CHILI, CHALK and COSTA Trenches. Activity also opposite "the Nose" considerable, in left Coy. front. Small enemy mining party dispersed by L/Cpl. ___	
"	29th		Work continued repairing trenches where blown in. Enemy activity above normal - At 4 p.m. enemy opened heavy barrage of all calibres on our support trenches and C.T.S. Several direct hits were obtained. At about hour a party from 10 to 12 attempted to raid our Sap No 8 Post. in D Coy area on left, but they were driven off by rifle fire of Lewis fire and rifle grenades before reaching our line. The S.O.S. was put up and our artillery within a minute had placed a heavy barrage on the enemy lines opposite front. Half an hour all was more or less back to normal, and no other action followed - night was quiet.	W.B.T

Army Form C. 2118.

WAR DIARY
or
INTELLIGENCE SUMMARY.

(Erase heading not required.) Vol. XII. 6/7th Royal Scots Fusiliers

Instructions regarding War Diaries and Intelligence Summaries are contained in F. S. Regs., Part II. and the Staff Manual respectively. Title pages will be prepared in manuscript. November 1918.

Place	Date	Hour	Summary of Events and Information	Remarks and references to Appendices
GREENLAND ALL SECTOR.	30.		Enemy activity above normal. Between 1-30 p.m. and 1-50 p.m. enemy put down barrage on our front and support trenches and also on Communication trenches, the latter having received direct hits – no infantry action followed. There was also some gas shells put over but smell was only slight. Enemy aeroplanes also very active, flying very low over our trenches, in some cases firing into them – all driven off by A.A. Lewis gun fire and rifle fire. Work was carried on repairing damaged trenches. Orders were later for our relief of Battalion by the 9th Black Watch.	E. I. O. Porter Lt. Col. 6/7 R. Scots Fus.

Secret Copy No 2

6/7th R.S.F. Operation Orders No. 20

Ref. 51B NW.   Appendix I
French Map.

(1) The Battalion will be relieved tomorrow, 2nd inst, by the 8th Bn Seaforth Highrs.

(2) Disposition

"C" coy, S.H, will relieve "C" coy R.S.F.
"B" "   "   "   "   "B" "   "
"A" "   "   "   "   "D" "   "
"D" "   "   "   "   "A" "   "

(3) Guides   for "A" & "B" coys S.H.

(a) 1 per platoon and 1 for Bn HQ. will be at Ars. Siding at 3.40 P.M. Lieut. McKenzie will take charge and will reconnoitre tomorrow morning the shortest route from here – There is a Bridge across the river about this Siding which is approx. H.22.600.20. These guides will rendez-vous at Batln HQ at 3 PM. where Lt McKenzie will collect.

(b) Guides, 1 per platoon, for C coy. S.H, will be at same place as in para (a) at 4.40 P.M. These will be under an officer who must reconnoitre the route before hand.

(c) D coy, S.H, (Stirling Camp) will be leaving Arras at 1.30 PM.

(4) On relief coys will move by platoons at usual distances to Oil Factory, Place St Croix. They will take over same billets as when last there.
Advance party of 1 NCO per platoon will proceed in advance – They will parade at Bn HQ at 12.30 PM.
Lieut G.A. Mavis will proceed in the forenoon to take over Stores etc – The inventory will be carefully checked – An officer from "C" & "D" coys will proceed in the forenoon to check inventory of their HQ which is detached & not in Oil Factory.

(5) Transport Officer will arrange.

(1) 2 limbers for use of B, D & HQ coys to be at point on road near Bde HQ. at 3.15 PM to collect Lewis guns Mess Kit & dixies.

(2) 1 limber to be at Camouflage Screen for same kit of "B" coy at 4.30 PM. Mess cart to take requirements of "A" coy at Stirling Camp.

(3) Officers chargers of B & D coys at Bn HQ at 5.15 pm. Bn & A coy at Bde HQ at 6.45 pm. For CO & Adjutant at Bde HQ at 5.45 pm.

(4) Blankets, valises, mess kit, Orderly Room boxes etc. to be taken to OIL FACTORY.

(5) In absence of QM, arrange for hot meal for coys on arrival in billets.

6. The incoming Battn. will relieve R.A. gun in the afternoon. On the coy will have guide ready on their arrival — gun mounting & pole but not sights will be handed over and receipt obtained.

7. (a) All trench stores will be handed over & receipts obtained. These will be forwarded to Battn HQ by 9 pm on 2nd.

   (b) Stores in Reserve position will be taken over & receipt given.

8. Relief of work parties is issued under separate cover.

9. Attention is drawn to ARRAS TOWN ORDERS and Battn. orders thereon.

10. All positions will be handed over in a clean and sanitary condition.

11. Relief complete will be reported by the word LEAF.

12. Acknowledge.

1st November 1917
Issued as per Routine Orders.
1 Copy OC 8th Seaf Highrs.
1 "   CO
1 "   War Diary
1 "   File
1 "   War Diary

D. Stephen
Capt Adj
6/7 R.S.F.

SECRET.   6/7th. R.S.F. OPERATION ORDERS. No. 21.   Copy No.

Ref:-
    5 I.B. NW. 1/20,000.   *appendix II*
    And Trench Map.

(1). The Batt. will relieve the 10th. Scottish Rifles in the
Right Sub-Section, Divisional Front, tomorrow 10th. inst.

(2). **Dispositions.**

    "A" Coy. R.S.F. will relieve "D" Coy. S.R. on Right Front.
    "D" "   R.S.F.   "   "   "A" "   "   " Left   "
    "B" "   R.S.F.   "   "   "C" "   "   " Support,
                                                   (Curb Switch)
    "C" "   R.S.F.   "   "   "B" "   S.R. on Reserve,
                                                   (Musket & H. Valley).

    Batt. H.Q. junction CURB SWITCH RESERVE & ORCHARD RESERVE.

(3) **Guides.**

    1 per platoon and one for H.Q. will be at junction
of JOHNSON AVENUE & LANCER LANE at 3.30 p.m.

(4) a. Order of march will be "A" "D" "B" & "C" Coys'. HQ
    b. The leading platoon of "A" Coy. will march off from here at
    (1.15) 1.45 p.m.   Platoons will march at 5 minutes intervals.
    c. As the relief is a daylight one, every precaution will be
taken to conceal movement. Lewis Guns, rifles etc. will
not be carried in such a way that they prject over the
parapet.

(5) No.1 & 2 Posts garrisoned by "A" Coy. consists of 1 N.C.O.
and 6 men in each post, with a Lewis Gun in No. 1.
1 N.C.O. and 2 men for each post will proceed this evening
and will parade outside Orderly Room at 9.30 p.m. The N.C.O.
for No. 1 Post will be the No. 1 of the Lewis Gun. 2/Lt.
J.O. Deans will proceed with this party and will post the men
and reconnoitre the patrol route to 4th. Division Post on
our Right.   The Scottish Rifles will leave half the
garrison of each post in, till relieved tomorrow night. The
men in these posts will wear gum boots which will be issued
at Right Coy. H.Q.
Guide for this party will be at junction of JOHNSON AVENUE
and LANCER LANE at 12 midnight tonight.

(6) Advance Party to take over Stores which will be carefully
checked will proceed tomorrow morning and will be met by a
guide at junction of JOHNSON AVENUE & LANCER LANE at 10.30 a.m.
1 N.C.O. per Company for this purpose will parade at Orderly
Room at 8.0 a.m. L/C. Fairbrother will take over for H.Q.
but will proceed this evening, parading at Orderly Room at
9.30 p.m. with 2/Lt. Deans's party.

(7) **Cooking Arrangements.**

    a. All cooking is done in Cookhouse in LIME AVENUE close to
R.E. dump in HAPPY VALLEY. Cooks will proceed with their Coys'
detaching as they come to Cookhouse.   1 cook will proceed
in advance and will parade at Orderly Room at 8.0 a.m.
tomorrow.   He will take over all particulars as to cooking.
Sgt. Wyeth will detail.

    b. 20 Other Ranks to carry meals and rations to Front Line Coys'
will be found from "C" Coy. in Reserve. Sgt. Wyeth will
supervise despatch of all meals. These men will stay with
Reserve Platoons in HAPPY VALLEY.

(8) a. All Lewis Guns will proceed with their Coys'.

    b. The 3 remaining No. 1s of Lewis Guns of "A" Coy. plus the
No.1 of "B" Coy. gun attached to "A" Coy. and the 4 No.1 of
"D" Coy. Guns will proceed in advance and will parade at
Orderly Room at 8.0 a.m.   They will take over the

(contd). 2.

(8). b. the/ sites for their gun. Guide will be at junction of JOHNSON AVENUE & LANCER LANE at 10.30 a.m.

(9). Rations will come up nightly from "Q" dump at 4.0 p.m. arriving B.403 station at 6.0 p.m. approximate. The usual trolley parties will push from there to HAPPY VALLEY.

(10). a. Blankets will be rolled in bundles of 10 and stacked by Coys' in COOKER SQUARE at 11.0 a.m.

b. Officers' valises will be loaded at 12.0 noon.

c. Officers' Mess Cart will be forward at 12.15 p.m.

(d) " Changed at OIL FACTORY.

(11). Transport Sgt. will detail:-
a. 4 Limbers, 1 for each Company, to be at OIL FACTORY at 12.30 noon/M This limber will carry Lewis Guns, cooking utensils and Company Officers' mess kit.
They will proceed to junction of LANCER LANE & CUTTING (CAMOUFLAGE Screen) and Coys' will make their own arrangements to collect from there.

(12) Rations for 11th. inst, will n t be carried on the man but will be taken to "Q" dump at 3.30 p.m. They will be taken by train which arrives at B.403 station at 6.0 p.m. O.C. "C" Coy. will meet and bring to H.V. where Batt. H.Q. Support & Reserve Coy. will draw. Rations will be taken up to "A" & "D" Coys' by "C" Coy.

(13). ~~per Coy. will remain in details. This party will remain behind in charge of Lieut. Dick till Batt. moves.~~ Lieut. Dick will receive certificate that billets are clean, forwarding same to Batt. H.Q. by the following days rations. ~~No. 0 RUE du BLOC. Details will be accomodated in~~ ~~XXXXXXXXXXXXXXXXXXXXXXXXXXXXXXXXXXXXXXXXXXXXXXXXXXXX~~

(14). 10 Signallers will remain behind for training and will be accomodated ~~with details~~ O/QM Stores. When Batt. moves off they will parade ~~with details~~ under Lt. Dick. Sgt. Hutton will act as instructor. Separate orders have been issued him by S.O. Names of Signallers will be issued later.

(15). Relief complete will be reported to Batt. H.Q. by the code word "TRIFLE".

(16) Receipts for all trench stores, maps, Defence Schemes, work programmes etc. will be forwarded to Batt. H.Q. by 9.0 p.m. tomorrow 10th.

(17) Work programme issued seperately.

8th. November. 1917.

Capt.
Adjt, 6/7th. Royal Scots Fusiliers.

Issued to:-
1 Copy Commanding Officer.
1 " O.C. 10th. S.R.
1 " O.C. "A" "B" "C" & "D" Coys'.
1 " War Diary.
1 " Transport Officer.
1 " File.

SECRET.   OPERATION ORDERS NO. 13.   Copy No.
                       6/7th. Royal Scots Fusiliers.   Appendix III

1. a. The Battalion will be relieved by the 13th. Batt. The Royal
      Scots, tomorrow 14th. inst.

   b. On relief the Battalion will move into Brigade Support.

2. Dispositions.
   "B" Coy. Royal Scots will relieve "B" Coy. R.S.F. Right Front.
   "D" "   "   "   "   "   "C" Coy. R.S.F. Left Front.
   "C" "   "   "   "   "   "D" Coy. R.S.F. Support.
   "A" "   "   "   "   "   "A" Coy. R.S.F. Reserve.

3. Guides.
   a. 1 Per Platoon for "B" & "D" Coys. Royal Scots will be at
      junction of ORCHARD RESERVE & CURB STITCH SOUTH at 8.45a.m.

   b. 1 Per Platoon for "A" & "C" Coys. Royal Scots & 1 for H. Qrs.
      will be at junction of JOHNSON AVENUE and DANGER LANE at 8.30a.m.
      These will rendezvous at B.H.Qrs. at 8.45a.m. and proceed under
      Lieut. O.A. Kessle.

   c. Guides for Right Front will be informed at 8.40a.m. whether
      BRIDCON can be used for Right Coy. relief.

4. a. Nos. 1 & 2 Posts of Right Coy. will be relieved before dawn
      tomorrow. 2 Guides, one for each post, will be at junction of
      ORCHARD RESERVE and CURB STITCH at 12 midnight.

      O.C. "B" Coy. will arrange that Gum Boots are available for
      these men for use in the Posts.

   b. Observers of Royal Scots will take over by 8a.m. tomorrow.
      Guides for these will be got at B.H.Qrs.

5. a. On relief Battalion will be disposed as follows:-
      B.H.Qrs., "A" & "D" Coys.   STIRLING CAMP.
      "B" Company   JOHNSON AVENUE.
      "C" Company   HAPPY VALLEY, with garrisons
                                      in "G" & "H" Posts.

   b. Lieut. K.S. Dick, with 1 N.C.O. from "A" & "D" Coys. details
      will report at STIRLING CAMP at 7a.m. and take over accommodation.
      Lieut. K.S. Dick will check over Stores and give receipt.

   c. O.C. "B" & "C" Coys. will each send down 1 N.C.O. per platoon
      to take over their accommodation, at 9a.m. tomorrow.

6. a. 1 Limber for "A" Coy. and 1 for "D" Coy. will be at steps on
      embankment, near Left Brigade H. Qrs., at 11.30a.m. This will take
      Lewis Guns, Dixies, and Mess Kit.

   b. Horses will be at same place for:-
      O.C. "A" & "D" Coys. at 11.30a.m.
      C.O., Sec. In Command, and Adjutant at 1.15p.m.

   c. Valises and Blankets for H. Qrs., "A" & "D" Coys. will be
      at STIRLING CAMP at 12 noon.

   d. Rations for "B" & "C" Coys. will come up to B.405 Station as
      at present. Coys. will ration themselves.

7. All trench Stores will be handed over, and taken over, and
   receipts forwarded to B.H.Qrs. by Cp.m. Care will be taken in S.O.S.
   Iron Rations, and Gum Boot Stores.

8. Gum Boots for the use of Right Coy. Royal Scots will be at
   drying shed near Cookhouse at 8.30a.m. These will be donned and
   checked there before Coy. moves up. O.C. "A" Coy. will detail an
   Officer to distribute and obtain receipt.

9. Code Words will be issued later.
   a. .... reported by the word "HERRING"

OPERATION ORDERS NO. 43.
6/7th. Royal Scots Fusiliers.

Issued to:-

    Commanding Officer.
    O.C. "A" "B" "C" & "D" Coys.
    Transport Officer.
    O.C. 13th. The Royal Scots.
    War Diary.
    File.

                          Capt.,
                Adjt., 6/7th. R.S.F.

Secret.   8 -v 11th Royal South East Lancs.   Copy No.
                           OPERATION ORDER No. ?   appendix IV

1. The Battalion will relieve the 10th. Batt. Royal Berks in
    the Right Sub-Section, Divisional Front, tomorrow 14th inst.

2. Dispositions.

        "D" Coy. R.S.E.L. will relieve Right Front Coy. R.B.
        "A" "   R.S.E.L. "   "   Left   "   "   R.B.
        "B" "   R.S.E.L. "   "   Support Coy.   R.B.
        "C" "   R.S.E.L. "   "   Reserve Coy.   R.B.

3. Guides.
    a. Guides, one per Platoon for "A" & "D" Coys. R.S.E.L. will be
        at junction of JUNCTION AVENUE and LANCHE LANE at 12.45 pm.

    b. There will be no guides for "B" & "C" Coys, who will move
        into their old positions.

    c. "A" & "D" Coys. will move off from HAPPY VALLEY at 1. p.
        "D" Coy. leading.

4. a. Nos. 1 & 2 detached posts on the Right will be relieved
        before daylight tomorrow. Garrison of each post one N.C.O.
        and 6 men.

    b. No.1 post has a Lewis Gun in it.

    c. A guide for each post will be at Junction of MACHINE AVENUE
        and MAIN AVENUE, (Battalion Headquarters) at ?am. tomorrow
        19th. inst.

    d. O.C. "D" Coy. will arrange at Battalion H. Qrs. with R.B.
        this evening as to Case & Post for these posts.

5. a. Observers will take over their post by ? . tomorrow. They
        will parade at Batt. H. Qrs. STIRLING CAMP. at 7a.m. catching
        7.15 a.m. train at A.? Siding.

    b. 1 Officer per Coy. will take over stores at ? p.m. tomorrow.
        Those from "B" & "C" Coys. will catch the 7.15 a.m. train at
        A.? Siding.
        Particular care will be taken in checking over S.O.S. and
        Gas Rockets. The Master Gass will take over the Hot Food
        Containers at HAPPY VALLEY.

    c. All records (in single) will be forwarded to Batt. H. Qrs.
        by 6p.m. tomorrow, 13th.)

6. a. H. Qrs., "B" & "C" Coys. will move in that order, from
        STIRLING CAMP.

    b. H. Qrs. will move off at 12.45 p.m. the remainder followed
        by platoons at short stated intervals.

    c. The Camp will be left in a clean and sanitary condition.
        The Company Officers will report Camp clean at ? . ? m.

7. a. Cooks will move with their Coys.

    b. One limber per each Coy., to take Lewis Guns, Mining and
        Bomb Kit, will be at STIRLING CAMP at ? . ? m.
        "D" Coy. limber will take S. Arms Amn Kit in addition.
        These limbers will proceed to dumps at embankment ? entrance to
        Coven Lane, and await Coys. there.

    c. Blankets of H. Qrs., "B" & "C" Coys. will be loaded on G.S.
        ?

7. Cont'd.

d. Officers valises will be loaded at 11.30 a.m.

e. Officers Mess Cart for surplus Mess Kit will be formed at 12.15 p.m.

f. Rations will come up in the evening at usual time to B. H.Q. Station. O.C. "C" Coy. will arrange as per before.

g. O.C. "C" Coy. will supply the carrying parties for meals for Front Line Coys.

9. Work parties will be found as per Separate Table.

10. Reliefs complete will be sent by the code word "Leah".

11. Acknowledge.

18th. November 1917.

Issued to:-

O.C. "A" "B" "C" & "D" Coys.
O.C. 15th. The Royal Scots.
Commanding Officer.
Transport Officer.
War Diary.
File.

Capt.,
Adjt., 6/7th. Royal Scots Fus.

Secret.   Copy No. 8

9th R.S.F. Operation Orders No. 30.

Appendix V

(1.) The Battalion will be relieved to-morrow, 26th inst, by the 7th Battn. Cameron Highlanders.

(2.) (a) Battalion will move into OIL FACTORY, ARRAS.

(b)
Top Floor	C. Coy.
Second Floor	D. Coy.
Third Floor	A. Coy.
Fourth Floor (Bottom)	B. Coy.
H.Q.	as before

(c) <u>Officers' Messes</u>

A. Coy where	C. Coy was
B. Coy "	D "
C " "	A "
D " "	B "

(3.) (a) Companies will move off to-morrow in order C, D, A, B Coys, H.Q. "C" Coy will move off at 2 p.m. the others following at 5 minute intervals.

(b) Cookers, Watercarts, Medical cart etc will move in a body 300 yards in rear of H.Q.

(c) Companies will enter by the Back Door of FACTORY. The SQUARE will not be used.

(4) (a) Blankets will be stacked at Company Stores by 9 a.m. and each Coy will load their own blankets on arrival of G.S. Wagons.

(b) Valises will be loaded at 12 noon.

(c) Officers Mess Kit will be collected by Mess Cart at 1.30 p.m.

(d) Officers chargers will be forward by 2 p.m. Commdg. Officer and Adjt. by 2.45 p.m.

(5) An advance party to take over billets and unload blankets etc., on arrival will proceed in advance. 1 Officer per Coy. will proceed to check over their inventory. A duplicate for all furniture signed will be kept with the receipt of the Town Major's representative thereon. These Officers will proceed 12.30 p.m.

1 N.C.O per Platoon will parade at Orderly Room at 12.15 p.m. and proceed in advance. Lieut G. A. Massie will take over for H.Q. and give receipt for all stores.

(6) The Orderly Officer will hand over Camp to representative of incoming Unit and obtain receipt of cleanliness.

(7) The Camp will be left scrupulously clean.

                                                   Capt. & Adjt.

Issued to   6/7th Royal Scots Fusiliers
1 Copy O.C. 7th Cameron Highrs.
1 ,, C.O.
1 ,, War Diary
     File.
1 ,, O.C. A. B. C. & D. Coys.
1 ,, Q.M. & T.O.
25th November 1917.

6/7th Royal Scots Fusiliers.

WAR DIARY

From 1st December 1917   To 31st December 1917.

Vol. XIX.

WAR DIARY or INTELLIGENCE SUMMARY

Army Form C. 2118.

Vol. XIX 6/7 t Royal Scots Fusiliers

December 1917

Place	Date	Hour	Summary of Events and Information	Remarks and references to Appendices
ARRAS	1.		Orders issued to-day - see O.O. Adt I, for relief of Battn. by the 9th Bn. Black Watch in the left Sector, Centa Bartalion, of the Divisional front.	App. I
"	2.		Church Service. Church of Scotland in the SALLE de CONCERT at 11A.M. Church of England in the Theatre at 11A.M. and Roman Catholics in Catholic Club at 10:30A.M.	
"	3.		Parades. 9A.M - 1P.M. "A" Coy. ARRAS Moat Range. 9-11:30A.M. "B" Coy. on old British and old German trenches just E. of ARRAS - training includes Extended Orders Drill, Company Drill, Physical Training & Bayonet fight. 1pm - 2pm Baths - "C" Coy. 9-11:30A.M as for "B" Coy. 12 noon - 1pm Baths - 9A.M - 10:30A.M "D" Coy. on Bayonet Course in Billet - 11A.M-12 noon Baths - 5-30pm - 7pm "A" & "D" Coys. Patrol work on old trenches E. of ARRAS.	
"	4.		Parade. 9. 10A.M. "A" & "D" Coys. On ground near BUTTE de TIR Rifle Range - training includes Physical Drill, Bayonet fighting, Coy. Drill & c. 8:30A.M - 9:30A.M. Assault Course in Billets. 10:15A.M. "A", "B" & "D" Coys. Route March - ARRAS. ST POL Road. 9A.M - 1P.M "C" Coy. CITADEL RANGE.	
"	5.		Parades. 8:45A.M - 9:45A.M. "A" Coy. Assault Course in Barracks. 10A.M - 11A.M "B" Coy. Assault Course in Barracks. 8:45A.M. "C" & "D" Coys. on ground E. of ARRAS. training includes Physical training, Bayonet fighting, Coy. Drill and musketry. 10:45-11:45 for "A" Coy. as for "C" & "D" Coy. 1-4 P.M "B" Coy. CITADEL RANGE. Draft of 20 O. Ranks reported to-day from depot - nearly all casuals.	
"	6		Parades. 9:15A.M. Rifle Grenadiers under D/L J. Walker - firing of rifle Grenades. 9:30A.M. - 11A.M "D" Coy. Assault Course in Billets. 1pm - 4pm BUTTE de TIR Range. "D" Coy. 9:15A.M. Route March - W.O. ABsitt Coy. ARRAS DOULLENS Road. 2-30pm "B" Coy. Rifle inspects by Armorer-Sergeant.	
"	7.		Parades. 9A.M - 12 noon. "B" Coy. On Citadel Range - 10A.M - 1pm "A" Coy. BUTTE de TIR RANGE. 9A.M - 1pm "C" + "D" Coy. Route March - ARRAS - BAPAUME Road. Rifle Grenadiers as for yesterday - 2 Visit of LtCol R.R. FLEMING reported to-day and is taken on strength of Battalion.	Sus?

WAR DIARY or INTELLIGENCE SUMMARY

Army Form C. 2118.

Vol. XIX. 17th Royal Scots Fusiliers

December 1917

Place	Date	Hour	Summary of Events and Information	Remarks and references to Appendices
ARRAS. MONCHY SECTOR.	8		Orders issued for move into line to-day relieving the 12th A.&S.H. with Right Sub section Right Sector Divisional Front. oo for Operation Orders No. 22. Dispositions same as follows:- "C" Coy with on right - Front. "B" Coy on left front, just S. of R.De A R.E. with "D" Coy in support in WELFORD RESERVE and "A" Coy in RESERVE in JOHNSON AVENUE. "D" Coy in support in JOHNSON AVENUE. Battalion H.Q. move in JOHNSON AVENUE. right was quiet - Patrols sent out no signs of enemy.	Appendix II.
MONCHY SECTOR	9.		Enemy activity confined to back areas - front quiet - Words received and orders issued for whole Battalion to "stand to" from 6.30 AM. until orders received from Brigade to "stand down". 12 Persons of "A" Coy moved up to 16 WELFORD RES. North at 6 AM in readiness - "STAND DOWN" was at 7.40 AM.	
"	10.		About 2 AM Enemy shells were fired over on our left Coy. front - Patrols went out and old dug-outs in no mans land - found them empty and mined the entrances - went on to point approx. I.25.a.55. so to suspected enemy post - found it unoccupied but brought back 300 enemy Very Lights. Patrol was fired on but no casualties. Night normal - Joint support line and E. Sap. and commenced digging new trench N. End of SCABBARD Support to LAGOON. Enemy shelling normal except for some S.g.6 on WELFORD and JOHNSON AV. between 4.30 p.m - 5.15 p.m. One man slightly wounded with this rear Batt. H.Q.	
"	11.		Joining of Support line and E Sap continued and digging of new Trench to LAGOON - Another new trench at N. end of WELFORD commenced - to be firesteps facing N.N.E. Patrols active throughout the night - no enemy seen - One visited German post as below, but again found it unoccupied. Day normal.	
"	12.		Work as for previous night. Companies changed over dispositions - with "A" Coy now on right. "D" Coy on left. "B" Coy in Support in WELFORD RESERVE and "C" Coy in RESERVE, in JOHNSON AV. Patrols out own no signs of enemy - use discharged gas at 8 p.m from Other Bombs from Support line - front was evacuated and reoccupied ½ hr. afterwards. a little gas shelling on our front - Information received 6.Day of 2/Lt. T.T.DAVIS to England (sick).	East

oo Telegram means to 27th Inf. Bde. No other retaliation on our front.

9) evacuation

Army Form C. 2118.

WAR DIARY
or
INTELLIGENCE SUMMARY.

(Erase heading not required.) Vol XIX 6/7th Argyll & Sth Feal'rs

December 1917

Place	Date	Hour	Summary of Events and Information	Remarks and references to Appendices
MONCHY SECTOR.	13.		Day very quiet - enemy inactive - a few hostile T.M's fell on our front line about 9.30pm. Patrols out found the enemy very quiet much on the alert and having listening posts out in no mans land.	
"	14.		Continued work on Front and Support trenches. Trench N. end of WELFORD RES. now completely duckboarded, also new trench from N. end of SCABBARD Supt. completed to LAGOON. Wire in front of support line now a good obstacle. Enemy activity below normal. Night very dark. Heavy Barrage N. of river at 2pm. our casualties nil.	
"	15.		Quiet day. Visibility very good. enemy artillery and T.M's very active - throughout the night reports barrage were put down on ROEUX and T.V. cross roads - No infantry action - Patrols active throughout the night, but reported no unusual enemy movement. Orders issued for relief tomorrow. See operation Orders No. 36.	Appendix III
GAVRELLE SWITCH.	16.		The Battalion was relieved by the 6th Cameron Highlanders, and on relief proceeds to Support position, with 3 Companies "A" "B" & "C" in GAVRELLE SWITCH, and "D" Coy in "K" L.T.M. Pots and 1 platoon in LANCER AVENUE - Major T.L. de Morillais having been appointed to Command Pte Cameron L.T. is absent attending course.	
"	17.		Day generally quiet. Parties were working on CORONA SUPPORT, CORDITE RESERVE, firestepping - also firestepping PEPPER TRENCH in Coy. area -	
"	18.		On 17 Inst. no shelling in the vicinity of area occupied by these Coys - D. Coy reports shelling of "K" Post in LANCER LANE, with 5.9.6. Two casualties - Owing to reinforcing front D. Coy. was relieved by one Coy 13th Royal Scots. and on relief proceeds to GAVRELLE SWITCH.	
"	19.		Continued work on CORDITE RESERVE. N. S. of CEYLON AVENUE. making of new Firestops. also continued firestepping of CORONA SUPPORT and PEPPER TRENCH. Orders issued today for relief of 114 C.M.O.S. 1 Coy. 13th Royal Scots in front line, immediately N. of River SCARPE.	Appendix IV

WAR DIARY or INTELLIGENCE SUMMARY

Army Form C. 2118.

Vol. XIX. **1/7th Royal Scots Fusiliers**

November 1917

Place	Date	Hour	Summary of Events and Information	Remarks and references to Appendices
ROEUX & SECTOR	20.		Dispositions were as follows:- "A" Coy. on left, relieved "A" Coy. A.&S.H. and 1 Platoon "D" Coy. A.&S.H. "B" - in centre, relieved "C" Coy. A.&S.H. and 1 Platoon "B" Coy. A.&S.H. "C" - on right, relieved "D" Coy. Royal Scots and 2 Pls "B" Coy. Royal Scots. "D" - relieved a Coy. Royal Scots in Support in CORONA CAVE. A.O. R.S.F. in CRETE TRENCH.	
"	21.		General situation quiet – no great activity by enemy artillery. a few air-darts on Corona Support about 11 A.M. visibility very bad – troops on front line trenches carried on – also wiring of front line. Gas Support trenches. Patrols saw no signs of any enemy in No Mans Land. Capt Rodriquez left Battalion for six months tour of duty at Home.	
"	22.		Generally quiet – supports out on extreme right of position – Several and Important COLOMBO and CORONA Tunnels made their débris up in Otway Point. Divisional wire in front "posts 8 and 9" and 5 between Posts 2 and 3. Patrols out during night. Examined enemy wire and found it no armour obstacle. No enemy patrols or unusual movement seen. Captain Rennie to day for relief of Battalion by the 9th Black Watch – Major Hannay, 1st Cameron Highldrs in Command, while C.O. was acting Brigadier.	
" and ARRAS	23.		Day normal, except for enemy barrage on Support line about 11 A.M. for which retaliation was asked and was given. Otherwise nothing unusual to report – Work of strengthening wire in Support was carried on – General survey of all Trenches and wire in Battalion area was made to day and report forwarded to Brigade – On relief, the Battalion moved to ARRAS occupying the ECOLE de JEUNES FILLES. Just after relief, enemy opened very heavy barrage on our night messages sent out to Bde. for orders. but as our immediate front was not affected Battalion move out. On arrival at ARRAS, Lt. Col. Rostron again assumed Command of Battalion.	Appendix VI
ARRAS	24.		Battalion employed in cleaning up equipment and being refitted. Preparations for leave were also made.	
"	25.		Voluntary Church Service – No work was done in order that Brigadier-General Jnr. Corps sit down to dinner at 12-15 P.M. and the other two at 1-30 P.M. In the evening the Battalion had a Cinematograph entertainment and concert. Heavy fall of snow after darkness fell.	E.15

Army Form C. 2118.

WAR DIARY
or
INTELLIGENCE SUMMARY.

(Erase heading not required.)

Vol. XIX 6/7th R.S. Fusiliers

Place	Date	Hour	Summary of Events and Information	Remarks and references to Appendices
ARRAS	26.		Parade. 9-10 AM. "C" Coy. Assault Course & Rifle - 9-12.30 pm. "A"-"B". "D" Coys. Route March - Bapaume Road. - 1-4 pm. "C" Coy. Butts at T/R Rifle Range.	
"	27.		Parade. 9 am - 1 pm. "B" Coy. Moat Range. also all Lewis Gunners at MOAT RANGE. "A" "C" "D" Coys. Route March - BAPAUME ROAD.	
"	28.		Parade. 9 am - 1 pm. "D" Coy. Crodel Range. "A" "B" "C" Coys. Route March as for yesterday. In the afternoon and evening - working Parties. The following officer admitted for duty. 2/Lt. J.M.CORREY. and is taken on strength of Battalion.	
"	29.		Parade. 9 am - 12-45 pm. Lewis Coy. arrangements. Training to include Physical Drill and Bayonet fighting - Assault Course. "A" Coy. - 1 pm - 4 pm. CITADEL RANGE. All Fire Repairs were 16 days examined on following officers reported to day for duty and are taken on the strength by Bull. Room Office. 2/Lt. J.W. McDONALD Shot. J.A. BURNS, Lieut. R.M. HOWATT, on strength of Battalion.	
"	30.		Church Service. Church of Scotland 11 Am in Divisional Cinema. C.E.E. at 11 AM in Theatre and Roman Catholic at 10.30 am in Catholic Club. Draft 2 O.Ranks joined to day (Canada).	
"	31.		Parade. 9 am - 1 pm Route March All Coys including all Rifle Grenadiers at practising with live grenades under Bull. Bombing Officer. Orders issued to-day for move to Corps Reserve. Battalion moved to WANQUETIN.	

E.H. Falcon
Lieut. Col.
Commdg. 6/7th R.S.F.

Secret 1/R.F. Operation Order N° By x Koly 16

(1) The Battn. will be relieved today, 1st Dec, by the 9th Bn. Black Watch in accordance with attached table.

(2) The Black Watch party of 1 O Rank per platoon who reconnoitred route last night will rendez-vous at Bn HQ at 3.15 P.M. — They will be despatched from there to act as guides. OC Coys. will warn these men to parade as above.

(3) Every precaution will be taken to conceal movement or noise during relief.

(4) All movement will be by platoons at 300 yds. interval — on relief the Bn will move to billets in ECOLE des JEUNE FILLES.

(5) Transport Officer will arrange
   (a) 1 Lumber per coy. to be at CAM VALLEY BOARD on ATHIES RD. at 7.30 P.M.
   (b) Horses for OC B & C Coys at same place 7.30 P.M
       "   "   A & D.   "   "   "   "   8 P.M.
       "   "   CO & Adjt "   "   "   "   8.15 P.M.

(6) Quarmr. will arrange
   (a) Valises & Blankets to be taken to ECOLE des JEUNES FILLES.
   (b) Officers Valises and mess kit   " " " " " "
   (c) Orderly Room Boxes   " " " " " "
   (d) Hot tea for men on arrival in billets

(7)(a) All trench Stores, Battalion Defence Scheme, air photographs, trench maps (except 1 per officer) position cards & programmes of work will be handed over & receipts obtained — These will be handed in to Orderly Room by 9 AM tomorrow at ? end.
   (b) Quarmr. will take over training stores & equipment (if any) in ECOLE.

(8) There will be no advance party — Quarmr. and details are taking over billets. Guides, 1 per platoon, will be at the ROND PT. at 9 PM to guide coys in.

(9) Completion of relief will be sent by 'phone by Coys

Word "JAR" - Op Lines "DIS" by runners

(10) Acknowledge.

In the field 1-12-'7
Issued to all recipients OO.

W Pettigrew
Capt OC
AMBUSH.

Plt/Sect - Issued with 4 rds - Section One 4-1

Coy	Manned By	Destination	Notes to be Taken	Remarks
D Coy	D Coy R.H.	Relief the forward pickets	Notes to be shown, Battery Locns, Enemy & friendly	2nd Brick check para friendly & enemy Rdvs Hts/Gds DP at 30m.
A	A Coy R.H.	-ditto-	-ditto-	
B	B Coy R.H.	-ditto-	-ditto-	
S	R.V.		Logistics Battle Pn/Valley Athmes	
HQ	R.V.		-ditto-	

Notes:
(1) Battery Grp Guns used to Accompany Troops
(2) Each day coy duties to avoid posn burnout affect troop in search to stay & ensure 4 to strengthen, 24hrs to Coy reflect when necessary given the factors

* Machine gun - Rum from MSAM Church HSA Again Chrisk AK, Chruck HSAC Chrisk MSA Rolls it ABS CALF rcs, V alter HTZ GBS (operation/Chrk TBS guns USDS or fromat (delivered)

Secret   O/y in R.C.F. Operation Order No. 32.   Copy No

Appendix II.

① The Battalion will relieve the 12th H.L.I. in the Right Sub-section, Right Sector Divisional Front, tomorrow 8th inst, in accordance with the attached table.

② All trench stores, Defence Schemes, Air photographs, trench maps, position calls & programmes of work will be taken over & receipts given. — Receipted list of trench stores will be sent to Bn. HQ by 9 P.M.

③ Every precaution will be taken to conceal movement during the relief from hostile observation. Lewis Guns Rifles etc. will not be carried in such a way that they project over the parapet. — Should the enemy observe the relief & commence shelling, Commanders on the spot will stop the relief till later in the night. — Should low flying hostile aircraft come over in daylight, whilst relief is in progress all movement will cease at once, and will not be resumed till the aeroplane is out of view.

④ Completion of relief will be sent by 'phone by the code word "BEE" if lines "DIS" by Runner.

⑤ Advance party as under will proceed to take over stores. — They will parade outside Orderly Room at 8.30 AM & move by march route. —
     B & C coys   1 Officer and 1 Sig. each coy + NCO of Lewis Guns
     A & D coys   1 Senior NCO and 1 Sig. each coy
     HQ   NCO to be detailed by RSM. —

⑥ The Quartermaster will hand & check over stores etc, bullets to incoming Battn. & receive chit of cleanliness. — The Band will stand by as extra fatigue party at his disposal.

⑦ Transport Officer will detail 1 limber per coy & chains to take up Lewis Guns, officers Mess Kit, to CORPS Steps at EMBANKMENT. — Limbers will be forward at 1.15 P.M. prompt. — HQ mess kit will go with A coy limber.

⑧ @ Packs & blankets (in bundles of ten) will be loaded as follows:-   HQ, A and B coys   11 AM
                                              C and D coys   11.45 AM

(b) Officers Valises will be loaded at 12 noon.
(c) Officers Mess cart will collect Kit for stores at 1 P.M.
(d) Officers chargers will be forward at 1.30 P.M.
(e) Canteen & Orderly Room stores will be collected last under arrangements Transport Officer.

(9) Rations for 9th inst. will come up to dump at CHINSTRAP LANE at 9 P.M. — "D" coy will ration themselves & B & C coys. HQ will ration themselves. OC 'A' coy will arrange to collect his own at junction of CAMOUFLAGE SCREEN & road (near LANCER LANE junction with RLY) at 8.30 P.M.

On the night of the 9th & thereafter rations will come up by rail to B403 Stn where they will be met & pushed to H Valley, & there carried to Front Line Coys. OC A coy will detail this pushing party & will find ration party for ~~Bn~~ A, B, & C Coys ~~the Support Coy~~ ~~Battn, with the exception of~~ HQ & D Coy will ration themselves.

(10) Water and Ammunition dumps etc will be notified later.

(11) 10 Signallers ~~with~~ Cpl McIntyre as instructor ~~and~~ 1 per platoon for training in Lewis Guns with instructor to be detailed later will remain in details. Names of Signallers and LG instructor will be submitted Corps later.

(12) All billets will be left scrupulously clean.

(13) Acknowledge.

Relief Table. round with 4th R.S.F. Operation orewards.

Unit	Destination	Relieving	Guides	Remarks
C coy	Right Front	C coy HLI	1st Platoon at Junction JOHNSON AV & LANCER LANE at 4 P.M.	Leading Platoon marches off 1:30 PM to center INVERNESS LANE via CORPS STEPS by 3:15 PM
B coy	Left Front	A coy HLI	ditto	Follow C coy as above — Also attached from "A" coy 1 L.C. for AA Post
D coy	Support (WELFORD RES)	B coy HLI	ditto	Follow B coy as above
A coy	Reserve (LANCER LANE)	D coy HLI	The Malson Junction INVERNESS LANE and LANCER AV 3:30 PM	Follow A coy — OC A coy will attack 1 K.C. & them to B coy 6 minutes halt
HQ	JOHNSON AV	HQ HLI	None	Follow D coy

(a) Cooks will move with their coy/s.
(b) East of a N & S grid line between "C" & "H" Squares, swet tu by Platoons at 6 minute intervals.
(c) There will be no stragglers. Platoons must move as the face of the slowest man —
(d) Order of move is as above table —

Secret. R.S.F. Operation Order No 36. Appendix III Copy No.

1. The Battalion will be relieved tomorrow (16th) by the 6th Cameron Highrs.

2. Dispositions
   A coy R.S.F. will be relieved by B coy C.H.
   D "   "   "   "   D "   "
   B "   "   "   "   A "   "
   C "   "   "   "   C "   "

3. Guides 1 per platoon, will be at junction of JOHNSON AV. and LANCER LANE at 4.30 PM. These will rendez-vous at Bn HQ at 4.10 PM.

4. On Relief. D coy will be in LANCER LANE manning K, L, M Posts with 1 platoon in each.
   A B & C coys will be in PUDDING TR. (GAVRELLE SWITCH) taking over from like coys of the Camerons. HQ will be in PUDDING TR.

5. (a) Advance parties from 6th Camerons will be up in the forenoon to take over stores etc. - No 1 of Lewis Gun for front coys will be with this party. The A.A. gun at present manned by B coy will be relieved early to allow of team joining coy. and moving out with them.

   (b) An advance party of 1 per platoon for A B & C coys and 1 for HQ will proceed in advance under Lieut Gammessie. These will take over coy area & return to act as guides later. They will parade at Bn HQ at 9.30 am tomorrow. Guides of A B & HQ will return in the evening and meet coys at junction of JOHNSON and LANCER at 6 PM. C coy guides will return in the afternoon to their coy. & and act as guides in the evening. OC D coy will send down advance party at his own convenience to take over. An officer will take over stores & carefully check all iron rations in posts.

6. C coy with 3 platoons will relieve platoons of D coy of Camerons in K, L & M Posts at 2 PM. The stores in these posts will be taken over by D coy officer and

6. C coy with 3 platoons will relieve ~~D coy of~~ platoons of D coy
in K & L & M posts at 2 PM. — The stores in these
posts will be taken over by D coy officer and platoons will
be relieved by D coy R.S.F. later in the evening —

7. Defence Schemes (with Addendum issued this evening)
trench stores, aeroplane photos etc will be handed
over & receipts obtained —

8. (a) Rations for tomorrow will come up to RIDDING TR.
for A B C & HQ and for D coy to CAMOUFLAGE SCREEN
foot of LANCER LANE at 9 PM. — Each coy will
ration itself

(b) Water is drawn in petrol tins from KAMPOUK —

9. The following work party will be found
tomorrow by OC B coy — Strength 2 NCOs and
20 men to be at KAMPOUK LOCK at 5 PM — work —
clearing spoil — Guide from 9th Gordons will meet.
An extra man will be sent with advance party
by B coy to return in the afternoon & proceed with
this party to act as guide on completion of
their task —

10. Completion of relief will be acknowledged by the
word NIB.

A.d.C. W.S. Pettigrew
Capt & Adjt.
6/7th R.S.F.

15/12/17

Secret   R.C.F. Operation Order No 36   Copy No

1. The Battalion will be relieved tomorrow night by the 1st Cameron Highrs.

2. Disposition
   A Coy RCF will be relieved by B coy C.H.
   D   "   D   "
   B   "   A   "
   C   "   C   "

3. Guides & perplications meet at junct of JOHNSON AV and LANCER LANE at 4.30 pm. These will rendezvous at Bn HQ at 4.10 pm.

4. On relief D coy will be in LANCER LANE, manning K, L, M Posts with 1 platoon in each.
   A, B & C coys will be in PUDDING TR (GAVRELLE Sw) taking over from like coys of the Camerons.
   HQ in PUDDING TR

5. (a) Advance parties from 1st Cam. High will be up in the forenoon to take over stores etc. No 1 officers & men per front coy will be with this party. The AA gun at present manned by B coy will be relieved early to allow of team joining B coy & moving out with them — (for A B & C)

   (b) An advance party of 1 per platoon & 1 per HQ will be proceed in advance under Lieut G A Maccie. These will take over coy area & return to act as guides.

Guides of   They will parade at Bn HQ at 9.30 am tomorrow.
A & B   will return in the evening & meet coys at junction of JOHNSON & LANCER at 6 pm. C coy
            Guides will return this afternoon to their coy & act as guides in the evening — OC D coy will send down advance party at his convenience to take over. An officer will take over stores and carefully check all iron rations in posts —

SECRET.   6/7th. R.S.F. OPERATION ORDERS No. 35.   APPX N: 4
                              Appendix 4   War Diary

1. The Battalion will relieve the 11th A. & S.H. and 13th R. Scots
   in the Front Line at present held by them, to-morrow
   20th inst.

2. Dispositions.
   As laid down for A. B. & C. Coys. in map issued
   herewith.
   D. Coy. in CORONA CAVE with H. Qrs. in BURMA
   CAVE.
   Bn. H. Qrs., H.24.c.80.85 (CRETE TRENCH)

3. Guides etc., as per attached table.

4. (a) Advance party to take over stores, 1 N.C.O. for each
       coy., and 1 for Bn. H. Qrs. and 1 Signaller per coy.,
       and 1 for H. Qrs., will parade at C Coy. H. Qrs.
       to-morrow at 9 a.m.
   (b) Observers will parade also as in (a) & proceed in
       advance, reporting at Bn. H. Qrs. A. & S.H. CRETE TRENCH.
       2 Observers will report at Bn. Hqrs. R. Scots,
       CRETE TRENCH, & take over post in CORONA SUPPORT,
       near CORSE CUT.
   (c) O.C. C Coy. will despatch personnel (a) – (c)
   (d) 2 Lewis Guns and teams for night posts in CRUMPET
       TRENCH will proceed in advance under Sgt. Tonner
       and will move off at 2 p.m. reporting at Royal Scots
       H. Qrs. CRETE TRENCH by 3 p.m.

5. Cooks will proceed with their coys., a guide being
   given them at rendez-vous, SINGLE ARCH.

6. All trench stores, rifts, work in hand will be
   carefully checked and taken over. Work in hand by
   coys. now will be forwarded to Orderly Room by 12 noon
   to-morrow, for handing over purposes.

7. Trench Shelters & dug-outs will be left scrupulously
   clean.

8. Relief complete to be reported by the code word
   WALK.
   10th Nov. 1918

	RELIEVING	GUIDES	REMARKS
C	D Coy R Scots and A Coy 2 Police, B Coy R Scots.	1 Pr Inds at/or Recrd Kalom at Single Arch at 4-4.5 PM	To march 1/4st - 15 M York Lane Beam Post Athies Row & holding Now have only to have close guards throughout H18 and as above to AB Dugouts and beam sentries
B	C Coy, A Coy SH + 1 Platoon 2nd at Starting Pt of B Coy and SH	— Acco —	To follow C Coy.
	A Coy A - SH I & Platoon Icn down of B Coy HQ and B Sr RAMC	— Accs —	To follow B Coy Aye with D Coy & can't carry stretchers
D	Coy R Scots in Corona Cave	1 Pr Ala Coy Single Arch at 4.45 PM	No follow A Coy
HQ	H.Q. Bn S.H Creek Th	1 Guide at Single Arch at 5-5.15 PM	To follow D Coy

(A) Descent at 300 yds will be manned between Posts to CRU-12 Wharf - D Coy will form
(B) Interval [illegible] 50 yds between [illegible]

Secret.   6/7th R.S.F. Operation Orders No. 37.   Copy No. 1

Reference:-
PELVES TRENCH MAP
1/10,000.
GREENLAND HILL 1/10,000.
51.D N.W. 1/20,000.

1. The Battalion will be relieved by the 9th BLACK WATCH, in the Left Sub sector of the Right Section, Divisional Front tomorrow evening 23rd inst.

2. "A" Coy. 9th B.W. will relieve "A" Coy. R.S.F.   Left Front Coy.
   "B"   "   "   "   "   "   "B"   "   "   Centre Coy.
   "C"   "   "   "   "   "   "C"   "   "   Right Front Coy.
   "D"   "   "   "   "   "   "D"   "   "   in Support.
                                                    (INDIA CAVE.)

3. Guides 1 per post for front line Coys and 1 for A.C. "C" Coy HQ. with 1 guide for "A" Strong Point and 1 guide for "B" Strong Point will rendezvous at Battalion H.Q. at 8.50 P.M. Daytime guide per platoon and 1 for Coy. H.Q. will rendezvous at same place and time. O.C. "D" Coy. will detail an Officer to be in charge and to take all guides to SINGLE ARCH, where they will await the incoming Battalion. One guide will also be sent for Battn. H.Q.

4. Observers and 1 N.C.O. per Coy. are reporting at Battn. H.Q. from the 9th B.W. to take over all stores etc. at 11 A.M.

5. All Trench Stores, Battalion Defence Scheme, air photographs Trench maps, position calls, programmes of work, anti-aircraft poles and mountings will be handed over and receipts obtained. These latter will be handed in to Orderly Room at 9 A.M. 24th.

6. On relief the Battalion will move to Billets at ECOLE des JEUNES FILLES, ARRAS, proceeding by following route:- SINGLE ARCH - FAMPOUX - ATHIES - ST. LAURENT BLANGY -

7. Every precaution will be taken to conceal movement during the relief from hostile observation. Lewis guns, rifles etc. will not be carried in such a way that they project over the parapet. Should the enemy observe the relief and commence shelling, Commanders on the spot will stop the relief until shelling dies down.

8. O.C. Coys. will make necessary arrangements to prevent straggling when parties leave trenches and proceed along a road. All movement E. of a N. & S. grid line between "G" and "H" squares will be by platoons at six minute intervals.

9. Completion of relief will be notified by wire, or runners if lines "dis", of the code word "TAR".

10. The Quartermaster will arrange:-
    (i) To take over ECOLE, and stores.
    (ii) To have hot tea ready on arrival of Companies.
    (iii) To have all Blankets and Officers' Valises and mess kit at ECOLE.

11. The Transport Officer will arrange:-
    (i) To have Officers' chargers for A.D.C. and "D" Coy at X Roads in H.7.c. just S of YORK LANE at 6.30 p.m.
    (ii) To have 1 Limber for each Coy Lewis guns, missiles, and officers mess kit at same place at 6 p.m.
    (iii) To have cookers, water carts and medical cart taken to ECOLE.

12. Acknowledge.

                                        G. Albert Davies
                                               Lieut & Adjt.
                                                 6/7th R.S.F.

Issued to all recipients
of Battn. R.O.
and 1 copy to 9th Black Watch.
    1 : to File.
    1 : . War Diary.

22nd December 1917.

6/7th Bn. Royal Scots Fusiliers.

WAR DIARY

From 1st Jan. 1918.   To 31st Jany. 1918.

Vol. XXXI

2nd Febry. 1918

WAR DIARY or INTELLIGENCE SUMMARY

Army Form C. 2118.

Vol. XX. 6/7th Royal Scots Fusiliers

January 1918.

Place	Date	Hour	Summary of Events and Information	Remarks and references to Appendices
ARRAS	1st		Orders were issued for move to WANQUETIN, the Division going into rest. The battalion paraded at ECOLE du JEUNES FILLES at 12.30pm and proceeded by march route. The day was cold but dry. First line transport accompanied Battalion - only one team fell out on march, with sprained ankle. An advance party under Lt. FIFE took over billets. The Battalion arrived and was in billets by 5pm.	
WANQUETIN	2nd		Parade. 9am - 1pm. Section and Platoon Training on training area at Eastern end of VILLAGE. Football and other sports were carried on in afternoon. Cleaning of equipment and improvement of billets also carried on.	
"	3rd		Parade 9am - 1pm. Section and Platoon training on training area. 15. F.& N.C.O's having reports over without on leave to U.K. in attack off Ouinghet of Battalion.	
"	4th		Parade 9am - 1pm. Section & Platoon training - Exercises 1 and 2 pr laid down by Brigade. Afternoon spent in Short Training and Football.	
"	5th		Parade. 9am - 1pm. Platoon training continued - Exercise 2,3 + 4. All signallers under signalling officer for instruction - a draft of 65 other ranks joined today. One boy was wounded and the others went on of a great cheer.	
"	6th		Church Service. Church of Scotland. 11.30am. Church of England 9.30am. Roman Catholic. 10.45am. Capt. A.H. FERGUSON rejoins from Six Corps. Hqrs. and now before its Command "A" Coy. Three N.C.O's instructors were attached to Battalion, one for P.T. & B.F and one as musketry instructor. Platoon training carried on. Exercise 3,4 & 5 and 6. being gone through. Signallers under signalling officer from 9am - 11am. One Company fires on range - application, rapid & snapping at 100 yds.	
"	7th		Platoon training - continued. Exercises 5.6.7 & 8. One Coy. on range firing above practices - as weather was very bad, very little shooting was done.	
"	8th		Platoon training - Indoor Coy. arrangements in Huts - as heavy fall of snow made training outside almost impossible - no shooting done.	
"	9th		Parade. 9am - 1pm. As weather had improved, outside training again carried on as for 8th.	
"	10th		Parade 9am - 1pm. Commenced firing ARA Competition with "C" Coy. other Coys. doing exercises 8, 9 & 10.	
"	11th		Brig. Gen. Amos. Pres. Inspected Coys. 6 day. A & B Coys. in Marching Order and C & D Coys in Battle Order.	

WAR DIARY or INTELLIGENCE SUMMARY

Army Form C. 2118.

Vol. XX. 6/7th Royal Scots Fusiliers. January 1918.

Place	Date	Hour	Summary of Events and Information	Remarks and references to Appendices
NANQUETIN	12th		Parade 9 am - 1 pm. Platoon training and Bayonet 9 - 13. Another Company fires its practice in A.R.A. Competition. Afternoon - sports and other Coy field A.R.A Competition	
"	13th		Church Service. As for last Sunday. Baths were allotted to Coys. in afternoon. Three other ranks (Cavalry) joined B. Coy, and are posted to their former Companies.	
"	14th		Parade 9 am - 1 pm. B, C & D Coys. Platoon training with 1 hour each Live Bombing - "A" Coy on range - firing practices 1, 2, & 8. At 2 pm Final of A.R.A. Competition between Coys. when No.1 and 8 Platoon Bombs were used. They represented Battalion in Bde. Competition. A team of 40 from Battalion won the Bde. Coys Country race in afternoon, and became the Btn. representatives in Divisional Cross Country race.	
"	15th		Parade 9 am - 1 pm. "B" Coy fires on range 6-day practice 1 - 3. "A", C" & "D" Coy. continued Platoon and Company training and Exercises 13, 14, 15 & 16. Signallers were under Drapnalling officer from 9am to 11 am. "D" Platoon were used as enemy. Paraded again afternoon for Lecture on Lewis demonstration, by divisional Gas officer. At 5 pm there was a Lecture to all officers by Divl. Gas Officer. At 11am "C" Coy Rifle Bombers paraded under 2/Lt Watson, for practice in firing live rifle grenades and "C" Coy paraded at 12 noon.	
"	16th		Parade 9 am - 1 pm. "B" Coy allotted ranges, took Rifle as Lewis Gun, but no firing done owing to bad weather. Other Coys. training in Huts. S? Swimming & Gas Respirator Drill being carried on.	
"	17th		Inside & outside training impossible. Preparation made for divisional inspection in Mot. Scrubbing of equipment and general cleaning of all kit. Kit Inspections were made.	
"	18th		"B" Coy on range "A", "C" & "D" Coys. one hour Bombing and Rifle Bombing at others working. 2 pm. BR. Coy paraded for Inspection and Drill. Exercises 13, 14, 15 & 16. Lt. Col. No. J. B. Borton, who guided Command of the Battalion to-day, hearing him appointed to take Command of Bn. Royal Scots Fusiliers. Major H. P. Hart, D.S.O, who has been acting as Second-in-command since beginning of month assumed command of Battalion on from this date. Capt N. Jope M.C. from Command of "D" Coy, takes on duties as Second-in-command and is promoted Major. Lieut. D.C. Brown takes over command of "D" Coy.	

WAR DIARY or INTELLIGENCE SUMMARY

Army Form C. 2118.

Vol. XX. 6/7th Royal Scots Fusiliers
January 1918

Place	Date	Hour	Summary of Events and Information	Remarks and references to Appendices
WAN QUETIN	19th		Parade. 9 Am - 1 pm. "C" Coy on Range firing practices 1, 2, & 3. Application, rapid & snapping & at 10 yds. "D" Coy followed "C" Coy on Range, when latter has finished. "A" Coy. Company training. "D" Coy. when not on range did specialist training. "B" Coy. Live bombing and rifle bombing for 1 hour, and afterwards Company training. Football were carried on in afternoon. Inter platoon competition. Church Service. - as for last Sunday. In the afternoon, companies kit & arrangements for inspection.	
"	20th			
"	21st		Parade 9 am - 1 pm. "D" Coy on range. Shooting practices 1, 2, & 3. 9.10 am "A" & "C" Coy specialists hour. 10 - 1 pm. Company training. Afternoon football & sports. 5.30 pm. Lecture to all officers on map reading by Capt. A.W. FERGUSON, having been appointed Staff Capt. of 2nd Inf. Bde. & attack of Strength & Limits and fund. N.R.H. Hutchison assumed command "A" Coy.	
"	22nd		Parade. 9 - 10.30 Am. "D" Coy on Range. 10.30 - 11.30 am. "A" Coy. Range. 11.30 am - 1 pm. "B" Coy Range. Coys and training carried on when not on Range. 6.30 pm. Lecture on Communication hour officers and 8 N.C.O's per Coy. at SIMENCOURT.	
"	23rd		Divisional Commander inspected Battalion on Parade, including transport. Very satisfactory. The Transport and Cookers were particularly complimented. No. 5 Platoon was what was required. After inspection, Companies carried on with training.	
"	24th		Parade. 9 am - 1 pm. Details of our Coys. first platoon stage in Bn Respirator Musketry Competition. And Coys. Companies paraded under their Company training continued. And again - Companies - games by Commanding officers. At 5.30 pm All officers on "Organisation" - given by Commanding officer. Concert at 6.30 pm by mens Bandh. Platoon Competition carried on in afternoon.	
"	25th		Brigade Scheme. Battalion moves to an exercise by Brown, landing out 7.45 am. On completion of exercise. Battalion returned to billets by Busses.	
"	26th		Battalion horse race. Battalion forms up in trench system to the east of village. In the afternoon the final of the A.R.A. Competition was fired.	
"	27th		Church Service. - as for last Sunday. three Canadian 2nd Battalion to day and are taken on strength.	

Army Form C. 2118.

WAR DIARY
or
INTELLIGENCE SUMMARY.
(Erase heading not required.) Vol. XX 6/7th Royal Scots Fusiliers

Instructions regarding War Diaries and Intelligence Summaries are contained in F. S. Regs., Part II. and the Staff Manual respectively. Title pages will be prepared in manuscript. January 1918.

Place	Date	Hour	Summary of Events and Information	Remarks and references to Appendices
WANQUETIN	28th		Parade. 9am – 1pm. "A" Coy. Ranges - Practice 6 & 7. application & rapid at 300 yds – 9-10 am "B" Coy. P.T. r.B.F. and Lise bombing. 10 – 11 am. D.Coy. P.T. r.B.F. & Live bombing. 11-12 noon "C" Coy. Live bombing – Other Coy. Company training – 2-4 pm Heats for Regimental Sports and musketry. 5-30 pm Lecture by Commanding Officer on organisation.	
"	29th		Battalion sports – Field training in training area. In afternoon heats for Regimental Sports. 5-3opm Lecture on Trench Feet by Medical Officer – Sent with Phimulic and fruit. Men must remember to say for duties and are taken on strength.	
"	30th		Parade. 9am – 1pm. "B" Coy. Ranges. Practices 6-7 am for 28th October Coy. co-op for 28th Other Coy. on 5-30pm. Lecture to section Commanders by C.O. & later. platoon football competition.	
"	31st		Parade 9am – 1pm. "C" Coy. Range. other Coys. one hour specialist training and other hour Company training – Battalion Sports in afternoon.	

Major
Commanding 6/7th R.S.F.